Chinese Merchant
Families in Iloilo

Chinese Merchant Families in Iloilo
Commerce and Kin in a Central Philippine City

John T. Omohundro

Ateneo de Manila University Press
Quezon City, Metro Manila

The Ohio University Press
Athens, Ohio
1981

Library of Congress Cataloging in Publication Data

Omohundro, John T.
    Chinese merchant families in Iloilo.

    Bibliography: p.
    Includes index.
    1. Chinese—Philippines—Iloilo.   2. Iloilo
(Philippines)—Social life and customs.   3. Iloilo
(Philippines)—Commerce.   I. Title   II. Title:
Shang chia.
DS689.I44O48   305.8'951'05995   81-1143
ISBN 0-8214-0441-5   AACR2
ISBN 0-8214-0619-1 pbk.

Printed in the United States of America.

ACKNOWLEDGMENTS

This monograph is a revised version of my dissertation in anthropology and a product of eighteen months' fieldwork in Iloilo City, Philippines, from October 1971 to March 1973. The research was supported by a National Institute of Mental Health Combined Fellowship and Field Grant.

To my doctoral committee and especially to Professor Aram A. Yengoyan, I owe my graduate education and the inspiration for this work.

Special thanks go to my hosts in the Philippines, the Ateneo de Manila's Institute of Philippine Culture and the Central Philippine University, for their many resources and help in making my research and residence successful.

To my friends and helpers — Robert Young, Benjamin Yap, Sy Bunhong, Po Seng-ka, and Dominga Conejar — I owe the preponderance of interesting and accurate data that I was able to collect.

Among the numerous friends and colleagues who gave me encouragement, hot tips, and advice, I wish to thank Father Charles McCarthy and Pagkakaisa sa Pagunlad, Inc., Professor See Chin-ben, Mr. Bernard Go, Reverend Floyd and Beverly Roseberry, and my research methods class at Central Philippine University. Geographer Doug McDonald at State University of New York College at Potsdam made my maps and Dick Bitely prepared the photographs.

The Chinese community in Iloilo, both officially and informally, graciously tolerated me in their shops, churches, homes, schools, and clubs for eighteen months, answering thousands of questions and granting hundreds of requests. My heartful thanks and best wishes for prosperity, longevity, and peace of mind are herewith extended.

I am deeply grateful to my wife, Susan, who participated in all aspects of the research, and in the preparation of the manuscript for publication, sharing all of the trials and collecting few of the rewards.

Finally, I dedicate this book to my parents, who gave me the opportunity to see the world, discover the variety of cultures, and wonder what makes people tick.

CONTENTS

Chapter

1   THE PHILIPPINE CHINESE 1
     Merchant Families Outside Manila 2
     The Chinese as an Ethnic Group 4

2   HISTORY OF THE CHINESE IN ILOILO 15
     The Spanish Regime: 1570-1898 15
     The American Regime: 1898-1930 17
     The Pattern of Immigration: 1898-1949 21
     Facing the Problems of the 1930s 29
     The Japanese Occupation 31
     Postwar Recovery 32
     Life in the Philippines: 1946 to the present 34
     Growth of the Chinese Community 41

3   CHINESE BUSINESS LIFE 46
     Merchant Society and Merchant Culture 46
     The Chinese Presence in Iloilo's Economy 47
     Distribution of Chinese Merchants 50
     The Chinese and Iloilo's Distribution System 52
     Hiring, Labor, and Employees 57
     Money Handling 62
     Contracts and the Law 74
     Investing 76
     Real Estate and Storefronts 78
     Consumption Patterns 80
     Economic Advantages of the Social Structure 83

4   ORGANIZING FOR BUSINESS AND DEFENSE 89
      Chambers of Commerce 92
      Specialized Business Associations 96
      Political Clubs and Family Associations 99
      The Music Club and the Catholic Women's Association 104
      The Organizations and Their Interrelations 105
      Principles of Leadership and Organization 109
      Intercommunity Sanctions 116

5   BUILDING A FAMILY 121
      Immigration 122
      In-marriage, Incest, and Intermarriage 125
      Household Composition 134
      Postmarital Residence 136

6   THE FAMILY AND BUSINESS 139
      Division of Labor and Control 139
      Transmission of the Business 145
      Business Training 146
      Inheritance 149
      Recruitment and Alliances 156
      New Developments in Affinal Business Relationships 162

7   LO'S FAMILY DRY GOODS STORE: A CASE STUDY 169
      Early Beginnings 169
      Business Expansion and Family Problems 171
      Lo's Control of Finances 177
      Future of the Store 178

      EPILOG 181

      BIBLIOGRAPHY 195

      INDEX 200

1

THE PHILIPPINE CHINESE

THIS STUDY OF THE CHINESE COMMUNITY of Iloilo City, Philippines, is organized around three themes of both social and economic import to the contemporary Philippine nation. First, the organization and operation of Chinese business life is portrayed to support my contention that like the fisherman, hunter, or farmer, the merchant has a culture which owes much of its structure and distinctiveness to his livelihood. Second, the family business, as the basic social unit of the Philippine Chinese, is examined for the complex interplay between social and commercial needs and desires. Finally, running as an undercurrent throughout the book and receiving careful scrutiny in the epilog, is the prospect of Chinese integration into Filipino society. Momentous changes have occurred in the Philippines in the last few years. By directing attention to the Chinese as ethnic merchants, organized into family businesses, we can best foresee how those changes will affect integration.

Compared to other Southeast Asian Chinese populations, that of the Philippines is small (about 300,000 people) and a small proportion of the total population (about 1 percent). Compare these figures to those for Malaysia's Chinese (3,000,000, or 30 percent of the total population) or Thailand's Chinese (about 2,500,000, or 8 percent of the total population). In spite of its small size, however, Philippine Chinese society has frequently been the subject of anthropological studies. The structure of the Philippine Chinese family and its patterns of marriage and intermarriage have been treated a number of times (H. Reynolds 1964; I. Reynolds 1964; Liu, Rubel, and Yu 1969; Amyot 1960; Tan-Gatue 1955). The structure and history of community organizations, including the lineage and other kin groupings, have also been described (Amyot 1960; Weightman 1960; Blaker 1970). Some of the myriad works on the Philippine Chinese operations in the economy have also attempted to comprehend the specific internal workings of local Chinese marketing practices (Wickberg 1965; Doeppers 1971) and the intra-community network of business connections and market information (Weightman 1960). The urban ecology of Chinese neighborhoods (Doeppers 1971) and the position of the Chinese as a class in the colonial and post-colonial socioeconomic orders (Wickberg 1965; Ravenholt 1955) have also been carefully researched.

From these social studies as well as from the more general works on the history and political status of the Philippine Chinese emerges a vivid picture of the condition of this overseas Chinese community compared to others in Southeast Asia. George Weightman (1960:10) has summarized this position as follows. Philippine Chinese constitute a smaller percentage of the population of their host nation than do most Southeast Asian Chinese enclaves, yet their economic position is still very strong. Overall, they are a remarkably homogeneous and well-to-do group, with an almost nonexistent peasant or proletarian element. They comprise only two speech groups, the Cantonese and the Fukienese. They are more urban than any Southeast Asian Chinese group, except that in Singapore, and enjoy a standard of living higher than most. They are more literate than most, more Christian, and operate a number of high quality news services, schools, churches, and public relations activities. They are more exclusively pro-Kuomintang than most Southeast Asian Chinese, at least in public, reflecting the anti-Communist bias of the Filipinos. Finally, unlike the Chinese of Malaysia and Indonesia but similar to the Chinese of Thailand, Philippine Chinese have not maintained any distinct intermediate ethnic groups of the Peranakan or Baba Chinese type.

Chinese Merchant Families Outside Manila

Because of the relative homogeneity of the Philippine Chinese group, the relative abundance of literature about them comes closer than in other countries to a faithful portrayal. Yet there are still some rather large gaps in our knowledge which my research has sought to fill.

First, most scholars have concentrated their attention on Manila, whose greater metropolitan area contains about one-half of the Chinese citizens and probably a similar proportion of the ethnically Chinese Filipino citizens (Purcell 1960:494). The remaining 50 percent of the Philippine Chinese are not well understood in either their own community organization or in their relation to Manila.[1] For this reason Iloilo province and Iloilo City were selected as the site of this research. As we shall see in chapter 2, Iloilo is one of the largest, oldest, most active, and most conservative of the Chinese concentrations outside of Manila. On the other hand, because of the homogeneity of the Philippine Chinese, many of the conclusions regarding business practices, family life, intermarriage, and so forth that I shall set out here should be fairly applicable to the Chinese in Manila, Davao, Cebu, Zamboanga, and other Philippine cities.[2]

Second, there have been few attempts to examine and analyze the economic activities of the Philippine (or any Southeast Asian) Chinese at the local level. Precisely what is the operation of the "airtight system of financing and credit, cooperative purchasing, and interlocking ownership" (Alip 1959: 69) which is frequently alleged to be characteristically Chinese and the source of their economic advantage? What is the connection of Chinese enterprise to Filipino capital, to Filipino labor, to the Filipino agricultural hinterland? Precisely how do Chinese organize and operate their businesses? What resemblance does this bear to the way Americans or Filipinos might operate? There are many barriers to this sort of inquiry, some of which involve the Chinese businessman's understandable reticence to be investigated in these matters. Other barriers involve the theoretical tools which economists bring to their task. Philippine Chinese writers themselves, beneficiaries of the best inside information, tend to be most interested in macroeconomic questions. They shun the local study, which demands a sociocultural approach and thus veers away from the patterns of economic tests. Inclined to work with official statistics and usually working within the same paradigms of economic activity as their official sources, the conventional economic students are at a loss at the local level where statistics are virtually unavailable and the macroeconomic categories appear far less relevant. The approach of the economic anthropologist, who is prepared to gather his own facts and to invent more of his own categories (or accept those of his subjects), seems preferable on the local level, even when working in a community of thousands of Chinese located in a matrix of hundreds of thousands of Filipinos.

A third deficiency in the study of Philippine Chinese is the failure to correlate the institutions of their society. That is to say, Philippine Chinese economy, religion, political behavior, and family life, for example, have been the subjects of good research. However, these different aspects of Chinese community life are usually presented as isolates. Also, data collection is often a remote questionnaire procedure, at best. Yet residence in a community of Philippine Chinese shopkeepers will quickly show the researcher that there is a definite social organization to Chinese economic activity and that a heavy burden of economic function is placed upon the social organization. For this reason I have presented and defended the term "merchant society" as a label for the Philippine Chinese (chapter 3). This "merchant society" label serves to emphasize the interrelationship between the social area and the economic area of Philippine Chinese behavior. Second, this label will draw attention to their place in a worldwide presence of "marginal trading communities," "resident strangers," or "immigrant shopkeepers," as they are variously called (Nash 1966; Weightman 1960). In *East-West Parallels*, W. F. Wertheim (1964) has already argued for a view of the overseas Chinese within a worldwide phenomenon of "minority trading communities." However, Wertheim has dealt exclusively with assimilation and racial harmony. In a wide variety of contexts, writers have made reference to the similarity between European Jews, Levantine traders in Africa, and Indians and Chinese in Southeast Asia, but these were only passing references.

Comparisons of the economic activities of trading minorities and their family structures still beg to be done.[3]

A central theme of this book is the interaction of family and business in Iloilo Chinese merchant society. The family business, as the ubiquitous social unit of Philippine Chinese communities, is here considered as both an economic unit and a kinship unit. The shape the family takes is a product of culture exported from China and reworked in the Philippine environment (the subject of chapters 2, 5, 6 and 7). The strengths and weaknesses of this commercial unit stem in a large part from its familial base. At the same time, the shape of the family is influenced by the needs of business. This latter process has been given much attention on only two occasions, Maurice Freedman's (1957) Singapore Chinese work and Donald Willmott's (1960) study of Chinese in Semarang, Indonesia. I have expanded their treatment of some topics, for example, the business effects of marrying a native wife, and in several places my findings do not agree with theirs.

The importance of family organizational principles, kinship, and commercial concerns in Iloilo Chinese life can be seen in chapter 4, where I attempt to discern a pattern and purpose in the complex and flexible political organization the Chinese have raised since the Second World War.

Finally, the close bond of family and business is the key to understanding the future integration of Chinese into Filipino society, the subject of the epilog. I cannot pretend to foresee the future, but some trends are perceptible and some conditional statements are possible.

The Chinese as an Ethnic Group

The Chinese living in the city and the province may be labeled an ethnic group, but choosing an appropriate definition of that term immediately introduces inevitable and pervasive biases. On the one hand, we shall find it useful to define the Chinese as those within a certain residential area, or breeding population, or those possessing certain culture traits imported from China. On the other hand, we might usefully allow the Chinese to define themselves in terms of who thinks he is Chinese or in terms of the behavioral strategy exercised (in this case, being a sojourner or minority merchant). Even this dichotomy does not illustrate the full range of possibilities for defining the group. Sometimes the Chinese talk of themselves as a statistical sum of individuals and businesses qualifying as culturally Chinese, and at other times they speak of a Chinese identity giving particular shape to a person's actions and thoughts. Lastly, J. Clyde Mitchell (1974) has pointed out that not only might the ethnographer and the actors have two (or more) different conceptual frameworks for defining the ethnic group, but each might also have his own ways of interpreting the behavior of the actors.

This complexity should not be cause for dismay. The problems of defining and explaining ethnic groups have finally broadened to join anthropology's older debates on the core notions of culture and society. Anthropologists are no more in agreement on what an ethnic group is, how it should be studied and explained, and what its boundaries are, than they are agreed about their older term, culture. Now that the study of ethnicity by anthropologists has intensified in recent decades, theoretical rumblings in one area are bound to jostle the other.

In this study, the several notions of ethnic groups are used like interchangeable lenses on a microscope, each revealing different ways light is shed by the subject. At the outset, the population approach and culture trait approach will provide convenient overviews.

According to Bureau of Immigration statistics, Iloilo City's alien Chinese community of 2,200 stands fifth behind Manila, Cebu, Davao, and Cagayan de Oro, in order (Philippine Census 1960). However, Iloilo has the third largest number of Chinese business establishments registered in the Chinese business directories (*Filipino-Chinese Chambers of Commerce Yearbook* 1965). In the opinion of Filipinos and Chinese, the Iloilo Chinese are considered to be a more visible, more active, more conservative, and more ancient Chinese community than any but Manila and Cebu. There are more Chinese associations and Chinese schools in Iloilo than anywhere but Manila and Cebu. By most measures, then, Iloilo ranks in the top three or four Chinese communities of the Philippines.

Iloilo itself, at the southern tip of Panay Island in the western Visayas region (map 1), is a town of about 250,000 Filipinos. It is the capital of Iloilo province, one of the oldest Hispanic developments and the third greatest rice-producing region in the nation. Iloilo City plays the dominant role in the western Visayas as accumulator of agricultural products and distributor of imported and manufactured goods. It has served in this capacity since the seventeenth century, thus providing fertile ground for the growth of a Chinese merchant community. Until the rise of Cebu in the twentieth century, Iloilo was the second most important and second largest Spanish settlement in the country after Manila, earning the title "Queen City of the South."

The Chinese community of Iloilo province is based in Iloilo City, where about 90 percent of their number reside and operate businesses. The vast majority of combined business-and-residences are in the downtown business district on five or six main streets (map 2). Unlike the Binondo-Santa Cruz area of Manila, which is called Chinatown, Iloilo's downtown does not constitute a Chinatown in the sense that the businesses hire predominantly Chinese or cater predominantly to Chinese or that residence within the area is limited to Chinese or that residence outside the area is restricted for Chinese. It is simply that the majority of downtown businesses are owned and lived in by Chinese.

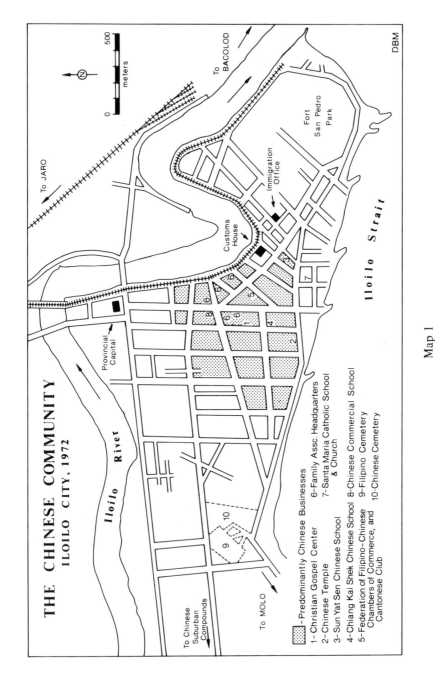

Map 1
Chinese in Iloilo City

In defining Chinese individuals for demographic purposes, I shall include all ethnically Chinese individuals, regardless of citizenship. An ethnic Chinese was born in China or attended Philippine Chinese schools, can speak Chinese, and has traceable descent from Chinese ancestors. This operational definition allows me to include Philippine-born Chinese and mestizos and yet exclude the pure Filipinos who attended Chinese school and can speak some Chinese. It begs the questions of political allegiance, assimilation to Filipino culture, and personal identity for the time being.

Official Philippine government recognition of the Chinese community is by means of statistics on race, mother tongue and citizenship of individuals. According to data recorded at the Office of Immigration in Iloilo in 1973, Chinese citizens of the Republic of China comprise about 1 percent of the city's population and 0.3 percent of the total provincial population. In the 1948 census, the last to record "race," there were 2,487 individuals of pure "yellow" race in Iloilo province and about 1,200 mestizos. The racially pure Chinese, then, constituted 0.3 percent of the total population. In the Philippine census of 1960, 2,032 or 0.2 percent of Iloilo's provincial population spoke Chinese as their mother tongue (first language learned). So, by race, language, or citizenship, the Chinese are between 0.2 percent and 0.3 percent of the total provincial population and about 1 percent of the city's population.

When the Filipinos speak of the Chinese, officially or unofficially, they estimate their number at 2,000 to 3,000. When Iloilo Chinese estimate their own numbers, confidential estimates often range to 10,000 (whereas officially Chinese accept the Filipino figures to play down their presence). The Chinese are apparently counting by quite a different method than are the Filipinos. For the Chinese, a man is *lán-lâng* ("our people") if he meets the flexible set of criteria which I mentioned above as a working definition of ethnic Chinese.

There are numerous ways to estimate the cultural Chinese population, but one of the better methods is to extrapolate from the Chinese school population.[4] In Iloilo the assumption that all cultural Chinese will send their children to Chinese school is reasonable, since I conducted a survey of Iloilo's schools and found only 3 percent of the racially pure Chinese children not in Chinese school. The main flaw in extrapolating the population from the school age population is that the Chinese population pyramid is not symmetrical due to immigration patterns.

In Iloilo City's four Chinese schools the enrollment in 1972 included 710 pure Chinese, 1,277 mestizos, and 500 pure Filipinos, a total of 2,489 children. Eliminating the pure Filipinos and the students who board because their families live in other cities but adding the small number of dropouts each year gives a total of 1,950 to 2,000. Now, what percentage of the total population do these children represent? Alien registration figures for the province suggest schoolchildren are 22 percent to 34 percent of the total number of Chinese, which is far too low.[5] In a standard population pyramid school-age children are about 40 percent, and in Iloilo they may constitute 50 percent. Thus, Iloilo's ethnic Chinese population is roughly 5,000.

Comparing this total to my previous figures on citizenship, we may conclude that about 40 percent of the ethnic Chinese are Chinese citizens. In a genealogical survey of 70 families, the proportion of Chinese citizens more closely approached 50 percent. Applying this same formula to the national figure of 150,000 Chinese citizens results in a population estimate for ethnic Chinese of about 300,000 to 375,000 (Philippine Census 1960). Estimating the national ethnic population directly from Chinese school enrollment figures of 65,000 in 1971 (McCarthy 1972) gives 195,000.[6] Thus, the ethnic Chinese population of the Philippines is probably between 195,000 and 375,000. With far less care in computation, estimates of 500,000 to 1,000,000 Chinese have been published by the mass media and the government.

Government definitions of citizenship can give misleading results for research purposes. Alien certificate of registration figures copied during fieldwork in 1972 reveal that 49 percent of the 2,221 people shown as Chinese aliens in the province are Philippine-born minors. Forty individuals are pure Filipino women who married their Chinese husbands officially and, thus, lost their Filipino citizenship. Also, there are a large number of mestizo minors who have not yet officially filed for acceptance as Filipino citizens as is their right through their Filipino mothers. So about one-half of all aliens registered are not the "stereotypic" aliens, that is, China-born adults of pure Chinese race, and some do not even qualify as ethnic Chinese.

In the final analysis all government figures, social surveys, and extrapolations therefrom are only estimates and should not be made to carry much burden of proof.

Although the Chinese community is about 50 percent Chinese citizens, the distribution of aliens among the generations is highly skewed. First-generation immigrants, whether they arrived in the 1920s or 1950s, very rarely acquire Filipino citizenship. Each subsequent generation, born and educated in the Philippines, acquires Filipino citizenship at rates of 25 to 50 percent per generation. My collection of sixty-eight genealogies of ethnic Chinese in the city shows that families whose third generation is now about forty-five years old have the highest proportion of Filipino citizens, but immigrant families of more recent arrivals have acquired Filipino citizenship at the fastest rates. Overall, the community is predominantly alien for persons over forty-five and predominantly Filipino citizens for persons under forty-five years old.

The Chinese community is racially heterogeneous, also. Data I gathered from seventy Iloilo Chinese families concerning racial composition by sex and generation show that racial variety has increased with each generation. An

Map 2
Panay Island, Philippines

overall average of 80 percent pure Chinese is thus an excessively coarse measure. The schoolchildren in 1972, it will be recalled, were 64 percent mestizos.

Of the province's cultural Chinese, 90 percent live in Iloilo City, but about 500 (including 300 aliens) reside and work in provincial towns and crossroads. The number of aliens in proportion to the number of ethnic Chinese is larger in the provincial towns because a greater proportion of men marry Filipinas. The subsequent mestizo generations lose contact with the Chinese community of Iloilo City faster than do pure Chinese or urban mestizos. The 1960 census showed that twelve Iloilo provincial towns had more than twenty, but fewer than eighty, Chinese citizens (thus forty or more ethnic Chinese). About two dozen other towns and barrios had one to twenty Chinese citizens.

In general, the populaton has grown faster in Iloilo City than in provincial towns, and a number of provincial towns have actually dropped in population (Census of the Philippines 1903, 1948, 1960). In the 1903 census, Iloilo City contributed 10 percent of the province's Filipino population, while in 1960 it contained over 18 percent. In both 1903 and 1960, the Iloilo City Chinese constituted 85 percent of the province's Chinese population. But the economic prominence of provincial towns with Chinese populations, like Janiuay, Sara, and Balasan, has declined. So, although the percentage of Chinese outside Iloilo City has not decreased, their importance clearly has. In addition, a look at the origins within the Philippines of Chinese migrants to Iloilo City's Chinese community reveals that about two-thirds of the Chinese who come to town have come from provincial areas or smaller Chinese communities. Likewise, those who leave Iloilo's community generally head for the bigger cities such as Manila, Cebu, or Davao. The overall migratory pattern for Filipinos and Chinese alike is, therefore, one of urbanization.

The Chinese community of Iloilo consists of about 490 business families in the city and perhaps 40 or 50 business families in the provincial towns, excluding families without any independent business, such as teachers, salaried executives, and salesmen. The number of households is somewhat fewer than 490, because some families combine into extended families and other large households. My genealogical survey reveals that average family size in terms of surviving children is 5.7 children, which is slightly below the Philippine national average of 6.7. Not all these children are now living in Iloilo with their parents. Average urban household size is 7.5 related Chinese family members, exclusive of nonrelated Chinese, servants, resident employees, and visitors. To include these latter categories of household residents would raise the average to 10 or more people per household.

As we have seen, the Chinese community is residentially concentrated in the downtown business area, operating over 400 shops, services, and offices. The three contiguous neighbor municipalities of Jaro, Molo, and

La Paz each have about 15 to 30 Chinese combined business establishments and residences.

Residence and business are not coterminous now, although they were until the Second World War. From a sample of sixty-three residence histories, I find only 54 percent of the families are living over their downtown businesses, 19 percent are living in apartments elsewhere in the city, and 27 percent are living full-time in country houses, Chinese compounds, or haciendas in neighboring Molo, Jaro, and La Paz. Almost all of these suburban residences were acquired after 1960.

The Iloilo Chinese are immigrants or descendents of immigrants from Fukien and Kwangtung provinces. Depending upon the method of estimating, the Fukienese comprise between 80 percent and 90 percent of the community, with the remainder composed primarily of Cantonese, plus a tiny handful of Swatow and Shanghai Chinese. Doeppers (1971) specified ratios of Cantonese and Fukienese for a number of Philippine cities. By those figures Iloilo is intermediate in its regional diversity, Davao being the greatest Cantonese area (36 percent of its Chinese are Cantonese), and some small towns such as Vigan and Laoag the least heterogeneous (3.5 to 5.7 percent Cantonese). Such variation occurred because Cantonese migrated to towns in demand of their regional occupational specializations, such as tailor shops and restaurants, and to towns where relatives and friends were available to receive newcomers.

To review the definitions of this ethnic group so far, statistics on parentage, citizenship, and residence patterns reveal a population aggregate in the city which can be called Chinese. The operational definition of Chinese used here, involving birth and language, is close to the one Chinese would use for themselves as a group. However, by my count there are 5,000 Chinese; some Chinese estimate their own numbers as high as 10,000. The Philippine government, not interested in counting other than Chinese citizens, arrives at a more conservative figure of 2,200 to 3,000. We may assume that three such disparate figures in the minds of different parties occasionally generate rather different behaviors.

Though actual counts vary widely, population aggregate figures for defining the ethnic group are fairly straightforward. Pinpointing the Chinese as a social structure or an identity group is more complex, partly because these criteria do not define the same groups. Note, for example, the disparity between Iloilo Chinese as a population and as a formal institutional structure. Although the Chinese have 10 to 25 percent of their number distributed about the province and suburbs, the actual seat of the community's cultural activities and organizations is clearly Iloilo City, where almost all provincial Chinese have homes, apartments, or branches of their family business; where their school-age children are enrolled; and where they will be buried in the Chinese cemetery.

Organizationally, Iloilo's Chinese community is defined by its Chinese Buddhist temple, a Chinese cemetery, three nonsectarian Chinese schools, a Jesuit Catholic Chinese school, two competing chambers of commerce, six family associations with four buildings, and numerous other clubs, associations, and business guilds. A synoptic chart of all these institutions is impressive (see chapter 4); also, many organizations make a visible impact in the town with their clubhouses with large identifying signs. The Chinese culture is frequently displayed and renewed during the many large group activities, such as when some Chinese celebrate weddings, honor their deceased, or celebrate Chinese New Year. In small daily behaviors, too, such as breakfasting on *lu kao* (rice porridge) or offering oranges to the household shrine of Koan-Im, the Chinese ethnic group may be identified.

Last, and most germane to this study, the Chinese ethnic group may be recognized by its maintenance of a distinctive merchant culture, a variant of ancient and modern Chinese and Occidental business practices and concepts, modified by the exigencies of the Philippine economy. The thesis developed in chapter 3 is that participation in this merchant culture is one of the best operational definitions of the Philippine Chinese ethnic group, for in Iloilo to cease to be a merchant is to cease to be Chinese.

Self-definition of individuals is the last definitional principle to be examined. Some scholars would argue that an ethnic group like the Philippine Chinese is what the members think it is (Barth 1969:10). In such a case the ethnographer and the actors may perceive the group differently. Some Iloilo Chinese—as I might define them—actively renounce official connections with the Chinese community as an organization and identity group. They avoid participation in social functions and associations./As individuals these people meet the objective criteria of ethnic Chinese, yet they eschew membership in the cultural Chinese community. Filipino and Chinese usage, and thus my own, still considers such individuals Chinese, though in truth they cannot be considered part of the "Chinese community" as I have studied it. Regardless of the reasons behind their self-banishment, such Chinese individuals are not part of the Chinese community, as a locus of organizational and informal social action and as an identity group.[7] Membership in the Chinese community, in practical terms, involves allegiance to Chinese language and culture as Iloilo's Chinese understand it at present: financial contributions to projects, participation in ritual and social events, and priority offered in all activities to members of the group over the wider Filipino society. The definition of Chinese individuals to analyze a Chinese community by population aggregate, on the one hand, and the definition of organizational forms and social action to analyze a Chinese community as a cultural phenomenon, on the other hand, will lead to some contradictions.

Despite the fact that there is no Chinatown and no exclusive neighborhoods and that there is social, geographic, and marital mixing with the wider Filipino society, the Chinese community is still quite visible, active, and self-aware. There is still very much a feeling of "community" among the ethnic Chinese.

One final problem that has not been faced yet in this consideration of definitions of the ethnic group is that of situational variability. In some multiethnic societies, groups and individuals manipulate their ethnic markers or redefine their ethnic boundaries depending upon whom they are addressing, what aspect of daily life is involved, and what goals are being sought (Despres 1975; Nagata 1974; Berreman 1972). Although the Philippine Chinese are not an extreme case of this situational variability, it is a factor in their adjustment to the Philippines. Situational variability of ethnicity seems to be most pronounced in societies where ethnic groups frequently interact and, perhaps also, where the character of that interaction is changing. This is true of Iloilo's Chinese and Filipinos. There is great variety of encounters in which these two groups might meet each other: at the Rotary Club, the mayor's office, a Chinese wedding banquet, a cockfight, on the street, in the market or store, and so forth. In these encounters, the motives of the actors, their self-definitions, and their selection from their repertoire of behaviors will vary. Social scientists are increasingly acknowledging this variability in ethnicity, which has resulted in a sharper distinction between what relationships are evolving between ethnic groups and what is, by nature, merely in flux. I shall return to this problem in the epilog.

In summary, there are at least three distinguishable methods for delineating who or what is Chinese: the population aggregate, the social institution and social action, and the identity as self-defined. Each has a reality and should be referred to when the fullest interpretation of Philippine Chinese cultural behavior is the goal. This eclectic approach is also tempered by the knowledge that definitions of Chinese may be situationally variable as well as in the process of evolving.

1. Exceptions to this statement are the general community studies of Ilocos Chinese (H. Reynolds 1964; I. Reynolds 1964); family studies of Cebu Chinese (Liu, Rubel and Yu 1969); and the urban ecology of Chinese in Dumaguete, Dagupan, and Davao (Doeppers 1971).

2. George Weightman (1960) has suggested that Filipino-Chinese relations in areas of Muslim Philippine culture can be quite different from other areas, so the inclusion of Zamboanga here is tentative.

3. Notable for their rarity are D. Stanley Eitzen's (1968) comparison of Philippine Chinese and Polish Jews; Burton Benedict's (1968) study of family firms and economic development, which includes several overseas merchant minorities; and Edna Bonacich's (1973) model of ethnicity and economic success for merchant minorities. Ivan Light's (1972) comparison of U.S. Black, Japanese, and Chinese commercial success is also excellent, but his attention to the merchant family is slight.

4. I owe this idea to Professor See Chin-ben of De La Salle University, Manila, who briefed me before I began work.

5. That is, compared to my own census surveys.

6. I have assumed that as many as 20 percent of the ethnic Chinese students are not in Chinese schools, following the advice of Father Charles McCarthy and Professor See based on their knowledge of other areas of the country.

7. Personal reasons for self-banishment usually involve a desire to protect one's Filipino citizenship against anti-Chinese sentiments. Occasionally, prospective leaders drop out because of personal feuds with members of the community's leadership.

2

HISTORY OF THE CHINESE IN ILOILO

THE CHINESE HAVE BEEN TRADING with Filipinos in the Iloilo area since perhaps the Sung Dynasty (960-1279 A.D.). Pre-Hispanic Filipino gravesites in the neighboring municipality of Oton have been unearthed containing Sung and Ming porcelains. The first permanent Chinese trade settlements did not arise until the Spanish began colonizing the Iloilo area in the sixteenth century and built fortified compounds which would protect the Chinese from Muslim pirate raids from the southern islands.

The Spanish Regime: 1570 — 1898

There is more documentary evidence of the Chinese colony in Iloilo when the Spanish began keeping tax and court records and other government documents concerning the Chinese.[1] Until the 1860s all Chinese in the western Visayas were confined to the ghetto, or *parian,* of Iloilo's neighboring town of Molo, where the Spanish fort and port were located. They introduced *meng,* or mongo beans, and peanuts to the area, and they were the original builders of the simple muscovado sugar mills and bricked salt-evaporating operations. In the seventeenth and eighteenth centuries, the Chinese concentrated in crafts, importing Chinese goods, and exporting Philippine products to China.

Large communities of mestizo Chinese arose around the Chinese parians of Molo, Cebu, Samar, and Manila. These mestizos were the active processors for the Spaniards of export crops and of native products shipped to Manila, and they were distributors of products around the Visayan area (Wickberg 1965:29). The mestizos, not residentially restricted like the transient Chinese, were thus more economically flexible and developed the towns of Molo and Jaro, where they were the most wealthy and politically dominant permanent residents (Wickberg 1965:34). The Spanish colonies of Molo and Jaro before 1860, then, were composed of a Chinese transient population in a ghetto and an economically dominant, residentially permanent mestizo community managing the towns (Wickberg 1965:28). Iloilo City in that period did not exist, the area being only a salt swamp.

In the period 1855 to 1861, Iloilo and Cebu were the first areas outside Manila to be opened by the Spaniards to international trade. By 1865 the residential and travel restrictions on all foreigners, including the Chinese, were loosened (Loney 1964). Foreigners built the port of Iloilo City, and the Chinese filled it with shops (Loney 1964; Bowring 1859). It was during this midcentury period that the whole colonial economy of the Philippines began gearing up for greater import of manufactures from Europe and mass export of agricultural and raw products. The Chinese began to shift their role in the economy and to supersede the mestizos. The Chinese shifted from being artisans and importers of Chinese goods to coastwide traders, middlemen, and wholesalers. Their system of wholesale-retail marketing networks, the *cabacillo*-agent system, helped deal the fatal blow to the mestizo wholesale trade (Wickberg 1965:77). The mestizos, encouraged by European capital, moved into the pioneer sugar business in Negros island. They also developed weaving and the professions. As the economic take-off of Iloilo occurred in midcentury, then, the Chinese were given an opportunity to profit from it, and they moved strongly ahead.

By 1870 the improvement and increased frequency of transportation made immigration from the ports of Amoy and Macao much easier and cheaper, and Chinese immigrants began to swell the heretofore relatively stable Iloilo Chinese population (Wickberg 1965:61). Government figures show Iloilo's Chinese population by 1881 comprised about 4 percent of the total Chinese population in the Philippines. The Iloilo Chinese themselves estimated their number at about a thousand (*Golden Jubilee Anniversary Yearbook* 1961).

There is little documentary evidence regarding Chinese community life in the late Spanish era, but there is mention of some internally and externally oriented governing organizations. A Cantonese Club or Kng-Tang Hōe-Koán; was established in 1870, and a Hok-Kièn Hōe-Koán is mentioned about the same time (*Golden Jubilee Anniversary Yearbook* 1961).[2] In 1878 Iloilo province's Chinese pressed for and obtained the right to elect a government as liaison to the Spanish colonial bureaucracy (Wickberg 1965:184). Prior to these developments, political organization among the Chinese were primarily a monopoly of ganglike *tong* organizations, or secret societies with politico-religious allegiances (Wickberg 1965:182-84). There were no Chinese schools in the Spanish era; any child who could afford an education returned to the mainland.

During the Spanish era and into the American period after 1898, the Iloilo Chinese community was virtually all male immigrants who left their wives in their hometowns and returned to them as frequently as possible to sire children, visit relatives, and invest their savings. Since men often took Filipino women as common-law wives (and were sometimes encouraged to do so by hometown Chinese families), the subsequent mestizo population was of a balanced sex ratio. Among the pure Chinese, however, as late as 1903 there were only 13 Chinese females per 1,000 males in the Iloilo community (Wickberg 1965:174).

Of the Iloilo community 90 percent were Fukienese. About 50 percent of these were from Chin-kang (Chin-ch'iang) County, Fukien, carrying the same surnames which predominate today: Tan, Uy, Sy, Ong, Chua, Go, Lim, Yu, and Yap (Wickberg 1965:172).[3]

In the second half of the nineteenth century, the growth of Iloilo's economy, the displacement of the mestizos in trade, the development of a Filipino and mestizo *ilustrado* class, and the beginnings of a Filipino nationalism all had a cumulative effect on Filipino-Chinese relations. Wickberg (1965) and A. Tan (1972) have covered the character and history of this relationship in detail. Suffice it to summarize their reports by saying that both the Filipino and Chinese communities began to grow more self-aware, more politically organized, and more competitive with each other in the economy. The Filipinos were developing the ability and the interest in taking control of the Philippine government and economy, and this meant they would be taking a harder appraisal of the Chinese "marginal trading community" in their midst. The Chinese, too, were feeling the "slings and arrows" of imperialism in homeland China and were developing a strong sense of national pride and cultural identity.

The American Regime: 1898-1930

With the signing of the Treaty of Paris in 1899 the Americans became the dominant force in the Philippines. They were slow to have an impact on Iloilo, where, for example, the Spanish language endured as a principal commercial language almost until the Second World War. The parian of Molo was essentially dissolved by the American era, and the Chinese population of about 1,600 were distributed heavily in Molo, Jaro, La Paz and Iloilo City, as well as dispersed into Iloilo province and neighboring provinces on the island. The Americans officially restricted Chinese immigration, but enforcement was lax and means of evading the regulations were numerous (K. K. M. Jensen 1956). The Americans required all immigrants to be family members of merchants already established in the islands. So the Chinese developed a brisk business in illegal documents to demonstrate kinship to Chinese merchants in towns like Iloilo. Every time a merchant returned from a visit to his Chinese hometown, he declared the birth of a son to immigration authorities. The certificate he received was then given or sold to some young man of the right age so that he might immigrate to the Philippines. Contemporary informants estimate over 50 percent of today's China-born adults came to Iloilo under such pretexts. Thus, many Chinese use at least two names: their original surname, by which fellow Chinese know them, and their *teng-ki-toa^n-li,* or the alien registration certificate name, by which they deal with government officials. To this confusion may be added the Filipino names many Chinese have acquired since the Second World War through baptism and the Chinese nickname or "store name" by which acquaintances address one another.

Once the upper levels of Spanish society were removed, the Iloilo Chinese and mestizo communities accelerated their divergence. The mestizos were primarily a Catholic group whose economic interests had changed considerably since their competition with the Buddhist Chinese in the Spanish era. The booming sugar industry of Negros Occidental was the main attraction for the mestizo business sector. Politically, the mestizos had become part and parcel of the ilustrado nationalistic movement by the time of the arrival of the Americans.[4] The ilustrados were not merchants but government and professional figures with families in small landholding positions; thus, they were similar in economic base to the Spanish aristocrats before them.

The Chinese on their part became more self-conscious and coherently organized as political developments on the mainland brought the end of the Ch'ing Dynasty and the establishment of the Republic of China in 1911.

In 1911, representatives from the new Republic of China visited Chinese communities in the Philippine cities of Manila, Iloilo, Cebu, Zamboanga, Sulu, and others, seeking loans to shore up the government (Tan 1972:216-18). In 1914 Sun Yat Sen sent Li Ch'i to Iloilo to form the Tiong Hoa Ké-Mia^n Tóng under the guise of a "reading club" (Tan 1972:227). Leaders of the Iloilo business community founded the Iloilo Chinese People's Society in 1911 to assist the republic financially. They also elected representatives to the first Nanking Assembly and Election of Senators in Peking in 1912 (*Golden Jubilee Anniversary Yearbook* 1961). Within a year this People's Society became Iloilo's first chamber of commerce, the Iloilo Confederation of Chinese Businessmen.

Trade opportunities in Iloilo with large American and British corporations such as Marsman and Company, Ker and Company, and Pacific Trade enlarged the Chinese involvement in pan-Visayan native products and whole-sale-retail distribution. Before the First World War, Chinese virtually monopolized all wholesale-retail operations. By 1918 the Americans and others began to add large import houses to the top of the distribution chain for the Visayas. They connected Iloilo directly into foreign supplies and exported its crops of sugar, copra, and tobacco. While this put pressure on smaller Chinese operations dealing in European imports, the overall effect was simply to increase the number of levels of the Iloilo distribution system and to vastly increase the volume of merchandise moving through the city. Until the

1920s Iloilo was the main supplier of all imports and Manila manufactures to Panay island, Bacolod, and Cebu.

Some Chinese acted as employees, executives, and salesmen as well as distributors for the foreign houses, and other Chinese depended upon the American and English firms as loan guarantors or creditors. Also, the Euro-American firms bought almost all that the Chinese could collect of the native product crops like high-grade tobacco, abaca, sugar, and copra.

There was, however, no group of Chinese operating as *compradores* for the foreigners like those in the Chinese ports of Amoy, Fuchow, Macao, or Canton. In those cities, compradores were Chinese entrepreneurs who connected a foreign firm with its Chinese labor, raw materials, and accommodating officials. In Iloilo, Chinese executives in Euro-American firms were no different from other executives.

The Chinese could sometimes beat the foreigners at their own game. In the 1930s when the Filipino government opened bids for contracts to build the present-day pier around Iloilo's harbor, an American engineering firm bid a low ₱4 million. But a certain Mr. Tan, though not a professional licensed engineer, put his practical experience and the money of some prominent Iloilo Chinese on the line, and bid ₱1.5 million for the same job. The job was awarded to Tan, even though the American firm took the case to the Philippine Supreme Court. The present pier, thus, stands as a monument to Iloilo Chinese enterprise.

After the First World War, some Chinese began to bring their wives along (in some cases, a few of their several wives) to live with them in Iloilo. Before the First World War, among a Chinese population of about 1,160 there were less than a score of Chinese women in the city (Philippine Census 1903, 1918), but by 1918 their numbers had grown to over 140 in a total Chinese population of 1,460. The effect of these women on the community was profound. Foremost was the result that pure Chinese were now born in the Philippine setting. By 1926, about 10 percent of the present-day men and about 30 percent of the present-day women born that year were Philippine-born.[5]

The presence of women and the growth of Chinese families changed the structure of Chinese business. Later we shall see that the partnership system and the combining of capital in joint ventures were jeopardized by the frequent inequality of family status and family size of partners.

The growth of Chinese families and consequent presence of school-age children, coupled with growing cultural pride and political organization, prompted the building of Iloilo's Chinese schools for elementary education. The Chinese Commercial School began in 1911 as a trade school owned by the old Iloilo Confederation of Chinese Businessmen. Sixty students enrolled. The Sun Yat Sen School began in the Cantonese Club through a group of nationalistic Cantonese and Fukienese supporters of the Kuo-

mintang. A third school, the Chiang Kai Shek, was built in 1938 by the
Ong Family Association when one of its leaders effected a split from the
Sun Yat Sen School leadership. These schools were for the elementary
education of the poorer Chinese and mestizo children because most affluent
men sent their children back to China for education and inculcation of
Chinese culture, language, and values. Many Chinese sent some sons, usually
the eldest, to China for elementary education and kept others, usually the
younger ones, in Iloilo schools. This was called "balancing the family,"
since part of a man's family was in China managing affairs and making demands on him from there. Balancing the family distributed responsibility
and liability for children's care, satisfied relatives, and hedged one's bets
on local politico-economic vagaries that might endanger the family. In any
case, after elementary education, further education had to be sought in
China. These mainland-educated sons often returned to the Philippines
to assume control of the family business at the death of the family head.

As Antonio Tan (1972) has demonstrated for Philippine Chinese in general, Iloilo Chinese national consciousness was given direct expression and
reinforcement by vigorous organizing programs in the 1920s and 1930s.
The Kuomintang branch in Iloilo formed in the mid-1920s and helped
operate the Sun Yat Sen School. The Cantonese, as a close-knit minority and
as immigrants from the home province of Chinese nationalism, made the
Cantonese Club a leading community force. The cemetery and Buddhist
temple were built in the mid-1930s, and family associations began to form
and to raise buildings at that time. The Ong family, or Tai-Guan Tong,
began in 1926 and had a building by the 1930s. The Chua-Gua, the Tan
(Yu Uy Tong), and the Tiu-Gan Family Associations appeared and raised
clubhouses in the 1930s.

During this period of intense organizational activity, Manila's Chinese
community took increasingly active leadership over provincial Chinese
developments. Most of the family associations formed through encouragement from Manila's family association headquarters and the Iloilo clubhouses were built partly with Manila funds. The Chinese embassy was in
Manila, and many projects were realized through Iloilo's honorary Chinese
consulate as if through a chain of command.[6] In other words, Manila began
to assume political as well as economic leadership in relation to the provincial Chinese organizations.

From the late Spanish era into the 1920s, Iloilo's Chinese community
was led in matters formal and informal by its wealthy, relatively cultured,
high-living Amoy City Chinese like those belonging to the families of Yap
Tico, Lim Bun So, Tantoco, and a few others such as those surnamed Uy
and Yu. These families hailed from the Ho-san area — Amoy City proper
and Ke-Long-Su island — where European influence was strong and where
big city life and education had their cosmopolitan influence. Immigration

data from Spanish records (Doeppers 1976, personal communication) show these Amoy Chinese were a larger percentage of Iloilo's Chinese than they are now. These Amoy City families made their wealth in exports, textiles, native products, and shipping. They maintained mansions in Amoy, acquired numerous wives and concubines, gambled vigorously, and frequently succumbed to opium habits. As soon as they could afford it, men from other Fukienese countries would acquire houses on Ké-Long-Sū and claim parity with Amoy families. Dissipation, growth of family without commensurate economic success, troubles in China, and the world depression of the 1930s, all served to break up these Amoy families, destroy or disperse their wealth, and remove them from the Iloilo limelight. Many mestizo branches of these Amoy families merged into Filipino society. Some members moved to more enticing economic climates elsewhere in the Philippines, especially the sugar-rich areas or the cities. Some returned to China. Although a number of Iloilo Chinese can show descent from these picturesque clans, the families are clearly gone. With them have gone the small but visible, affluent, fast-living, semicultured, political, and economic elite of the city.

The Pattern of Immigration: 1898-1949

By the second decade of the twentieth century, the history of Iloilo's Chinese community concerns the lives of many of its contemporary members. The growth of the Iloilo enclave depended heavily on the flow of immigrants into its fold. Perhaps underemphasized in all studies of overseas Chinese communities, understanding the selection process is central to understanding this group's growth and structure. Which Chinese ultimately boarded the freighters and ventured abroad? Are the resulting enclaves atypical in some unanalyzed way of South China's culture and character?

The selection process whereby people left their hometowns and chose to live in Iloilo City is difficult to define. The Chinese themselves usually exaggerate and romanticize the randomness of their own biographies. One informant recounts his grandfather's erratic course to the Philippines in the typical manner:

My father's father lived in a village by the shore of a small bay in Fukien where bandits and pirates used to hide. One time a pirate who was befriended by my grandfather gave him a bamboo pillow. Sometime later my grandfather discovered that the pillow contained money. He took the money to Fuchow City to start a buy-and-sell business, but he lost it all playing *mah jongg* and returned penniless to his village and wife. Later, when times were hard, my grandfather consulted a temple fortuneteller and was counseled to seek his fortune in the Lâm-iû^n [Southeast Asia]. It was then he came to Luzon, bringing his wife and nine-year-old son, who became my father.

Less romantically inclined minds in the community will be quick to admit that venturing into the Lâm-iûⁿ was not an act of great courage. They note that for a hundred years most immigrants' voyages were carefully arranged through correspondence and middlemen in their hometowns. They were ushered to and through the big port city of Amoy by these middlemen, who may have been relatives or unfamiliar professionals. They often traveled with several relatives, friends, or townmates; were met in the Philippines by other relatives or agents; and ushered to the town where their benefactor awaited them with room, board, and the chance to learn a trade. James Watson (1975) has shown that an entire Hongkong lineage may organize itself to facilitate this international migration for business. It is very likely that southern Fukienese lineages operated similarly.

The modes of individual immigration are far from random, as will be shown below. But while the selection process sent a stream of certain kinds of men and boys (and in recent history, women, elders, and infants) to Iloilo's community, the community has also developed its form reflexively from its tasks of receiving, coaching, protecting, and organizing this stream of immigrants. In subsequent chapters it shall be noted that Iloilo's chambers of commerce and family associations, as well as its informal structures of business and family, have been geared to assist in this immigrant flux. Their structures and functions have changed in response to changes in immigration trends.

Returning for the time being to individual immigration, the method of one's arrival and sojourn has followed a definite pattern in the lives of most of the immigrants who comprise part of the community today.

Whether assisted in emigrating by his relatives or a professional agent, a young man would embark for the Philippines in his late adolescence or early manhood. If a young man were the first of his immediate family to come to the Philippines, he was on average somewhat older than peers who already had fathers or grandfathers *in situ* to take them in. The latter group had a more secure standing and brighter economic outlook in advance, despite their tender years. Jacques Amyot (1960) found that, on the average, the Manila immigrants came at ages twelve to sixteen. My data on Iloilo Chinese, acquired from immigration records of 324 men, found such a young age to be typical only of immigrants with one or two generations of relatives already in the country. Immigrants without preceding close family relatives in the Philippines averaged between nineteen and twenty years old. Conceivably, the difference in average age of immigrants between Manila and Iloilo is due to the smallness and marginality of a provincial community like Iloilo. A large community like Manila can provide more protection and more of the comforts and atmosphere of home for the younger immigrants.

Obtaining access to a visa to immigrate to the Philippines required one to show kinship to a merchant already present. For some men this meant purchase of the teng-ki-toa^n-li, or alien certificate of registration. Other men had relatives to claim them. Still other men (and some young women) were adopted by childless Chinese men in the Philippines. At least one of the foster parents was always Chinese; Filipinos did not adopt Chinese. These adopted (or phō-ê) sons and daughters became the heirs for their foster parents and assumed all the duties and privileges of natural children. Not infrequently a couple would acquire their adopted child from a brother or sister with many offspring, thus keeping the child within the family. Today some Iloilo families are composed exclusively of adopted sons and daughters.

The teng-ki-toa^n-li system, which was only a kinship on paper, did not constitute adoption; many men never met their supposed "certificate parents." But teng-ki-toa^n-li "brothers," entering the country as sons of the same man, though perhaps not mutually related, would sometimes develop close personal ties if they were employed together by their sponsor. Some strong lifetime brotherhoods between Iloilo Chinese leaders were created because of this propinquity in immigration histories.

Another system which brought some of the earlier Chinese women in Iloilo was the concubine, or mûi^n-tsai, system. In the 1920s and 1930s when many Iloilo men had no wives, some of the affluent had several — their official wives as well as several young concubines. The latter are technically retainers or handmaidens of one's official wife, but their position in Iloilo (and probably in China) was virtually identical to that of the concubine. Some of these concubines later became business and political matriarchs with the passing of their powerful husbands and rivals; others escaped or were released at an early age and married other Chinese in the community.

The places of embarkation in China were the steamship ports of Amoy City, Fukien, and Macao, near Kwangtung. Immigrants are officially registered as residents of those points. All Cantonese in fact are called Macaos by the Filipinos in Iloilo. Today about 10 percent of the Iloilo community are Cantonese or Cantonese-Filipino mestizos, though there is reason to suspect that before the Second World War they represented a larger percentage of the immigrants to Iloilo. The present Cantonese population has been decreasing relative to the rest of the community because proportionately more Cantonese than Fukienese have returned to China since the Second World War, or emigrated to Hongkong or the United States.

Iloilo's immigrants came from fairly specific areas within Fukien and Kwangtung. Wickberg's (1965) data from the Spanish era suggest that the composition of the Iloilo community in terms of regional origin has not fluctuated much. Table 1 lists the proportions of Fukienese immigrants from the most common counties. Included are comparative data from Doepper's (1971) study of other provincial Chinese communities. Iloilo has always consisted of 50 to 60 percent Chin-kang (Chin-ch'iang) County

immigrants, but other provincial towns differ quite strikingly in their composition. Iloilo also shows more heterogeneity than other communities,
with two other Fukien counties contributing over 10 percent each to
the population.

Table 1

Regional Origin of Fukienese Immigrants in Iloilo
City, Dumaguete, Dagupan, and Davao

Hsien (County) of Origin	Percent from each county			
	Iloilo City	Dumaguete	Dagupan	Davao
Chin-ch'iang	59.0%	8.5%	90.5%	6.4%
Nan-an	23.4	5.1	5.8	81.6
Ho-shan*	7.0	69.5	0.7	3.5
Tung-an	0.2	5.1	–	0.6
Lung-chi	–	–	1.5	4.4
An-chi	0.7	3.4	–	0.3
Hui-an	3.0	–	0.7	0.6
Other *hsien*	1.5	8.5	0.7	2.6
Total percent	99.8	100.1	99.9	100.0
N	554	59	137	343

NOTE: Data gathered from the Iloilo Chinese cemetery in 1972 by this writer. Data
on Dumaguete, Dagupan, and Davao were gathered by Doeppers (1971). Place names
are rendered in Mandarin.

*Combined with the total from Hsia-men (Amoy City), which is a separate district
within Ho-shan.

Iloilo has been stable in its regional composition primarily because immigration is a kin-based phenomenon. Each regional group in a Chinese
community attracts a proportionate number of its own kin and townmates.
The reason for differences between provincial towns is harder to pinpoint.
Doeppers (1971) attributes the differences to the towns' small size; random
factors as much as anything and a process akin to genetic drift provide
each town with a different starter population and a particular trend in regional recruitment.

   Iloilo's Cantonese minority are immigrants or descendants of immigrants
primarily from the *sse-yap*, or four-dialect region, of Kwangtung province,
which contains Tai-shan, Kai-ping, Hsin-hui, and En-ping. According to
tombstones in Iloilo's Chinese cemetery, which are not a random sample

but accord with my conversations about Cantonese origins, 56 percent of Iloilo's Cantonese are from Tai-shan County, and 34 percent are from Kaiping County. Next most common, at 6 percent, are those originating in the Nan-hai area. The prominence of sse-yap Cantonese in the Philippines and in all overseas populations can be attributed to their proximity to the ports of Hongkong and Macao, their overpopulation, and their meager agricultural resources. It was both urgent and easy to leave their homeland.

The same pattern applies to the Fukienese counties of origin. They are all contiguous and near Amoy's port. Fuchow, the capital city of Fukien farther north on the coast, though a larger city, has sent virtually no Chinese to the Philippines. The foreign steamship lines ran from Amoy City to Manila and Cebu or Iloilo, and the majority of Philippine Chinese came through this pipeline.

Because immigrants proceeded to locales where they had contacts to help them, each Philippine Chinese community represents not only various Fukienese counties but also certain townships and villages. There is an association of Iloilo's immigrants with specific townships within particular counties. Within a given Chinese village only a few surnames predominate, so villagemates who followed one another to Iloilo frequently have the same surname. The counties of Chin-ch'iang and Nan-an, from which many of Iloilo's Chinese emigrated, are represented by only a few townships, but these are responsible for large proportions of particular Iloilo Chinese surnames. Four Chin-chi'iang townships provide most of the numerous Iloilo Chinese surnamed Chu, Huan, Sy, and Ang. Four Nan-an townships provide most of those of the families Yu, Po, Lim, and Cheng, all but the last of which are numerous. Amoy City area has contributed large numbers of those surnamed Tan, Yap, Sun, and Lim. These four are the surnames borne by most of the prewar elite of Iloilo City.

These surnames which cluster into certain townships of origin are also the most numerous in Iloilo. There are about thirty-five Fukienese surnames represented in Iloilo, of which eight have at least 5 percent of the total: Tan (11%), Uy (11%), Ong (8%), Lim (7%), Chua (7%), Go (6%), Yu (5%), and Sy (5%). The remaining twenty-five or so names comprise 40 percent of the community.

When the immigrants from China touched land, they usually went directly to their predesignated sponsor's locale. After marriage they became quite sedentary. Of a sample of thirty-six immigrants to Iloilo, 80 percent came directly or by way of short stays in Mindanao or neighboring Bacolod. The Cantonese as a rule have had more varied migration histories, both outside and within the Philippines. Their immigration history often includes sojourns in Hongkong or North America, and ranges from Central Luzon to Davao within the Philippines.

Iloilo's Chinese community is not a temporary conglomeration of geo-graphically mobile families. Over 60 percent of the families have lived in the city throughout the present generation. Admittedly, a number of these families are Philippine-born. But the first immigrant generation among the sixty-four families averaged 90 percent of their lifetime in Iloilo City, the second generation averaged 72 to 80 percent of their life spent in the city, and the third generation 87 to 96 percent. Clearly, most Iloilo families are stable residents in terms of their own life histories.

The personal histories of the 20 percent of the community who have spent considerable time elsewhere in the Philippines practically defy generalization. Some men have lived in twenty places in the last twenty years, others in but one place, and some have lived in numerous places in just the last five years. Those who have come to Iloilo after a stay elsewhere generally come from one of three places. They come from Manila, the largest Chinese community in the country and the stopover place for most immigrants on their way to residence in the provinces. They may come from provincial Iloilo towns like Janiuay or Balasan, or from more distant towns of Panay island like Roxas City and Kalibo, reflecting the trend of migration to urban centers mentioned earlier. Internal immigrants may also come from Bacolod on nearby Negros island. It is a bustling sugar trading town originally pioneered by Iloilo Chinese and mestizos and, thus, has numerous business and kin ties to Iloilo.

When immigrants came to Iloilo during the American era and perhaps before as well, they sometimes resided near members of their own *tzu* (lineage) or village group. While not a predominant pattern, this residential clustering can still be detected in the slight clustering of Tans in textiles on one street, Cantonese in another block, Yus and Yaps in textiles along another street, and across the way a group of Chuas in hardware. On the edge of the city and in Jaro and Molo, too, family and villagemate clusters of *sari-sari* (general) stores and textile stores occurred, too. Most of these clus-ters, however, have been obscured by the growth of the city and mobility of family members.

Though settled in Iloilo City, an immigrant made periodic trips to his hometown if his financial progress allowed it or if a sponsor financed the trip. Informants recall that by the 1930s the world economic depression and vigorous competition between shipping lines had driven the fare to Amoy down to about ₱5 (about U.S. $2.50). Other informants wistfully recall the days of long credit from the big foreign trading houses in Iloilo. In the 1920s and 1930s, they claim, a man could get ninety days or more credit on goods, sell them at cost, speculate with the resulting cash usually in a loan at high interest, take a trip to his hometown on part of it, and return, all within the limit of the credit period. Apocryphal or not, the story suggests that China visits were frequent and not very difficult. Most men visited China at least once every two years. Their wives or sisters, if they immigrated to Iloilo, tended to take trips far less often. Once a man acquired a Chinese family in Iloilo, his roots in China greatly weakened.

As mentioned previously, sons were sent back to China for education, especially for the inculcation of Chinese values. Of a sample of sixty-two families, whether China-born or not, 13 percent sent sons back to Chinese hometowns, Amoy City, Hongkong, or to Taiwan for education. Women were not sent back for education, but in several cases men with Philippine-based families sent their daughters back to relatives so they would be raised and married in a Chinese environment.

In the years after the Second World War, there was a large amount of visiting in China by Iloilo families to check up on relatives and to survey war damage to their property. It was at this time, informants claim, that many Cantonese returned to China for good. Also at this time many Fukienese made family adjustments: bringing wives and sons out, taking daughters and grandparents in, leaving some relatives in Hongkong, and so on. They were adjusting both to the new politically independent status of the Philippines and the increasing civil war strife in China.

After the 1949 Communist victory, immigration flow between China and the Philippines ceased except for some emergency exodus and illegal immigration. Few if any immigrants came to Iloilo from Taiwan; some who escaped or immigrated to Hongkong did continue to arrive in the Philippines but only if they had immediate family to receive them or if they had forged papers. Many of the immigrants from China (and visitors to China) during the 1950s and 1960s appear to have been much older Chinese; they chose to be buried in China hometowns or they sought support from their children in the Philippines.

In the early 1970s, as Asian attitudes toward mainland China's government softened somewhat, it became popular for well-to-do newlyweds to take a honeymoon tour of China via Hongkong. Martial law in the Philippines in 1972 put a damper on this practice.

According to the older immigrants' point of view, the ultimate goal of venturing to the Philippines was to make a fortune and retire in comfort to one's hometown or the cosmopolitan life of Amoy and Ké-Lŏng-Sū island. In the twentieth century there was a partial reversal of this view. Success in business was such a heady thrill, and the political climate in China was so uninviting that many persons remained in Iloilo until they were about to die. It was during the 1930s that the Chinese cemetery began to grow, and from the impressive grandeur of its tombs, it is clear that not all wealthy people desired burial in China.

The most successful merchants were the least geographically mobile. A large income brought in a larger income, and with no ceiling in sight there was no desire to break the pattern. Those who moved away from Iloilo or returned to China before senility were usually those who had failed and had to move to save face or to repair to their village to recoup their losses. It is evident from the residence histories of a random sample of sixty-four Iloilo men, Philippine-born or immigrants, that those men who had difficulty starting were those who moved about the Philippines the most. The more one succeeded the more he entrenched his position, bringing over wives, sons, nephews, maids, and parents.

Even though Iloilo's families have been quite sedentary, the community lacks the genealogical time depth of Manila's larger Chinese enclave. Jacques Amyot's (1960) one-hundred-family sample in Manila found 29 percent to have a history of five or more generations in the Philippines. My survey of sixty-eight families found only 4 percent of that length. It is possible that Amyot's sample does not include full representation of newer immigrant families, as they were the hardest for him to interview. In any case, the number of five-generation Manila families still prompts the following conclusions. Even though Iloilo's Chinese community is as old as Manila's, the individual families who compose it do not seem to endure as long within its boundaries. The most logical explanation for Iloilo's shorter genealogical depth is that after about three generations Iloilo's Chinese leave the Chinese community physically or culturally. Iloilo's smaller size and lack of a defined Chinatown have meant its Chinese immigrants are more exposed culturally to Filipino society. Christianization, intermarriage, and change of occupation away from merchant culture have drawn some participants closer to Filipinos and farther from the Chinese. An alternate explanation, that the older immigrant generation families migrated to Manila where they can survive culturally intact, is not borne out by the oral history of the community.

As mentioned, the trend of immigrants to reside permanently in Iloilo City became more pronounced and more in opposition to the old Chinese ideal during the American era of Philippine prosperity. One of the developments forcing the hand of Iloilo's immigrants was the worsening political situation in China in the 1920s and especially in the 1930s, chronicled by A. Tan (1972). The Shantung Incident in 1929, the occupation of Manchuria in 1931, and the steady move toward their home provinces by the Japanese prompted many men to call their wives and children from China to the relative safety of the Philippines. By 1939 there were 841 Chinese women recorded in Iloilo province, bringing the Chinese sex ratio to 317:100, up from 1173:100 in 1918 (Census of the Philippines 1918, 1939). For the first time, Iloilo's Chinese community began to consist primarily of families. Fewer children were sent back to the unsettled mainland for schooling. Iloilo's Chinese schools grew and improved as their charges' parents donated funds for buildings and teachers. By 1939, the Chinese Commercial School's population was 500, and the Sun Yat Sen School had about another 500 students (*Sun Yat Sen High School Yearbook* 1963).

Facing the Problems of the 1930s

Three knotty problems became increasingly troublesome through the 1930s in Iloilo and in all Philippine Chinese communities. One was the influx of Japanese imperial business interests and the consequent building of a Japanese fifth column in Philippine cities. The Japanese brought cheaply manufactured goods and proved ferocious competitors in the department store type of operation, much as the Indians from the Bombay region provide competition in contemporary Iloilo. The Iloilo merchant corps was then further subdivided into a many-layered multinational operation with the large Euro-American import-export houses on top and the Chinese wholesale-retailers next. The Japanese cut themselves into this operation by short-circuiting the upper supply channels with their own merchandise. The Filipinos were the last in the distribution system as agricultural producers, marketers of livestock and fresh foods, and as retail customers.[7].

In addition to adding to the complexity and competition in the distribution system, the Japanese were alleged to be secret agents for the Japanese army, reporting on Filipino-American military status and recording anti-Japanese treatment by the Chinese. This allegation was subsequently justified, for the Chinese anti-Japanese boycott leaders and other resisters suffered heavily when war hit the city.

The second severe problem was worldwide: the depression on the international market of prices for the native products which were Iloilo's mainstay, such as copra, sugar, abaca, rice, tobacco and corn. A number of prominent families in Iloilo whose fortunes lay in these commodities went bankrupt. America's own severe economic depression and inability to buy Iloilo's goods made the depression even more immediately felt.

The third problem was particular to the Chinese: the development (or suspected blossoming) of Communist sympathizers among a Chinese community which predominantly favored the Kuomintang. A. Tan (1972) reports that Chinese labor unions were active in the Philippines as early as 1922, when they formed leftist-leaning branches in Iloilo and Cebu.[8] By the 1930s the Filipino and Filipino-Chinese newspapers alike viewed these Communist and leftist groups in Manila, Cebu, and Iloilo as an active threat to the Philippines.

The split between Kuomintang and Communist sympathizers became endemic in Iloilo, especially in the rivalry between two of the schools: the Sun Yat Sen, run by the Cantonese Club and KMT supporters, versus the Chinese Commercial School, run by the old Confederation of Chinese Businessmen who by then called themselves simply the Chinese Chamber of Commerce. The Chamber was apparently somewhat exclusive in its membership and insisted on a neutral political stand in contrast to the KMT's partiality. Yet some of the Chamber's members and some of Chinese Commercial's teachers were Communist sympathizers, according to contemporary members of the same organization. As the situation on the mainland worsened, Chinese common cause against the Japanese overshadowed these political differences. But the rivalry was intense and showed itself in numerous ways. Few marriages occurred between Sun Yat Sen and Chinese Commercial School graduates. Gangs of students from the two schools occasionally skirmished. Few, if any, Cantonese attended Chinese Commercial School. Personal rivalries among the community's leaders tended to drive them into opposite school boards to advertise their mutual animosity. One Kuomintang supporter and community leader, Mr. Ongcu, was unwilling to join his antagonists at Chinese Commercial when he clashed with his fellow boardsmen at Sun Yat Sen School. So he began his own school, Chiang Kai Shek, in 1939. It operates to this day as a small feeder school to Sun Yat Sen.

The plight of the Chinese mainland under encroachment by the Japanese during the 1930s intensified money-raising and patriotic activities among all of Iloilo's Chinese organizations. The honorary consul of Iloilo for Chiang Kai Shek's government, with the Kuomintang, channeled many projects through the Sun Yat Sen and Chiang Kai Shek schools. The Chinese Chamber of Commerce, through Chinese Commercial School, also undertook projects. In addition, a number of separate groups sprang up to solicit help for the struggling republic. Beginning in 1931 with the occupation of Manchuria, Philippine Chinese organized an anti-Japanese boycott, neither supplying nor purchasing Japanese goods nor dealing with Japanese stores. If Iloilo was typical, however, this boycott was not complete, for some men in the 1930s did extensive business with the Japanese in Iloilo. Generally, however, the boycott was influential, and Japanese resentment of it found expression during the Occupation.

The Chinese Aircraft Construction Corporation, a fund-raising group founded in Fukien in 1928-29, organized a branch in Iloilo in the 1930s. Board members included men from both Sun Yat Sen and Chinese Commercial's leadership. After the Shantung Incident of 1929 and the Japanese encroachment in Manchuria in 1931, the Filipino-Chinese Save the Country committees formed all over the Philippines, including Iloilo. The Committee pledged to build a war fund, and zealous Iloilo members pushed through a proposal to donate a certain percentage of their yearly income (Tan 1972). Other committees like the Filipino-Chinese Support the Anti-Japanese Campaign Committee established branches in Iloilo, intensifying fund-raising activities. The overseas Chinese quite justifiably felt themselves to be the main financiers of the 1911 Revolution and the founding of the republic, and the mainland's nationalists left no plea unspoken to utilize this pride in an attempt to save the republic.

The Japanese Occupation

When the Second World War came to the Philippines in 1942, Japanese occupation of Iloilo was fast and complete. After Pearl Harbor, the Euro-Americans, selling their stocks at base prices to the Chinese, had evacuated Iloilo. Realizing that war and probably occupation were imminent, the Chinese began stockpiling this merchandise, splitting up their families, burying their valuables, and preparing for escape to the mountains. Most quality canned goods and imports were buried. Cash was converted to coins, stuffed into lead pipes, covered with wax, and also buried.

The first part of the war, beginning in December 1941 and extending for six to twelve months, was a time of evacuation in which most Chinese closed up their shops and waited in provincial barrios to see what would develop after occupation. Some men, because of their strong Kuomintang ties or work with the Filipino guerrillas, remained in the mountains for the entire war.

After bombing the city into submission, the Japanese occupied Iloilo in April 1942. With the help of detailed intelligence from the Japanese economic interests in town, the Japanese army quickly hunted down and imprisoned the majority of the city's Chinese anti-Japanese movement. These leaders were interrogated, ransomed for large sums, and made to form a "provisional leadership" as a price control board and liaison to the Chinese. This organization, called the Overseas Chinese Cooperation Society (Hôa-Kiâu Ha̍p-Hōe), was also required to raise periodic "friendship" payments for the occupation army.

After occupation was complete, the Japanese issued commands for all Chinese to return to the city for surveillance. Delinquents were to be executed. Late in 1942 most of Iloilo's provincial and city Chinese returned to Iloilo and recommenced some semblance of "business as usual." Most informants today claim that the decision to comply was not hard to make: even if a Chinese avoided capture and execution by the Japanese by hiding in the barrios, he was constantly raided and his merchandise confiscated by the Filipino guerillas.

Chinese did participate in the Resistance, however. The Chinese Chamber of Commerce surreptitiously supported a group of Chinese guerrillas and contact men and a rescue team for downed Allied fliers (*Golden Jubilee Anniversary Yearbook* 1961). The Kuomintang also acted as middlemen to supply goods and information to guerrillas. A large number of proguerrilla Chinese camped in the mountains near Passi, Iloilo province, were ambushed and massacred in September 1943. According to one of those who escaped, eighty-five Chinese died. The monument to those massacred stands in Iloilo's Chinese cemetery.

The Japanese closed all the town's banks and froze their funds. Travel for commercial purposes to Manila and other supply centers was slow, restricted, and dangerous. Chinese with funds in the banks and suppliers in other cities were forced to fall back on other means of support. Some with large stocks rationed them out for sale. Most Chinese moved into the transportation and distribution of agricultural produce, the black market, or cottage industry manufacture of soap, cigarettes, shoes, and other such basic commodities.

The war years' hardships brought the Filipinos and Chinese into closer mutual dependence and closer social relations. The Chinese supplied Filipino guerrillas, but many Chinese were also dependent on Filipino friends and godparents whose wealth was in their land and, thus, still accessible. Long and lonely residence in the barrios prompted many Chinese men to marry local Filipino women, both for protection and for companionship. The ensuing kin ties to Filipinos throughout the province are still recognized and sometimes active today. Kin and fictive kin connections to important Filipinos in the occupation government saved the lives of suspected Chinese guerrillas and resisters on numerous occasions.

Most Chinese lived out the war in a tenuous middle ground. They lived in the city and were required to entertain and do business with the Japanese army, on the one hand, and to harbor, support, and inform the Filipino guerillas, on the other.

In the last two years of the war, even the most abundant Chinese stocks began running out. Japanese Occupation currency (called "Micky Mouse" money) became wildly inflated, thousands of pesos being required to purchase a sack of rice. Coastal shipping was treacherous due to submarines. Harsh treatment of Chinese by ever more desperate guerrillas in search of supplies was also common. When Allied Forces bombed the city in 1945 to drive out the Japanese, much of the business district was again destroyed.

Postwar Recovery

American armed forces arrived in Iloilo in 1945. Their appearance meant war reparations money, G.I. surplus goods, a vigorous black market in commodities, back pay for guerrillas, and a new supply of money-laden American customers, all of which the Chinese moved to tap. The Chinese were welcomed by the G.I.'s as barbers, launderers, cooks, and middlemen. Chinese dug up whiskey and opened impromptu bars for American soldiers, receiving American cigarettes and canned goods in payment. They sold Chinese memorabilia as souvenirs. Many Chinese guerrillas, both legitimate and bogus, appeared on back payrolls. G.I. hardware, machinery, lumber, and foodstuffs passed through Chinese hands on the way to wildly profitable sales in provincial areas that only the Chinese could reach. With a return to safe shipping, Chinese set sail in all manner of skiffs and scows to revive the flow of Iloilo's native products to the starved southern islands and the eastern Visayas. These shipping ventures, filled with war surplus on the return trip, quadrupled capital with each voyage.

The postwar years were an enormous boom time for Iloilo due to her major role as distributor of imports and Manila goods throughout the Visayas. Even simple retail sales of textiles could net 30 percent profit regularly. Some men discovered that they could ship small, profitable department store items to their Iloilo stores by air freight, beating the competition and multiplying profits. Most of Iloilo's richest and most prominent men today made their fortunes in the flow of G. I. goods and consumer items in the early postwar years.

The Chinese community regrouped immediately after the war to restore schools, clubhouses, customs, and internecine feuds. There was a torrent of visits to hometowns in China to survey damage to family and possessions there. Banking operations between China and the Filipino-Chinese reopened and remittances to war-ravaged Canton and Fukien recommenced.

The internecine feuding within Iloilo resumed as the obstacles to Nacionalist versus Communist enmity in China dissolved. Members of the Chinese Chamber of Commerce, Kuomintang, and a number of independents constantly flung accusations at one another of collaboration with the Japanese. Informants recall that Communist propaganda and fund-raising efforts were intense in the early postwar years and centered on some of the personnel of Chinese Commercial School. When the Communist takeover of China was complete in 1949, it coincided with an anti-Communist atmosphere in the Philippines under President Magsaysay and set the scene for some vigorous scapegoating and a rightist backlash. Backed by the Philippine Constabulary, the Kuomintang, through its embassy and consulates, went in search of Communist sympathizers. Members of the Chinese Chamber of Commerce and some of Chinese Commercial School's teachers were especially persecuted. Leaders of the Chinese Commercial School were accused of misuse of anti-Communist campaign funds. Some were drummed out of community leadership positions, and others encouraged to leave town. Teachers and others suspected of inculcating Communist sympathies were arrested and detained in Camp Crame, Manila. Many of these were subsequently released without charges. But the Nacionalist embassy, in partnership with the Filipino-Chinese schools, revoked these teachers' credentials and so some were forced to leave the country. The hard feelings between community factions because of this partisanship and subsequent persecution rankle among Iloilo's Chinese even today.

The foundation in 1954 of Iloilo's branch of the Federation of Filipino-Chinese Chambers of Commerce, which was oriented to the embassy of the Republic of China, solidified the split between the factions. This federation was ostensibly a clearing house for the half dozen or so business guilds within the city and a liaison to a central Manila Federation of Filipino-Chinese Chambers of Commerce. But the effect of its creation was to solidify the split between the schools, chambers of commerce, and political ideologies within the Iloilo community.

To further complicate the organizational picture of the town, refugee Jesuit priests from China constructed the Santa Maria Chinese Catholic Church and School in 1954 with support from a few Chinese who embraced Catholicism. This school was implicitly meant to serve as a neutral meeting ground for the Chinese, and to this day it is a neutral territory.[9] However, because of pressure from the Nationalist faction and because of its proximity to Sun Yat Sen School, Santa Maria is under the school's informal tutelage for Chinese education.

Life in the Philippines: 1946 to the Present

Regardless of political allegiances, all of Iloilo's Chinese were hard hit by the 1949 Communist victory, which meant a virtual severance of contact with China. Pro-Nationalist banks closed and evacuated to Taiwan, and many Iloilo investors never heard further about their deposits. Lands and houses in Fukien and Kwangtung were confiscated by the new mainland government, and mainland branches of Iloilo businesses closed. Men were cut off from their families. Though it was still possible to get remittances to China (ignoring the danger of this in the anti-Communist climate of the Philippines), men could no longer return for visits or investments nor send their sons for education. Taiwan replaced China as the seat of education, but far fewer men availed themselves of this replacement. Iloilo's Chinese schools added high schools in 1949 (Sun Yat Sen) and 1955 (Chinese Commercial). Most residents faced with resignation the prospect of no more immigration or personal contact from China.

With the closing of the mainland and the isolation of China from the rest of Asia, provincial Southeast Asian Chinese communities have turned more to their own national primate cities, such as Manila, Singapore, or Bangkok, where the larger, richer congregations of Chinese serve as cultural exemplars and as sources of leadership, funds, and marriage partners.

The change in relations with China was only one of the major readjustments necessary after the Second World War. Equally important was the Philippines' new political independence and the growing Filipino nationalistic desire to restrict Chinese business operations in the Philippines. George Weightman (1960) and K. K. Myint Jensen (1956), among others, have carefully chronicled the growth of nationalistic sentiments and legislation regarding the economy.[10] Suffice it to observe here that not since the pre-1865 Spanish era had such sweeping economic legislation been aimed at a national minority.

Few discriminatory acts were enacted against the Chinese during the American regime until the Philippine Constitution was instituted in 1934. Americans had attempted to restrict immigration but were not particularly successful. The Bookkeeping Act had been   passed in 1921 but because of appeals was not administered until 1938. The law required Chinese to keep their books in English or Filipino as well as Chinese, or pay a translator to prepare them for tax auditing. The Coastwise Shipping Trade Act theoretically cut the Chinese out of coastal shipping in 1923. Provisions in the new Commonwealth Constitution of 1934 excluded Chinese citizens from owning agricultural land, timber, mineral lands, utilities, or inheriting the same, and limited their control of corporations to less than 40 percent (Alip 1959). Banking services were nationalized, requiring a majority of Filipino citizens on their boards. Selling in public markets was restricted to Filipino citizens. In 1938 an Anti-Dummy Law sought to prevent Chinese citizens from using Filipino citizens as "front men" for their business ventures with the object of circumventing the law. In 1954 a prosecuting board was appointed to police these ownership activities and enforce the Anti-Dummy Law.

The Import Business Nationalization Act of 1953 specified that no aliens could apply for licenses and that no current alien importers would be allotted any more   dollars for foreign trade. Aliens were also prohibited from being licensed as engineers, architects, chemists, pharmacists, dentists, accountants, nurses, optometrists, and lawyers. This restriction incidentally had the effect of driving many talented Chinese citizens back into commerce, intensifying their role in business.

The most crucial nationalization acts with the widest impact were the Retail Trade Nationalization Law of 1955 and the Rice-Corn Nationalization Act of 1960. The Retail Trade Law forbade any alien to acquire new retail licenses and required present alien holders of licenses to liquidate upon death or retirement. Partnerships or corporations of aliens were to be dissolved within ten years. New retail corporations required 60 percent Filipino citizen ownership. Later riders to the bill stipulated that no Chinese citizen could be employed in retail trade. The Rice-Corn Nationalization Act proceeded in like terms for the operations of all wholesale, retail, warehousing, and transportation businesses involved in rice and corn. Because in Iloilo virtually all large-scale commerce in agricultural products was handled by Chinese and because this business constituted the wealth of the province, the Chinese businessmen were acutely affected.

The laws in print were not identical to the laws in execution, and there was still some breathing room for the generation of businessmen already in commerce in the 1950s. For the first time, Chinese actively sought Filipino citizenship, an act which in prewar years was viewed with disdain. A man could have his son, Philippine-born and Philippine-educated, awarded Filipino citizenship, then turn the enterprise — on paper only, of course — over to him. Technically a violation of the Anti-Dummy Law, this common practice was viewed as necessary to preserve the son's birthright. Most dummies in Iloilo were and are of this sort. In the late 1950s and early 1960s the Filipino-citizen proportion of the Chinese community grew rapidly: in 1963, 4 percent of the graduates of elementary school were Filipino citizens, but in 1972, 60 percent of the student body were Filipino citizens. Aliens drop from the city's immigration records through transfer of citizenship at the rate of only forty a year, but larger proportions of Filipino-citizen babies are born in the community each year because the naturalized Filipino citizens are precisely those of childbearing age.

Laws were flexible in execution in individual cases, too, because of the relationship between the Chinese business community and the local government. Not only were there personal *utang,* or debt, relations between high officials and individual Iloilo Chinese which resulted in useful connections, but the bureaucracy made a routine practice of collection *tong,* or bribes. In this way a number of laws were stricter in the books than in practice.

The formation of specialized and full-time lobby organizations to meet with government officials, mediate the new rules, and collect tong increased the organizational complexity of the Chinese community. A Rice and Corn Dealers' Association appeared after the Rice-Corn Nationalization Act of 1960. After the imposition of a new city cigarette tax in 1971, the Cigarette Dealers' Association of Iloilo formed to protect its members from individual extortion. In addition to these specific associations, all organizations in town, whether chambers of commerce or family associations, created public relations offices. The public relations officers were Filipino-citizen Chinese who were versed in Filipino customs, had contacts, and were fluent in the Ilongo dialect and English. The creation of nationalization laws, or even the threat of such laws on local or national levels, produced a flurry of organizing, public relations, lobbying, entertaining, and petitioning by Iloilo's chambers of commerce and business associations. As we shall see in chapters 4 and 5, the organizational ability of the Chinese and the flexibility of the Filipinos meant that most Chinese businessmen could adjust their procedures and their lives slightly and continue with business as usual, in spite of the apparent formidability of the postwar nationalization campaign.

Although migration to and from China had come to an end, the Chinese did not cease their migratory habits entirely but adjusted them to correspond with national and local conditions in the Philippines. Because of the stiff nationalization campaign, many Chinese began to look elsewhere for security and prosperity. As the Filipinos became caught up in a mass migration to the United States, Philippine Chinese were in the vanguard, sending sons and daughters as nurses, engineers, and doctors to America, Canada, Europe, Hongkong, and to a lesser degree, Taiwan. By 1972 many Iloilo Chinese families had established individuals and family branches in such countries. The Cantonese, who often have friends and relatives in the United States, have an immigration rate to the U.S. higher than the Chinese average. Very few Chinese emigrate to other Asian or Southeast Asian countries.

Although Iloilo's Chinese population is relatively sedentary, there is nevertheless some internal migration in the Philippines as men attempt to improve their lot. In Iloilo this migration takes the form of a constant outflow of people to more prosperous cities like Manila and Bacolod. One informant estimated that one-quarter of his 1962 high school graduating class at Sun Yat Sen School left town for economic opportunities elsewhere. Although the Philippine Chinese are ideally strictly patrilocal, the pattern is often broken when Iloilo sons marry brides from Manila and remain in the more prosperous city.[11] Thus, not only do families send members to America and Europe, they also frequently lose members to Manila and Bacolod. On the other hand, few Chinese are arriving in Iloilo from other parts of the Philippines. As revealed by a tabulation of birthplaces of the registered aliens of the city as of 1972, only 14 percent of the 1,100 Philippine-born aliens were born outside the province.

Philippine government figures indicate that the alien Chinese population is diminishing in Iloilo province. Whereas in 1960 the provincial census recorded over 3,330 Chinese aliens, the 1972 alien registration was fewer than 2,200. The previously mentioned shift in the citizenship composition of the community accounts for this reduction. That some Chinese are Filipino citizens does not mean that they have left the ethnic Chinese community. In fact, the security and usefulness of Filipino citizenship may make a Filipino citizen of Chinese descent even more active and useful in the Chinese community than an alien. So although official figures suggest that the community is dwindling, a look about town will reveal that the community is as active as ever. Both Sun Yat Sen and Chinese Commercial are modernizing or building larger and more impressive facilities. The Uy and the Ang-King (Liòk Kui Tòng) family associations were organized in the 1950s; by 1972 the Uy family had a clubhouse and the Ang-King family had laid the cornerstone for theirs. The Ong and Tan family associations have built new buildings. The Chinese Chamber of Commerce has purchased new land for an extension of the Chinese cemetery. In the 1950s the Christian Gospel Center, an all-Chinese Protestant group, formed and raised a church. Santa Maria Catholic Church established an active Cursillo Movement of Chinese men in the late 1950s and in the late 1960s added an active Chinese Catholic Women's Association. As we shall see in chapter 4, the organizational complexity of Iloilo's Chinese chambers of commerce and trade guilds increased as relations with the Filipino government deteriorated and as intracommunity disagreements increased.

Furthermore, Chinese businesses are expanding and increasing in number. The Chinese of Iloilo are no longer prominent in the sari-sari, or corner-store, retail business, and the old-fashioned general merchandise department store filled with Chinese employees in baggy short pants is gone. But the Chinese have been quick in postwar years to move into new lines: automobile and machinery parts, electrical appliances, motorcycles, insurance and finance companies, stock brokerages, and Western-style department stores.

Iloilo's Chinese community is clearly not fading away. But of course, the community is not and could not be what it was in previous generations. Further illustration of this statement is contained in the epilog. In numerous ways Iloilo Chinese now resemble Filipinos and are socializing with Filipinos. The Chinese are also changing in ways which do not neatly copy any other culture. They continue their complex eclecticism of Spanish, Filipino, American, and Chinese traits. Even though each generation modifies these traditions somewhat, there are few signs of totally losing their distinctiveness among Filipinos.

Iloilo's Chinese, whether Chinese or Filipino citizens, continue to be carefully attentive to the international status of Taiwan and the mainland. In this way, too, the Chinese continue to respond to different stimuli than the wider Filipino society. Beginning about the time of Mao's Great Leap Forward in 1958, Iloilo Chinese official bias in favor of the Kuomintang and Taiwan began to melt. Heretofore quiescent for several years, Chinese Commercial School in the early 1960s began once again to advertise its independence from the Kuomintang and in subtle ways to proclaim its interest in mainland happenings. By 1966 the schools had again actively polarized along lines of interest in one or the other China. In 1966, the Chinese Commercial School burned in a large city fire. Construction of a large new school building rekindled school morale and interest.

By the time of the Great Cultural Revolution in 1966, the Chinese Commercial School was writing school posters in simplified characters and reading them from left to right, similar to the mainland practice and in contrast to Taiwanese tradition. Drawings by students included Mao and Nixon but not Chiang. By no means a Communist stronghold, the school was simply declaring, in a Philippine atmosphere more tolerant of Asian rapprochement, that it was independent of the Kuomintang and objectively interested in events on the mainland. The continuing factionalism between the schools and its modes of expression are clearly still Chinese or "Chinese-derived." In such ways does the community remain a separate social reality from Filipino society.

When President Marcos declared martial law in September 1972, the comfortable attitude toward the Chinese mainland and the likelihood of diplomatic relations with the Communists died quickly. The status of the Taiwanese embassy, of the Federation of Filipino-Chinese Chambers of Commerce which is allied with it, and of Iloilo's Sun Yat Sen School which is allied in turn with the Federation, all improved in official eyes at the expense of the independent status of Chinese Commercial School. As an illustration of the new imbalance of power, the Federation of Filipino-Chinese Chambers of Commerce of Panay is the exclusive channel for translation and dissemination of President Marcos's proclamations, and the opposing Chinese Chamber of Commerce which supports Chinese Commercial School has slipped into an inactive and less visible limbo.

The contemporary Chinese community of Iloilo is a separate society but not one independent from the forces which change or retard Iloilo City as a whole. The economic status and the reputation of Iloilo City vis-a-vis other Philippine cities parallel the reputation of Iloilo's Chinese compared to Chinese of other cities. Iloilo and her Chinese are both considered conservative, old-fashioned, and economically behind the times.

"What has been responsible for Iloilo's decline from the position of promise it occupied as early as a century ago? " asks Journalist Sixto K. Roxas III (1968:23), who answers his own question, thus:

> The shift of sugar production and shipping to Negros. The beginning of shipside loading of sugar on Negros Island. The establishment of bulk shipping facilities on Pulupandan. The labor troubles on the Iloilo docks. The deterioration of Iloilo's harbor facilities. The emergence of Cebu as an entrepot for international trade in the region.

Actually, Iloilo is not so much slipping economically as she is merely holding stable while neighboring cities grow. This can be demonstrated by examining the progress of Bacolod, Kalibo, and Roxas City, all merely agricultural provincial towns in the distribution network of Iloilo's merchants at one time. Iloilo's one-time customers are growing more independent of Iloilo as a distribution center. Since the Second World War all three cities have grown wealthier in cash crops, mainly sugar, and have established more direct trade with Manila, excluding Iloilo. Roxas City now receives many of its supplies directly from Manila via its own port. Bacolod is very likely in coming years to build a harbor within her city limits. Iloilo's own large port is vastly underutilized, due to a postwar history of labor union troubles complicated by big-boss party machines. These troubles coupled with high utility costs due to monopolies effectively exclude the possibility at present of Iloilo industrializing.

It is a common story told in Iloilo and Bacolod that well-dressed Bacolod Chinese with suburban houses and swimming pools come to Iloilo to seek credit from their one-time Chinese suppliers, who still live over their stores and work in their undershirts. Such a story reflects both Iloilo's passing prominence and the divergence of Iloilo and Bacolod Chinese life-styles today. It also underscores how the fate of Iloilo's economy and the Chinese merchant culture are interrelated.

The Euro-American companies never returned to Iloilo after the Second World War to help it return to prominence. The few remaining foreign companies are liquidating their assets and departing. Their places in the distribution scheme are usually taken by Chinese in Manila, leaving brokerages and branches to be run by Iloilo Chinese. Nothing new has developed in

Iloilo's postwar economy except a belated entry into the sugar industry and the construction in the province of a number of sugar centrals. The Chinese of Iloilo have taken the opportunity to enter this new field, as producer-landowners to international exporters. But sugar supplants rice, Iloilo's necessary and traditional main crop. A gain at one point, therefore, pinches Iloilo and the Chinese at another.

Iloilo's relatively stationary economy is reflected in the life-style and outlook of the city's Filipinos and Chinese. Iloilo's Chinese are referred to by other Chinese as *chin kiu-kiàm,* or penny-pinchers. Their nationwide image as conservative investors with great bank deposits goes hand in hand with their image as storekeepers in slippers and undershirts. Compared to the Chinese of Manila, Davao, Bacolod, or Cebu, they have been slower to buy houses and cars, slower to drop the political and clan feuds of bygone eras, slower to found corporations, slower to construct buildings and branches in other cities, slower to abandon Spanish as a commercial lingua franca, and slower to change in many other social and economic pursuits.

In the following chapters the nature of business and family life among Iloilo's Chinese will be examined in more detail. To what can we attribute their apparent old-fashioned and provincial outlook and life-style? Explaining a zeitgeist is filled with peril, but two explanations seem to stand out as reasonable. First, the Chinese are old-fashioned because the more progressive elements of their number have left the city. Second, the Iloilo Chinese are old-fashioned because the Iloilo Filipinos are old-fashioned. The Chinese merely reflect the ambience of the whole town. Generally speaking, these two situations exist because Iloilo's economy is agrarian, almost colonial, without essential change or diversification since Spanish times. Iloilo grows and exports sugar, rice, and copra, among other farm corps, to the rest of the country. In turn it imports manufactured and foreign goods from Manila and Cebu. The main economic roles fall to the middlemen and distributors of agricultural products flowing one way and imports flowing the other. These roles are the same that existed in the Spanish era of 1865 to 1898. The men who prosper in these roles and rise to positions of leadership, both within the Chinese and the Filipino communities, are the same kinds of men whose talents were in ascendance one hundred years ago. Unlike Davao and Bacolod, which have bloomed in postwar years, or Manila and Cebu, which evolved continuously during the American era, Iloilo has essentially the same economy it had in the Spanish era.

In addition, Iloilo Chinese are more old-fashioned than other large Chinese communities because their more progressive elements have left. As I mentioned earlier in this history, the Amoy Chinese who gave the city character before the war have all assimilated, dissipated, or moved to cities with more energetic economies. There is high competitive pressure today among Iloilo Chinese, who compete for markets and consumers that do not multiply as fast as Chinese businesses do. This competitive pressure discourages men who have bright ideas or new techniques. The creative men and those who prefer the executive employee life to the shopkeeper life leave Iloilo for newer economies filled with Western-style corporations pioneering in new industries or products. The mestizos of the nineteenth and early twentieth centuries who provided the political and cultural leadership of the city have for the most part separated from the Chinese and moved to colonize neighboring Bacolod, which thrives now in part because of their participation. Among the Chinese, the Filipinos, and the mestizos, then, those families which were able and willing to innovate removed themselves to other communities. Those who remained behind were practically by definition those who could not or would not change.

Iloilo's Chinese community is more old-fashioned than the other large communities because Iloilo Filipinos themselves are more old-fashioned. Iloilo's enclave has existed since the seventeenth century, and the Spanish made Iloilo their second most important city after Manila. Because of this, Iloilo is heir to a weightier Hispanic tradition after 300 years than most other towns. This is reflected in the greater proportion of Spanish words in Ilongo than in Tagalog, which is spoken in Manila. Iloilo's landowners and absentee aristocracy are mostly descendants of old families of Filipinos and mestizos who flourished during the Hispanic regime. Since these families' more progressive members have gone on to more prosperous cities, like the Chinese have done, those who remain behind are the most conservative Hispanic branches of the families.[12] Providing the customers, landlords, godparents, lawyers, and social contacts of Iloilo's Chinese, these old-family Filipinos have been the primary Filipino influence on them.

Growth of the Chinese Community

This historical perspective of Iloilo's Chinese community is a necessary amplification of the definition of community created in the last chapter. There, descriptive statistics, a definition of certain institutions, and comparison with other Chinese communities in Asia provided a variety of good but static ways of seeing the Chinese. Here, we acknowledge that the ethnic group also has a history. This capsule chronicle of the last hundred years adds to the group's definition a review of forces that have shaped it and suggests some directions it might go.

Marking out the recent history of the Philippine Chinese into four eras helps draw attention to the main influences in their Philippine sojourn. The four eras may be called the Ghetto Era, the Widening of the Niche, the Rise of Nationalism, and the Closing of the Mainland.

The Ghetto Era created a particular community form during the Spanish regime until the 1860s, when trade and travel restrictions on Chinese were loosened. Compared to the present, ghettoized Chinese were much more

isolated from Filipino society and more in contact with the Chinese mainland. Chinese were not totally isolated from the Filipinos, of course; but
the Spanish colonial government enforced their coresidence, limited their
occupations, granted them some self-government, and discouraged their
interaction with Filipinos outside the context of doing business. The community was virtually all-male, and family and farm were still in China.

The Widening of the Niche, at the end of enforced ghettos, began a loga-
rithmic rise in the nineteenth century toward total economic participation
for the Chinese. The niche referred to here is the economic role of marginal
trade, the useful pariah. Instead of importing Chinese goods such as porcelain
and exporting luxuries to China, the Chinese began dealing in local trade,
spreading out in the regions and in the distributional hierarchy of the old
colony's economy. Like a biological species coming into virgin territory
with few competitors, the Chinese multiplied and diversified to fill the
territory. They took up economic ventures too small, too distant, or involving too much work for the British and Spanish. They effectively dis-
placed the Spanish-Chinese mestizo commercial subculture, their main
competitors. The latter turned instead to government, the professions, and
landholding.

The last decade of the nineteenth century, with reformers from the
empress and radicals for the republic wooing the overseas Chinese, marks
the era of the Rise of Nationalism. Fund-raising, consciousness-raising, and
defense-oriented associations proliferated, solidifying the community in
some ways and increasing schisms in others. Undoubtedly, however, the
ethnic group's identity became an emotion-laden political as well as cultural
issue, and maintaining its distinctiveness from Filipinos increased in importance. The Chinese presence in the Philippines became more than an
economic nuisance to harried Spanish colonists; Chinese began to seem a
foreign political threat to the newly nationalistic Filipino population. By
the outbreak of the Second World War, Chinese communities like Iloilo's were
buzzing with the imminent Japanese occupation of their homeland and the
war between the Communists and Nationalists. The Filipinos, for their part,
began to protect themselves legally from Chinese economic hegemony and
their alleged political inflammability through restrictive legislation.

The closing of the mainland opened the current era; the Communist
victors began immediately to rework China in a way that was incompatible
with the bourgeois values and life-style of overseas Chinese merchants.
Since many merchants had settled their families in the Philippines, importing their wives during the last prewar years, few Chinese could point
to any gain in returning to their Fukienese or Cantonese homelands. The
recognition that the Philippines would be their home nation now grew
in the group. The diaspora has continued, of course, on a smaller scale,
to Europe and North America. But the vast majority of Chinese cease to

be sojourners, becoming instead immobile residents of particular Philippine cities. If they do not wax enthusiastic about their Philippine future, they at least make no plans to change. Some are enthusiastic about the accomplishments and future of the People's Republic of China, but they take their pride vicariously: few return to the mainland. In one way the current situation is nearly the reverse of that one hundred years before: the Chinese ethnic group is now cut off socially and politically from China and integrated into the Philippine society and polity.

By outlining these highlights of Iloilo's history and growth, I am suggesting that the city's Chinese community has been molded by four analytically distinguishable phenomena: the selection process of immigration, the response of the overseas community to this source of recruitment, association with the overseas sociocultural environment, and response to the Chinese homeland. Let us briefly review Iloilo Chinese history from these angles.

Immigration to Iloilo City appears quite selective in several respects. Only certain southern Chinese villages regularly sent immigrants. Only certain kinds of men and boys were likely to emigrate, being until recently mostly young bachelors eleven to twenty-five years old. The target of individual immigration was also selective: Iloilo's immigrants came from specific areas in Fukien and Kwangtung. The regional composition of the Chinese community has changed little since the nineteenth century. Because immigration closely followed social channels (well documented by Watson 1975), each Philippine town became disproportionately composed of particular kin groups and townmates. I have also speculated, but cannot document, that overseas life may attract immigrants of particular values and temperaments. The consequences of this selectivity in immigration have been to produce overseas enclaves that are not typical of their homeland and that vary among themselves in small but systematic sociocultural features. Recognition of this fact does not vitiate comparisons to China or among overseas Chinese themselves, but it should alert us to new sources of variability.

Any society which recruits new members primarily by immigration of individuals enculturated in another setting will have special organizational problems. Iloilo's Chinese society invented some organizations and behavior patterns, imported some intact from China, and modeled others after Filipino and colonial precedents. As I shall show in chapter 4, merchant guilds, music clubs, Catholic churches, and Chinese schools, among many others, contributed to the major tasks of organizing geographic mobility, aiding commerce, preserving Chinese culture yet facilitating acculturation sufficiently to do business in a foreign setting, and defending themselves against external threats.

The third phenomenon shaping Iloilo Chinese history has been their adjustment to a niche in a foreign environment composed of Filipinos, Spanish, and Americans. By different methods and for different motives, the Spanish, the Filipinos, and the Americans each contributed to the specialization of the Chinese in a merchant niche. Willingly, of course, the Chinese accepted this position. The result of one hundred years' single-minded devotion to the life of buy-and-sell in a Philippine setting is an ethnic group homogeneous in values and behavior and still distinct from its host majority. A merchant culture, built on such an historical foundation, will be a special type of edifice. Chapter 3 will explore this further.

Iloilo's Chinese have also made adjustments to the life-style of the Ilongo Filipinos they live among. The stabilized economy of exporting agricultural produce and retailing to a crowded rural province has influenced Filipinos and Chinese alike, in that their progressive elements have left the city. Further, the Chinese have acquired from their Ilongo environment a heavily Hispanized, economically conservative, politically factionalized life-style. Chinese social status in Iloilo province is also changing more slowly from the Hispanic tradition than it is in areas around vigorously growing Manila, Bacolod, Cebu, and Davao. This consonance is what Weldon (1974) has documented for Chinese in Indonesian cities of varying economic type: the majority's socioeconomic environment influences the Chinese minority position, too.

Finally, the Iloilo Chinese community has been shaped directly and indirectly by events within China during the last one hundred years. Ambassadorial and conspiratorial missions overseas, conquests, confiscations, and revolutions at home have all been felt in the lives of merchants in Iloilo. Their definitions of themselves as Chinese, contributing to their motives for remaining distinct, have varied as Chinese culture itself has evolved, and the image of their homeland becomes both more prestigious and more distant in their minds. Philippine Chinese treatment by Filipinos and colonial powers has always been hinged to the latter's relationship to China. Current Philippine diplomatic negotiations with China are having an effect on the lives of many Chinese who have never even seen China and have no desire to go there.

1. These documents, the *Chinos Provincianos,* are unanalyzed except in Wickberg's (1965) historical study. Most of my Hispanic era information comes either from Wickberg or from oral histories of Iloilo residents. Sir James Bowring (1859) and Nicholas Loney (1964), visitors and residents of Iloilo, both have some references to the Iloilo Chinese community.

2. The Iloilo community was one of the few to have a prominent Cantonese minority. Wickberg (1965:177) reports that by 1900 only two communities had sizeable Cantonese percentages: Manila (10 percent) and Iloilo (8 percent).

3. There are several methods for the romanization of Amoy Chinese. I have rendered most surnames and geographical names as they are written by the Philippine Chinese. All other expressions follow Douglas (1873).

4. See David Bernstein's (1947) historical review for a discussion of the emergence of the *ilustrados* and the Philippine Revolution.

5. These statistics are estimates derived from 1972 records of Alien Certificates of Registration from the Bureau of Immigration of Iloilo City.

6. Iloilo's consulate was created in the 1930s, and the post of honorary consul was awarded to Yap Kai-sing, a son of the wealthy Francisco Yap Tico family of Iloilo. This latter is mentioned in Wickberg (1965:90).

7. D. Doeppers (1971) and one of my Cantonese informants report a slightly different arrangement of prewar merchant niches in Davao. The Japanese specialized in importing Japanese goods and bought plantations of bananas and abaca. The Fukienese were strong in hardware and groceries, and the Cantonese specialized in tailor shops, bakeries, restaurants, and hotels. No mention is made by either source of the presence of Euro-Americans in this business scheme.

8. Members must have been mainly intellectuals because labor elements were few in cities like Iloilo.

9. As the only Chinese church of any size in town, Santa Maria performs almost all Christian baptisms, marriages, and funerals for the Chinese community, regardless of factional allegiances.

10. See also Alip (1959) and Liao (1964).

11. See chapter 5 for more discussion of postmarital residence.

12. G. M. Grageda (1966) of the *Philippine Free Press*, emphasizes in his sketch of Iloilo that the strong aristocratic classes of prewar Iloilo were depleted after Liberation when the big Filipino *hacendero* and industrial families left Iloilo for Manila and Negros Occidental.

3

CHINESE BUSINESS LIFE

THE WAY BUSINESS IS ACTUALLY PRACTICED   in the city, as well as the
Chinese norms for commercial life, exerts an enormous shaping influence
on the rest of community life. The community's institutional structure,
its kinship practices, and its family life are molded about the shopkeeping
life. Business activity for the Philippine Chinese comprises a principal "given"
to which their sociocultural life must adapt. So that this statement will not
sound unjustifiably materialistic, the concepts of "merchant society" and
"merchant culture" are introduced as perspective for the following chapters.

Merchant Society and Merchant Culture

When anthropologists study the overseas Chinese, they have two basic
viewpoints from which to examine the culture of their subjects. They
may adopt an historical viewpoint and ask, "How have these carriers of
Chinese culture come to diverge from people of their homeland? " Or they
may adopt an existential viewpoint and ask, "How does this group of immigrants interact with their host society? " Usually, of course, investigators
work with both viewpoints. It is virtually impossible to write an ethnography
of overseas Chinese without using these viewpoints, so they shape this study
as well.

What makes the Philippine Chinese peculiar for an anthropological ethnography is that they are predominantly merchants, or self-employed businessmen.[1] They are not farmers, fishermen, hunters and gatherers, pastoralists,
migrant laborers, or unemployed, but they are shopkeepers. They are not
part-time traders in a barter economy but full-time merchants whose fathers
lived by the buy-and-sell cycle and whose sons will very likely do the same.

Of course, in every complex society there is a group of merchants dedicated full-time to commerce. However, the Philippine Chinese are not only
almost all merchants, but they are also a cultural minority within another
society. They are what Manning Nash (1966:25) calls "resident strangers."

People of this type, distributed around the world outside of their home cultures in tribal and peasant societies, include Muslim Indians, Syrians, Lebanese, and Greeks, as well as Chinese.

When the Philippine Chinese were residents of China, engaged in commerce or farming, they were no different occupationally or culturally from other Chinese. Those who did engage in commerce were less exclusively merchants than they became overseas. In Lin Yueh-hua's (1947) *The Golden Wing,* no matter how the merchants Wang and Cheng fared, they were always allies to and agents for their family villages and farms. Their residence and labor fluctuated between the farm and the store. Ultimately, their fortunes were inextricably hinged to their agrarian ties and kinfolk.

But once they arrived in the Philippines, the Chinese immigrants' ties to their homeland began to weaken. Historic events in China and the Philippines have also nearly locked the Chinese into their merchant niche in the Philippines for the last half century. The Philippine Chinese are now very much a permanent part of the Philippines, socially and economically.

Writing with this in mind, George Weightman (1960) developed his historical study of the Philippine Chinese, describing them as a "marginal trading community." They are marginal in the sense that Robert Park (1928:881) defined the culturally "marginal man." Economically, however, they are dead center: the legendary middlemen. Besides being culturally marginal, they are definitely also a community, as I have shown in chapter 1. But what does it mean *culturally* to be merchants instead of farmers, hunters, or herders?

In this and the following three chapters I shall frame an answer to that question. In their marriage patterns, their superstitions and sayings, their inheritance practices, forms of reciprocity, political ranking, and even in their housing and household composition, Philippine Chinese society is rooted in the shopkeeping life. What served for them culturally in their rural life in China has undergone modification in transition to a shopkeeping enclave in a foreign culture's cities.

This is an ethnography of merchants, then, building upward and outward analytically from their occupation as businessmen. That they were Chinese and someday may become Filipinos, that they immigrated to their present home: these are crucial background themes and have been well treated by other investigators. The cultural and immigrant status of overseas Chinese is more variable than their status as merchants and businessmen. Therefore, I have organized this study of a Chinese merchant society and its merchant culture by emphasizing that which is most stable – their livelihood.

The Chinese Presence in Iloilo's Economy

The Filipinos of Iloilo City are sensitive to what they deem to be virtual monopolization of the city's business by the Chinese. Many Filipinos would agree with the following Ilongo journalist's impression of Chinese control:

> The Chinese, either as Chinese citizens or as naturalized Filipinos, own 9 out of every 10 retail stores, 8 out of every 10 eateries, 9 out of every 10 lumber yards and hardware stores, 7 out of 13 movie houses, 5 out of 8 huge rice mills and warehouses, and clutches of massage clinics, hotels, and lodging houses where they also subsidize prostitution by patronizing it at the ratio of 8 to 2 Filipinos. . . . Of an estimated ₱250 million business every year, the Chinese spawn 80% and own half the money involved in the other 20% (Zulueta 1968).

Notice that the writer includes naturalized Filipino-Chinese in his count of Chinese. If one counts only Chinese alien businesses, most of the 70 to 80 wholesale enterprises in the city are Chinese, but only 156 of 2,284 retail businesses are Chinese.[2] Relying only on the figures for aliens, government figures regularly underestimate the size of the Chinese population. The ethnic Chinese population is about double the city's alien component, as I have estimated. Even if Zulueta counts all ethnic Chinese, he still greatly exaggerates Chinese dominance of Iloilo business.

The only way to discover the extent of the ethnic Chinese community's business enterprises is to solicit the assistance of Chinese. One can assess Chinese presence by counting the percentage of the city's establishments which Chinese run or by estimating the percentage of the city's business taxes which they pay. With the aid of Chinese friends and Iloilo City records, I have collected information on both of these topics. In businesses with fewer than ten employees, which constitute over 90 percent of Iloilo's businesses, the cultural Chinese operate virtually all of some lines like wholesale textiles, groceries, and retail glassware, but they are involved not at all in other lines like motor and battery repair, dressmaking, or transportation. In only a few cases do they have the command of the market that Filipinos attribute to them. On the other hand, their involvement is enormous considering that they constitute less than 3 percent of the city's population.

Table 2 presents another view of the city's businesses. Regardless of the number of establishments they run, the Chinese pay about 35 percent overall of the city's business taxes. There is no reason to suspect this figure is too low due to tax evasion because Filipino businessmen practice evasion, too. It is possible that the Chinese pay more taxes than their share of the city's business would otherwise indicate because they are closely watched as an alien minority by the Bureau of Internal Revenue. In any case, the ethnic Chinese share of some businesses like banking, the professions, and agricultural mills is about 3 percent, or the same as their proportion of the population. Their share of the service industries, liquors, drugs and tobacco, and wholesale-retail transactions, on the other hand, is enormous.

Table 2
Business Taxes Paid in Iloilo City by Ethnic
Chinese Businesses, for January 1972

Business Category	Total Taxes Collected (in pesos)	Percent Paid by Ethnic Chinese
Transportation, real estate finance, insurance, brokerages, banking	179,905.22	1.5
Utilities, larger construction, manufacturing	26,447.61	28.3
Services (amusement, taverns and hotels, barbershops, etc.)	67,423.62	42.2
Small manufacturing, cottage industries, workshops, repair shops	16,172.96	31.6
Manufacture & wholesale/retail sales of liquor, drugs, tobacco	22,410.00	49.0
Professions	39,314.38	6.5
Native products processing (rice, corn, sugar, copra)	10,355.86	7.9
Sales taxes (all retail & wholesale businesses not listed above)	236,710.71	65.4
Income tax (personal & corporate)	194,715.95	12.2
Total	906,925.41	35.6

NOTE: Tax returns for January, the heaviest payment month, were recorded in the Bureau of Internal Revenue, Iloilo City, 1972. All taxpayers with Chinese surnames, regardless of citizenship, were counted. Figures probably represent minima because Chinese using Filipino names or paying through their Filipino dummies are not countable.

The Chinese are proportionately strongest in the city's middle range of businesses, that is, those with ten to fifty employees. Ethnic Chinese operate 40 percent or more of such establishments. Chinese businesses which hire fewer than ten employees are lost in a statistical sea of small Filipino retail operations. At the other end of the scale, there are eighty-three estalishments in Iloilo hiring more than fifty people, but these are owned mostly by absentee Filipino families, Spanish, and Americans.

Based on the Iloilo City tax returns of 1972, the ethnic Chinese paid 35.6 percent of the city's business taxes — an indication that they probably conducted that portion of the city's business. South Asians in Iloilo, numbering about sixty individuals in ten stores (Philippine Census Survey 1967), conducted 0.7 percent of the city's business, mostly in retail operations like shirt or variety stores. The British and Americans represent fewer residents and firms than the South Asians, but they conduct 3 and 7 percent, respectively, of the local business. The Spanish firms number about 6 or 8 and do 5 percent of Iloilo's business. There is one Lebanese in dry goods and tailoring. The Filipinos, well over 90 percent of the population, pay less than half the city business taxes.

Even though the Chinese do not have a monopoly of the city's business and, indeed, are not even represented in certain types of markets, they do have a remarkable stake considering their small numbers. They are present in large numbers in small businesses but have their largest impact in the middle range businesses. Their strongest and most visible role is in the retail-wholesale distribution scheme, from which 65 percent of the city's sales taxes are collected.

Distribution of Chinese Merchants

My field survey in 1972 recorded approximately 624 different establishments – stores, offices, workshops, theaters, factories, warehouses – operated by ethnic Chinese. Businesses were distributed about the province as shown in table 3.

The figures for provincial establishments are larger than those in the records kept by the town's Chinese chambers of commerce themselves, exceeding those listed in the Federation of Filipino-Chinese Chambers of Commerce *Business Directory* (1965) by about one hundred. This is because the national directory lists only businesses in the city proper and because the local Chinese only have records for establishments which pay dues and consider themselves part of the Chinese community. My survey figures include all businesses run by pure Chinese, regardless of citizenship, and many businesses operated by mestizos who are immediate descendants of pure Chinese. The criteria explained in chapter 1 for determining ethnic Chinese were also applied. Table 3 then is more inclusive than most tabulations because it counts all ethnic Chinese.

Two-thirds of the businesses of Iloilo City proper and its neighboring municipalities of La Paz, Molo, and Jaro are wholesale-retail operations. The service industries, native products, and small-scale manufacturing or milling each comprise about 10 percent of the establishments. In the provincial towns the breakdown is slightly different: among the six largest Chinese communities, about half the establishments are wholesale-retail, and one-fourth each are service industries or native-products dealers. The native products businesses are mostly farms or dealerships in sugar, copra, or fish. There is no Chinese manufacturing done in the province and very few milling operations are in Chinese hands.

That the Iloilo Chinese community is a merchant culture is evident in that over 73 percent of the working men are self-employed merchants, according to my survey of sixty-eight families in the city. Of the working men, 14 per-

Table 3
Distribution of Chinese Businesses in Iloilo City
and Province, 1972

Iloilo Provincial Towns	Ethnic Chinese Businesses Establishments/Town
Estancia	18
Passi	13
Pototan	8
Sara	6
Balasan	6
Janiuay	6
Dueñas	5
Calinog	5
Dingle	3
Barotoc Nuevo	2
Tigbanan	2
Others *	10
Total	84
Iloilo City Municipalities	
Iloilo City Proper	483
La Paz	28
Molo	18
Jaro	15
Total	544

NOTE: The survey was conducted by this writer, counting all Chinese regardless of citizenship. No data are available for Gigantes Islands, Guimaras Island, or other Iloilo provincial towns not mentioned in this table.
*Includes one establishment each in Banate, Barotoc Viejo, Cabatuan, Carles, Ajuy, Jordan, Nuevo Valencia, Lambunao, Oton, and Leon.

cent are white-collar employees, clerks, and salesmen; 9 percent are professionals such as doctors, teachers, and certified public accountants; and 1 percent work for the government. There is virtually no blue-collar labor force of Chinese in Iloilo.

The most common economic unit of Iloilo's merchant culture is the family-owned and-operated single proprietorship, which, as we have seen, generally has fewer than ten employees. Of the 544 businesses in the city, 87 percent are single proprietorships.[4] Family partnerships in which two or more related households participate comprise 6 percent, while nonfamily partnerships of two to six partners are 4 percent. Only 3 percent are officially incorporated, and some of these are simply Iloilo-based family businesses, too.

The Chinese and Iloilo's Distribution System

Iloilo's distribution system has four parts and the Chinese are involved in all of them. The first part imports foreign goods direct from overseas and distributes them over Panay island, western Negros, and sometimes northern Mindanao. Most of this distribution is handled by Chinese, with some competition from Americans, British, and Spanish. The second part of the distribution scheme makes of Iloilo a focal point for the interisland movement of native products for speculation and local consumption. This scheme also includes the collection of newly ripened native products from the province and their transport to Manila and Cebu for processing and export or consumption. The native products moving through Iloilo are rice, molasses and refined sugar, corn, copra, mongo beans, abaca, salt, tobacco, peanuts, fish, and livestock (Philippine Census 1960). The Chinese conduct 50 percent or more of the trade in tobacco, copra, copra oil, and cereals, and probably the other native products as well.

The third aspect of distribution is the manufacture of goods within the city or province and their distribution throughout the province and neighboring provinces of Antique, Aklan, Capiz, and Negros Occidental. Using manual labor or simple machines, small Chinese factories or cottage industries produce candy, candles, soap, shoes, soy sauce, cloth and netting, handicrafts, liquor, furniture, and custom jeep bodies, among other goods. Iloilo's Chinese are especially active in the liquor, furniture, candy and candles, and machine-shop production. They also produce the most popular locally sewn ready-made clothes for distribution as far away as Mindanao.

The fourth part of Iloilo's distribution system is the channeling of Manila-produced or Manila-imported goods through the city and into neighboring provinces. This is the vast area of wholesale-retail operations of which 65 percent are performed by the Chinese.

The presence before the Second World War of the large foreign import-export houses at the top of this distribution system focused the city's business more than it is today. American, British, and Spanish firms brought in a large percentage of the imports and purchased a large percentage of the native products for export. The collection of the native products and the distribution of imports over the province were left to the middle-range Chinese import-export concerns. But those who did business directly with the foreign firms received help in the form of credit. The third segment of distribution (the local manufacturers and cottage industries) produced for rural markets and had little association or competition with the foreign firms. The flow of goods from Manila was smaller before the war. The many franchises which produce these goods today were then under the direction of Americans who transported and sold the goods wholesale themselves.

With the foreign firms gone today, the flow of exports is no longer connected to the flow of imports and Manila goods. Direct foreign import is often handled by the Chinese import houses and separated from the flow of Manila goods or imports channeled through Manila. These Manila goods in postwar years have been competing with and replacing many of the items formerly produced in Iloilo such as clothing or soap. The market for consumer goods from Manila has extended into provincial areas, and Chinese who once ran shoe or candy factories now have closed down and distribute these Manila goods instead. Thus, Iloilo's postwar economy has actually become less "industrialized" and more dependent on regional imports.

Links to the Province and the Nation

The daily and seasonal fluctuations in supply of the province's native products — sugar, cereals, copra, dried fish, tobacco, beans, and salt — set the pace for the city's business life. Trucks filled with native products and busloads of provincial Filipinos arrive early each day at the city's market. By noon the trucks have returned to the hills and the swarms of provincial customers filling the city's Chinese businesses have evaporated. Through the dry season of March to June and into the rainy season of July and August, while the provincial farmers wait for the rice crop to come in, the city's Chinese businessmen are in their slowest season. All aspects of the distribution system slow down. By September or October the rice crop begins to arrive in town. Then not only are the native products dealers busy, but the whole Chinese merchant community begins its Christmas sales to attract the new money. Because the wealth of the province is regulated by the agrarian cycles, city business activity rises or falls by these cycles.

There is also a long-term trend toward growth or depression in the province's native products, to which Chinese fortunes in the city are pinned. For example, fishing in the interisland waters around Estancia in northern Iloilo province was very rich after the Second World War. In recent decades dynamiting and the lack of regulation have destroyed the fishing grounds and much of the industry has moved to Masbate province. Chinese who made money as fish brokers or as financiers for fleets have either followed the fleets out or shifted to *bangros* (*Chanos chanos*) which are raised in ponds and shipped on ice to Manila.

Since the postwar construction of four more sugar centrals in the province, Iloilo is gearing up for the high profits that Bacolod has enjoyed for decades. None of the sugar centrals are in the hands of Chinese, but many Chinese have made their living by supplying sugar centrals with raw cane, hardware, and vehicles or by purchasing sugar and molasses from them for sale or export.

The renegotiation in 1974 between the United States and the Philippines of price supports for sugar and other native products under the Laurel-

Langley Act threw large areas of Iloilo Chinese business into jeopardy. Not only have many Chinese become involved in buying and selling raw and refined sugar, but the city's agribusiness in selling trucks, parts, and machinery is partially in Chinese hands. The end of the sugar price support and the reconversion of sugar lands to rice by unregulated farmers threatened to produce a depression in Iloilo and Bacolod.

The conversion of land into sugar by Filipino farmers is not without drawbacks for the Chinese. There are no government regulations concerning land use, so as sugar fields increase, those plowed for beans, rice, and tobacco, in particular, diminish in number. The resulting rise in prices makes these latter products less saleable for Chinese brokers. The government's importation and sale at a loss of Thai rice further hinder the Chinese as rice merchants.

Though Iloilo's Chinese community is predominantly urban, it is highly dependent upon the flow and marketability of the province's native products. In addition to purchasing agricultural produce, the Chinese have five other links to Iloilo province and all of Panay. First, cottage industry consignments of handicrafts, weaving, or ready-made garment sewing are made to workers in the barrios around Iloilo City. Second, city businesses send trucks and salesmen into the province to supply regular retail and wholesale customers with the goods that are imported from Manila or overseas or that are manufactured in town. Some Chinese depend almost exclusively on this provincial merchandising from trucks. Third, Chinese finance Filipino farmers to build brick salt-drying beds, bangros ponds, and muscovado (crude) sugar mills or to plant tobacco and sugar. In return for the capital or equipment to begin, the farmers agree to sell back the bulk of their produce at discount prices. A fourth link to the province has developed in the 1960s and 1970s. Some Chinese, confident of their Filipino citizenship status, are purchasing haciendas of rice and sugar, and piggeries, chicken farms, or bangros ponds. Heretofore an area for investment but not ownership, these provincial farm industries are becoming more popular as Chinese realize that modern techniques and their own management skills can make them even more productive, especially since they can serve as their own outlets for sale. Finally, some Chinese are linked to the province through retail outlets or purchasing brokerages in order to be near the variable cash income of farmers and the supply of sugar, rice, and fish.

Goods move about Panay mostly by truck. Before the war and immediately after it, there was a great deal of retail sale in the province by truck when profit margins were high. This itinerant trade, called *bulante* by Filipinos and *a-hen-te* by Chinese, has diminished greatly in recent years. Narrower profits, highway robbers, and the expense of maintaining trucks have forced many Chinese to limit their provincial trucking to carrying native products and wholesale deliveries. There are a few Chinese in the truck transport business per se. Some are invisible owners because aliens are excluded from transportation. But there are no Chinese in Iloilo as there are in Bacolod who have invested heavily in trucks and buses, rationalized services – and prospered.

There is a Philippine National Railway train line from Iloilo City to Roxas City which, in addition to passengers, carries cargo such as eggs that Panay roads would destroy. But the train's proportion of provincial cargo is miniscule.

Virtually all movement of goods to and from Manila and other islands is by ship. Five of Iloilo's eight or nine shipping agencies are Chinese. These five are favored by the Chinese because they offer better claim service and various fringe benefits.

In the years following the Second World War the demand for consumer goods was so great and profit margins so high that some imaginative merchants began air-freighting goods from Manila. They received stocks sooner than their competition and, thus, could better keep up with demand. This practice ceased in the 1950s as the market became more saturated.

Before the war, when many Chinese worked as employees for other Chinese, the *pak-iau,* or provincial agent system, was the principal way of collecting native products. Throughout the American regime and probably in the latter part of the Spanish regime, the pak-iau was a traveling agent with a truck or wagon who was responsible for finding the produce, bargaining for a purchase, loading the produce, and returning it to the city warehouses of his Chinese boss. The pak-iau was usually a Chinese, a very trusted employee who handled money, goods, and vehicles without supervision. Since Liberation more Filipinos are filling these posts in Chinese companies because of nationalization pressures. But the posts are also becoming less common as collection techniques become rationalized and as the Filipino producers more often bring the goods to town themselves to get a better price.

Iloilo's prosperity has always depended on her focal position in the movement of goods in and out of the western Visayas. But old customer towns or cities like Kalibo, Roxas City, and Bacolod are continually improving their port facilities and their connections with Manila and are beginning to shrink Iloilo's hegemony as supplier to the provincial areas. For example, Roxas City in Capiz province is now receiving hardware, auto parts, and lumber supplies directly from outside sources. Roxas City is also serving as the outlet for its own crops of sugar, copra, and fish. This, of course, cuts into Iloilo's trade, and what hurts Iloilo's trade hurts Iloilo's Chinese.

Foreign imports received directly at Iloilo's port pass first through the import houses, many of which are Chinese. These imports are sold to the city's large wholesalers in bulk lots. Smaller wholesalers receive smaller lots at slightly higher prices. These smaller dealers often have retail outlets to improve their profit on the smaller lots. Almost all of these wholesalers are Chinese. Wholesalers sell the imported goods in small lots to city and provincial retailers, most of whom are Filipinos. The retailers may be fairly large urban stores or tiny rural sari-sari stores supplied once a week by truck from the city.

The foreign imports coming directly to Iloilo are mostly food commodities, nonperishable grocery store items purchased from the United States, Japan, Australia, and Hongkong. The vast majority of other goods come from Manila directly to the stores. If one merchant has an exclusive distributorship granted by the Manila producer or importer, he will be the sole wholesale outlet for Panay island. Piece goods like motorcycles or galvanized buckets may be handled this way. Other stores which retail the item in Iloilo must acquire it from this exclusive distributor. Other merchandise is ordered by wire, telephone, or personal visit to Manila. Outside the city, however, Chinese and Filipino merchants alike rely on the Chinese wholesalers in the city to supply them.

Provincial Chinese

Iloilo City Chinese are similar in their social and business life to the larger merchant enclaves of Manila and Cebu, but provincial Chinese life is quite different from these. Provincial Chinese merchants are neither the model of ancient Chinese merchants nor the indicator of future trends; they have always been an adjunct of Iloilo's urban Chinese society. The rural proportion of the province's Chinese population is holding steady, but rural Chinese economic success relative to that of the city's Chinese has diminished.

Because their market is smaller, Chinese in the province still operate the age-old general store, where everything from motorcycle parts to bakery goods may be sold. They often diversify by adding restaurants, gas stations, and auto repair shops, and by purchasing local crops for sale in Iloilo City. Provincial Chinese merchants more often marry Filipino women than do urban Chinese: if the wife has kinsmen and political stature in the community, the isolated Chinese man is assured of protection and good public relations.[5] Even though they are sent to Iloilo City's Chinese schools, the children of provincial merchants rarely become part of Iloilo's Chinese community.

Because of their small size, provincial towns develop a kinship group character as prospering Chinese invite in more relatives to help the business grow (see T'ien 1953). Before the Second World War, Janiuay, a town thirty kilometers from Iloilo City, was filled predominantly with families named Yu, Yap, and Tan, all intermarrying, just as their counterparts were doing in Chin-kang County, Fukien.

Even more a family town is San Jose, in Antique province, whose merchants throughout the twentieth century have been the Pe clan. Antique has always been an underdeveloped area of difficult access. According to a member of a family, a Pe first ventured into Antique as a pák-iâu, and opened a store sometime in the early twentieth century. Without competition, the man prospered, calling over more Pe kinsmen from China. Since it is a cash-poor area, most Antique Filipinos dealt with the Chinese by means of liens on their land. As mortgages were foreclosed for nonpayment, the land began accumulating in Pe hands. Antique land was fairly easy to acquire, unlike the rest of Panay island, where competition from old aristocratic landholding Filipino families precluded land accumulation by Chinese. The Pe group developed Antique farms, sugar fields, copra plantations, and simple sugar mills. They established a trucking company to carry these goods to Iloilo. Speculation in mining claims has hurt some of the Pe family but even today they represent a large proportion of San Jose's merchant community. Over the years they have both called for Chinese wives from the mainland and married the daughters of local Filipino families. Many families in Iloilo City named Pe can trace their histories through Antique.

Though widely dispersed, provincial Chinese keep in close contact socially and commercially with Iloilo City. The bigger provincial businessmen will join Iloilo's Chinese chambers of commerce and perhaps a lineage association. Their children go to Chinese school in Iloilo City (though Kalibo and Roxas City also have their own Chinese elementary schools). They may maintain an apartment or warehouse in the city where a branch of their extended family resides. When a provincial Chinese dies he will be buried in the city's Chinese cemetery. When his daughter marries, it will probably be to an Iloilo City Chinese boy. Though the wedding may be in the country, their new residence will surely be in Iloilo City.

The Chinese communities in San Jose, Roxas City, and Kalibo may be treated as an intermediate type between provincial Chinese and city Chinese. They resemble the urban Chinese in that they work and live closely together and form organizations, and they resemble the provincial Chinese in their common kin communities and their wide business diversification.

Hiring, Labor, and Employees

The labor and employee situation in Iloilo Chinese businesses has altered since the 1930s, when immigration from China was the main source of employees. The war, the closing of Chinese immigration, and Philippine nationalization campaigns have all worked to change the composition of labor in Chinese establishments from many to a few Chinese and to change the role relations between employer and employee.

The Apprentice System

Before immigration from China ceased, the Chinese employee was part of a strict but dynamic social system which brought men to the Philippines, trained them in business, and helped them start on their own. This apprentice system may have operated without much alteration for several hundred years.

The apprentice system worked as follows. A young man acquired his immigration papers (teng-ki-toa^n-li) from relatives or a professional middleman in China. His kinsmen corresponded with kinsmen or friends in Iloilo who had agreed to take the boy in. Sometimes the sponsor acquired the immigration papers or paid the boat fare from Amoy. Sometimes the sponsor also adopted the boy. Informants claim that document costs, bribes, fees to middlemen, and steamship fare in the 1920s and early 1930s totaled about ₱50 to ₱100 (U.S.$25-50), when employee salaries were about ₱25 a month.

Upon arriving in the Philippines, the young man was ushered to Iloilo and his new home with his sponsor's business. The sponsor took the young man as a *chiáh-tháu-lo* (employee) and assumed total responsibility for him. *Chiáh-tháu-lò* is the most common and generic word for employee. The boy became the bottom rung in a tightly run hierarchy of a business family and its retinue of employees. He began in the back of the store as cook's helper or janitor of the senior employees' quarters. His hours were long and he was at the command of his many superiors. Apprentices were sometimes segregated at meals and tea breaks from senior employees.

The novice's leisure hours were rigidly supervised by his sponsor and provided little opportunity for waywardness and vice. The crude baggy short pants, the "uniform" of employees of the period, were without pockets, ostensibly to discourage the spiriting away of money or merchandise. Should a young man incur the wrath of his paterfamilias sponsor and be fired, he was liable to be blackballed as disreputable by the entire community and be forced to migrate or return ignominiously to China.

In his first years an apprentice might receive only room and board and a sum of perhaps ₱10 a month to remit to his parents or wife. Even if wages were paid, they might be in the form of shares in the business or they might be accumulated as severance pay for when the boy struck off on his own. Senior employees received cash wages of ₱25 or so a month. When they had accumulated ₱200 every couple of years, they usually were allowed to visit China.

On his own time a young man often acquired tutors to train him in accounting, plus Ilongo, English, and Spanish as commercial languages. As their ability in languages and local customs grew and their trustworthiness was demonstrated, apprentices were promoted to work in the stockroom as *hoe-chhia*, or stevedore, as clerk, or as cashier.[6] They learned the inventory, ordering, prices, and money handling. In prewar years many more of Iloilo's Chinese businesses were general merchandise outlets, and an employee would be introduced to a number of different lines of merchandise, salesmen, and suppliers.

Trained employees might be shown great trust in their duties. They might be put in charge of warehouses or made pak-iau (traveling purchase agents). By this time in their careers, however, most apprentices would be very aware of the Amoy expression *"Chiah-thâu-lò lâng siá phō kiáh khang,"* or "An employee's compensation (in the account books) is a fixed sum." In order to make his fortune, especially if he already had acquired a family in China or the Philippines, an employee had to set off on his own. Some employees continued as minor partners of their original sponsor, but most became independent. They usually became an independent outlet for the goods they had been trained to sell. With long and liberal credit terms from their sponsor, with whom they had proved their worth, they acquired their stock with little capital. Their relation to their sponsor then entered a new phase, characterized in the Spanish era as the *cabacillo*-agent system (Wickberg 1965), which will be discussed later.

Postwar Chinese Employees

After the Second World War the Filipinos gained their independence and embarked on a nationalization campaign. Also, immigration from China was drastically reduced when the Communists took power and the Philippines responded by closing down immigration from the mainland. These two events had the effect of reducing the number of Chinese employees in Chinese businesses and increasing the number of Filipinos. Young unmarried Filipino labor was cheaper and better for public relations than older married Chinese men with families. The latter were more and more coming of age and becoming independent merchants. Legally, too, Chinese aliens could only be employed in alien Chinese businesses, which diminished in number in the 1950s because of the nationalization campaign.

In contemporary Iloilo Chinese society, most young future businessmen are trained in their fathers' businesses to replace them. If a father has no business or decides not to bequeath it, he will seek out friends or kinsmen to take in his son as a trainee. Thus, the apprentice system still exists today but in very modified form. The sponsor no longer exercises *in loco parentis* powers over his charge because the boy's family is present in town. He pays the boy a living wage and does not require him to start "in the back" because in all likelihood the boy knows Filipino language and culture better than his employer. The boy's father in some cases purchases a share in the sponsor's business as a bond of good faith. Thus, while the skills accrue to the son, the father may be collecting the wages and profits. This bond of good faith is becoming more necessary in Iloilo's tightly competitive merchant community because an employee whose family has money might be acting simply as their industrial spy while training in a man's store.

Roughly speaking, most Chinese and mestizo employees in today's Chinese stores are of three types: the minor partner, the potential competitor, or the charity case. The minor partner is usually an older man without family in the Philippines who rose through the ranks as employee to become a fixture of the business and virtually a member of the family. The potential competitor is the younger man described above who is being trained to start his own store. This type resembles the old apprentice system in its dynamism. But it is the charity case which most resembles the old apprentice system in its way of life. The charity case is either an old man without connections or a young man or woman from a poor home (often a mestizo) being given an opportunity.[7] These people may be assigned undemanding clerical or warehouse jobs and might never leave their sinecures with the families who have taken them in.

These types are not immutable. Sometimes a charity case or potential competitor will become a minor partner, or a minor partner may become an independent competitor. Potential competitors may also marry the boss' daughter or a mestiza charity case may marry her employer, in which case the employee has moved into the elite circle of the business family itself.

In the decades before the closing of the Chinese mainland, mestizo employees were valuable assets in Chinese businesses in much the same way that Filipino wives were for provincial Chinese. Mestizos were born in the area, fluent in the dialect, and knowledgeable concerning local etiquette, so they could deal with Filipinos in business. Mestizos were especially valuable as foremen of Filipino workers, salesmen, and pák-iãu. Connection through their fathers to the Chinese community makes mestizos *ab initio* more reputable than Filipinos, who would lack backing from within the Chinese community. There is a feeling among employers that the Chinese blood in a mestizo constitutes something like collateral for trusting him.

Because so many Chinese have raised families in the Philippines since the war, there is a large supply of young Chinese born and educated in Iloilo City and conversant in Filipino ways. These pure Chinese obviate the special usefulness of mestizos. Some mestizos still work in Chinese businesses today, of course, but it is for their sake more than the sake of the business. A common pattern today is for a Chinese business family to take in a few of its mestizo relatives from poorer branches of the family. By working for the Chinese, the mestizo will be educated in Chinese schools and retained somewhat within the Chinese community.

Throughout the American regime, there were always some Chinese who were employed in non-Chinese businesses. American and British trading corporations in Iloilo hired Chinese salesmen. Local branches of foreign oil companies have had Chinese executives. Since the 1920s, Chinese have been employed as special liaison officers to the Chinese by the Bureau of Internal Revenue, the city government, and the National Bureau of Investigation. No cases are known from the past of pure Chinese working in Filipino commercial firms. However, in the 1970s young college-educated Chinese are seeking executive positions in greater numbers than ever. Because there are only a few Chinese companies in Iloilo that need executive employees, the young Chinese are either forced out of town or into Filipino corporations, several of which have large Iloilo branches.[8] Some young Chinese are opting for the diffused responsibility of a corporate position and relief from the daily anxiety entailed in being shopkeepers like their fathers. Filipino corporations often eagerly seek young Chinese for liaisons to the Chinese merchant community and for their assumed commercial superiority. Employment in a corporation as an executive employee puts a person one degree removed from the town's Chinese merchant culture.

Filipino Employees

Today the vast majority of employees in Chinese stores are Filipinos. The Chinese have had Filipino employees as manual laborers, accountants, occasionally as clerks, and as labor for cottage industries and small factories in and around the city. Filipino employees have been primarily unskilled workers under careful supervision. Since the war, however, Filipinos are more often employed as salesmen and drivers of delivery trucks, both fairly responsible positions. Still, the vast majority of employees in Chinese establishments are manual laborers, clerks, or workers in small labor-intensive factories.

Since the 1920s labor unions have organized in Manila, Cebu, and Iloilo, among other cities (Tan 1972). Since 1946 the strength of Iloilo's labor unions has grown significantly. Iloilo politicians in alliance with labor unions have created an image for Iloilo of an aggressively unionized town and are one of the main reasons for Iloilo's decline in relative prosperity. Labor problems and strikes in the 1950s caused a number of Iloilo Chinese in labor-intensive manufacturing to close out. Labor problems combined with stiff competition from Manila products are still causing men to close down factories. For one or both reasons, local Chinese in noodles, furniture, construction firms, and cottage industries, among others, are cutting back operations or closing.

Sensitivity to labor problems is still high, as evidenced by the "riot" of 1970. Public anger at the recent floating of the peso and the subsequent rise in prices was first focused on the American oil companies and Filipino public transfortation fares. It soon shifted to the Chinese for alleged hoarding of commodities and ignoring the minimum wage law. Over ₱300,000 damage was caused by street crowds to the exteriors of Chinese (and some Filipino) businesses.[9]

Along with night crime, the unionization of Filipino workers is one of the main reasons that the Chinese no longer keep their grueling 6:00 A.M. to 9:00 P.M. hours. Conventional business hours today for the Chinese are 8:00 A.M. to 5:30 or 7:00 P.M.

Besides stevedores and factory workers, only the stores with the largest numbers of employees are unionized. Filipino employees of most Chinese shopkeepers become part of the wide family business menage and have no union. Not infrequently some employees will be from a Filipina wife's or mother's side of the family. This is one of the few ways Iloilo Chinese men will tolerate Filipino kin and in-laws becoming involved in their businesses. The Filipino employee is often a young relative who is receiving city schooling and room and board in return for his work.

Because they can work more smoothly with Filipino workers, mestizos and men with Filipino wives have more easily engaged in labor-intensive businesses. By 1972, however, pure Chinese are becoming equally capable of directly managing Filipino employees.

Before the Second World War, if a Chinese was an employer it could help in some ways to have a Filipino wife, but if he was an employee a Filipina wife was anathema. If a man was employed in a Chinese business and he took a Filipino wife, he was cashiered and no one else would hire him. Further, if he was self-employed he sometimes found it very difficult to obtain the credit on his otherwise unblemished reputation that he could have had, had he married a Chinese woman. His employees and suppliers operated on the not unfounded assumption that a man who married a Filipina was either already financially shaky, or soon would be, when Filipino relatives made their demands on him.[10]

Money Handling

The Chinese and Filipinos say that the strength of the Chinese storekeeper lies in his ability to give and get credit. Chinese financing is one reason why Chinese businesses appear practically overnight in a new region or product line. Financing also increases the attractiveness of Chinese merchants to Filipino customers seeking credit. In addition, a simple traditional bookkeeping system is valuable to Chinese merchants' money handling. Like financing, bookkeeping is based on personalistic factors like reputation and trust.

A great variety of financing methods have been available to Chinese merchants. There have been mainland banks with branches in Iloilo, local Chinese exchange companies, and modern Philippine Chinese banking corporations. Filipino banks have also been patronized by certain business lines and for specific objectives. In addition to such formal organizations, there exist the community leader philanthropists, the private moneylenders, and, especially, the cabacillo or patron (immigrant sponsor and ex-employer). The i-soa, or short-term friendly loan, and the "mutual plumping up" occur daily between friends and acquaintances in town. Except for specific dealings with the Filipino banks, all of these financial operations are highly flexible,

informal dealings heavily dependent on mutual trust and publicity of the
proceeding throughout the Chinese community. A man's solid reputation
earns him an inexhaustible supply of easy credit, and it is the reputation of
individuals which makes or breaks whole businesses. Partnership arrangements are another means of raising capital and skills, but they, too, are highly
flexible and informally contractual. Their volatility under social and family
pressures has made partnerships a somewhat dated phenomenon, and they
are apparently fewer today than in the past. The traditional bookkeeping
system is also based upon this personalism and primacy of trust. The
bookkeeping system symbolizes the high flexibility, informality, and indi-
vidualism that are the traits of Iloilo Chinese shopkeeper culture. The
appearance in recent decades of bonding for the younger Chinese and of
tighter credit and shorter terms for all businessmen is an indication of the
weakening of this personalistic environment as the Chinese become less
a closed ethnic community and as competition with one another increases.

Banks and Banking

There are numerous ways that Chinese acquire loans or credit. Since
at least 1900 there have been Chinese banks of varying degrees of stability
and visibility. Some of these, like the Overseas Trade Bank, were based in
Fukien and Kwangtung and established branches in cities like Iloilo. These
banks handled remittances of overseas Chinese to their hometowns and also
served as savings banks. Their branches in Iloilo might have been no more
than an individual who accepted the banking duties as a sideline to his main
occupation. Paperwork was rudimentary. Transactions were all among
Chinese and such banks kept a low profile to the Philippine government,
for they did not pay taxes. On the other hand, security was low because
there was no regulatory body. Most such banks ceased operations in the
Philippines by 1949 when civil war forced them to Taiwan or made them
lose their holdings. Records were lost, and some Iloilo customers lost considerable sums.

Banking firms were also founded in Iloilo City by its Chinese residents.
These banks, called exchange companies, would establish agents in other
Philippine and South China cities to handle remittances and the transfer
of commercial payments. Exchange companies facilitated the intercity
movement of money between Chinese and avoided taxes on such transfers.
A transfer operated as follows. A Chinese copra dealer in Iloilo loads his
cargo on a Manila-bound vessel and receives an immediate cash payment
from the exchange for the previously arranged price of the cargo. He offers
a simple handwritten receipt in return. The receipt travels by mail to the
Manila branch of the exchange. When payment is made for delivery of the
copra to some Manila buyer, the cash goes to the Manila office of the exchange. The receipt is returned to the seller in Iloilo and the debt terminated.

The exchange companies also functioned as loan banks. An Iloilo merchant who cannot get a shipment from Manila on the credit terms he needs appeals to the exchange. The exchange pays the man's bill with a Manila check. The merchant then pays installments of the debt to the exchange. This arrangement has operated until the present. Informants claim interest rates vary depending upon the reputation of the merchant, kin ties to the exchange company, and the risk of the loan.

The establishment in the last few years in Iloilo of two modern Philippine-Chinese banking corporations which pay daily interest and offer some free intercity transfer arrangements has cut into the business of the traditional exchange companies. These banks cater primarily to Chinese merchants — over 50 percent of the city's Chinese do some or all of their banking with them, and 80 percent of their clientele is Chinese. They are flexible in their rules, paperwork, and interest rates, and offer Chinese-speaking employees to improve rapport. Their primary use has been as savings banks and as advice and information centers. The managers are frequently called upon as middlemen to aid businessmen in preparing reports and government forms or as supervisors of some new investment. The banks and bank personnel are called upon as Chinese school trustees or club officers (especially when a club will soon need a loan).

Exchange companies have not disappeared, however, for the simple reason that some Chinese prefer their more personalistic methods or cannot qualify for a bank loan.

Mutual aid societies do not exist in Iloilo City and probably not at all in the Philippines. In these societies, members contribute to a common fund and draw lots for the use of the fund for a certain time at a certain interest rate. While Filipinos have sometimes suspected the business guilds of operating as mutual aid societies, the Iloilo guilds carefully avoid such use of their treasuries, which are meant for charity and protection. Iloilo informants claim that large Manila family associations have on occasion agreed to back some of their more illustrious members in financial difficulties. But family association leaders in Iloilo refuse to make business loans from association coffers.

Filipino banks have also been patronized, at least for the last forty or fifty years, especially by Chinese in big business, manufacturing, import-export, and native products. These Chinese, in order to acquire the bonding, licenses, and large sums of money needed in their lines, have operated through the same sort of official channels as their Filipino competitors. For example, rice and sugar dealers bond their warehouses to Filipino banks in order to receive low interest loans on crop purchases.

Business with Filipino banks lends an aura of respectability and patriotism to Chinese operations. Filipino banks furnish a way for a Chinese to invest in conspicuous enterprises without unduly alerting tax officials. For example, in one case a Chinese possessed the ₱200,000 requisite to build a hotel, but to avoid attention, he deposited it in a Filipino bank at 6 percent interest and drew a loan at 8 percent interest. For 2 percent the investor covered his personal wealth.

Credit and Loans

Until the advent of modern Chinese banking corporations in Iloilo in 1968, most of the commercial financing was a personal affair between Chinese individuals. Acquiring merchandise involved a traditional credit system, but buildings and other investments required personal loans.

The modern credit system is a descendant of the nineteenth century cabacillo-agent system described by Wickberg (1965:74). Often the patron of a man who has finished service as an apprentice employee will act as his supplier. The patron is familiar with the reputation of the new merchant and is likely to offer him the best credit terms and be most loyal in times of goods shortages. Unlike the nineteenth century cabacillo, however, the patron is not necessarily the sole supplier and "boss" of the agent's business. Many of a patron's wholesale customers may be his former employees, but they are independent of him. In fact, as T'ien (1953:44) confirms also for Sarawak, the Chinese customers are involved in a subtle power play with their Chinese ex-patrons to see whether it is the debtor or the creditor who determines the amount and frequency of credit.

Informants claim that it was not infrequent before the Second World War for a man to begin business with 100 percent credit on his merchandise. Terms for repayment were very flexible. Even foreign firms offered much credit and long repayment periods to Chinese. For most individuals with unsullied reputations, 40 to 80 percent credit used to be the usual range. By the 1970s only individuals with very good or very old contacts can expect as much as 50 percent credit, and the time allowed for repayment is shorter. Within the city, a week is the usual term for a casual debt. Debts of more than thirty days are not uncommon but are charged interest.[11] Debts contracted between men in Iloilo and Manila are usually for thirty days.

In the 1970s it is no longer possible to start a Chinese business in Iloilo with 100 percent credit. Apparently the value of one's reputation has declined as acceptable collateral in a town with more Chinese businesses and more competition than ever before. To start a retail-wholesale textile store, for example, requires ₱70,000 to ₱100,000 to pay bonds to suppliers, to pay rent and purchase stock, to pay official costs and bribes, and so forth. When the Chinese community was smaller and more closely knit and, thus, had stronger sanctions, personal reputation carried much more weight for building a business.

Even though there is a discount to Iloilo's shopkeepers if they purchase their Manila goods with cash, they prefer the leverage with their patron that credit dealing permits. Iloilo's wholesalers, by the same token, must offer their Chinese clients credit or lose business. As a result of these constant credit dealings, the Chinese informally classify their clients into four categories, depending upon their repayment habits. A *siōng-kheh*, or "top customer," is one who pays a down payment and always repays the remainder on time. A *hó-hêng*, or "good repayment," while he may not pay cash down, at least repays on time. Unpredictable is the *bōe-ti-tit* or "impossible sailing" for he is a customer who is constantly changing his habits about repayment and cash in advance. The *chhàu-kheh*, or "smelly customer" is one who does not pay in advance and constantly seeks extensions on his repayment arrangements. Such a troublesome customer is kept only because of extenuating circumstances — perhaps he is a kinsman.

When a Chinese customer becomes difficult about repayments and seems unconcerned about the malicious gossip his creditors spread about him, then sometimes a boycott is informally organized to pressure the delinquent into line. Such a man is liable to be without stock when supplies are limited, as they were in the lumber storage of 1971, when only hó-hêng and special friends could get the meager lumber from their suppliers.

Business dealings of Chinese with Filipino suppliers have long required bonding. For the first time in the 1960s and 1970s, Chinese suppliers are requesting new Chinese wholesale customers to post a bond in order to facilitate credit dealings. Most of the customers affected are young Philippine-born Chinese businessmen. Bonds are especially necessary for salesmen and native product dealers. Postwar cultural changes have greatly weakened the old sanctions and the sanctity of personal trust in the comunity. With each new generation of businessmen the Chinese community grows larger and less strictly demarcated. Businessmen are no longer totally dependent on their standing within the old reference group. Business relations with Filipinos, Filipino banks, and foreigners and a working knowledge of Western business practices and law have all contributed to put the younger generation on the periphery of the older Chinese business community.

Yet a break from the Chinese business community is the last thing an ambitious young businessman would seek. Some mestizo informants lamented to me that their inability to speak Chinese severely handicapped their business futures in town. Those mestizos who worked for Filipinos looked longingly at the large local markets closed to them because of their own inability to be accepted by the Chinese community. Some Filipino merchants even send their children to Chinese schools in an effort to draw closer to the Chinese and provide richer business futures for their children.

Besides the credit system between patrons and clients in a specific line, there is the much broader pattern of personal loans. As mentioned above, Chinese and Filipino banks are sources of loans for some of Iloilo's largest Chinese corporations, but most loans are negotiated on a personal basis.

Because the profit margins in most lines have shrunk in recent years due to heavy competition and interference from government officials, a number of Iloilo merchants have closed their shops or shifted to low-capital lines and put their surplus capital to work in private loans and investments. Credit is tighter for merchants now, especially for the poor risks, who will agree to the high interest which the private moneylenders require. Young Chinese starting out without backers often turn to these moneylenders. It is not uncommon for a man to borrow ₱10,000 indefinitely at ₱300 interest per month. These private transactions are always between Chinese or Chinese and mestizos — Filipinos do not participate.

In the first half of the twentieth century when immigrants from China entered the Iloilo business community, certain individuals and businesses, because of their large size and community leadership positions, served as $\bar{a}u$-$piah$-soa^n ("back mountains," or backers) for large numbers of immigrants. Both for philanthropic reasons and to acquire political supporters, certain prominent men funded newcomers in businesses without requiring collateral. For example, a certain Cantonese named A Hong was responsible in the 1920s and 1930s for helping a large number of today's Cantonese businessmen on the road to prosperous grocery, restaurant, and tailoring businesses. These beneficiaries were not his apprentices in the usual apprentice system. They were simply men to whom A Hong made generous loans at easy terms. This redounded to his political credit in the city. A number of Fukienese merchants also acted as loan sources for Fukienese immigrants. There usually was some specialization in such a man's loan activities. He might concentrate on help to townmates, sibmates, or his dialect group.

Men starting in business without adequate credit or skills usually formed partnerships. The combination of several men's skills and capital provided greater security in the treacherous early years of a business venture. However, as the Chinese say, "*Hàp ti phái^{n}siá*," "Cooperation is a hard word to write," for Chinese partnerships are quite unstable. Partnerships are admittedly only a way of acquiring capital. If a man had a reputation that would deserve an adequate credit line, he avoided partnerships and struck off on his own. Businessmen will claim "*Pat lâng khah hó pat chî^n*," Connections are more important than cash in the bank." Until recently a man could begin a store with nothing if his reputation with prominent men and his patron was intact.

Naturally, all else being equal, an affluent merchant could acquire a loan more easily than an impecunious one. Even merchants with money do much of their business on credit and with loans, for such arrangements provide more working capital. It is not an admission of weakness to deal on credit or with loans but a sign of good reputation for the man who successfully maintains his status as "top customer." A thousand pesos on credit, a thousand borrowed, and a thousand on hand make the enterprising merchant 200 percent more maneuverable than those who choose or are forced to deal in cash.

One of the most common forms of loan is the informal *í-soà* or "transfer," a euphemism for a short-term loan, frequently at low or no interest. The connotation of an *"i-soa"* is that the lender is not actually parting with his money but transferring it to work elsewhere at a *compadre's* or kinsman's business. The i-soa is negotiated casually and orally between acquaintances. The length of the transfer varies from a week to indefinitely, depending on the relationship between the loan parties. When Mr. Tan, a native products dealer, needs a lump sum to close a copra purchase on Saturday, he often turns to Mr. Go, a shoe store owner, who carries large amounts of cash on weekends for his store. On Monday when the banks open, Mr. Tan will withdraw money to repay Mr. Go and no interest will be paid.

When the í-soà arrangement of short-term loans continues regularly and reciprocally, it is called *sa^n-chiàh-khi* or "mutual plumping up." The two parties offer each other merchandise on credit or cash loans without interest or down payment. These patterns of "plumping up" and money transfer occur almost daily and push toward an equilibrium of cash reserves and merchandise among the Chinese at any point in time in the city.

Most loans, then, are a personalistic matter, but they are not private affairs. In a community the size of Iloilo all financial negotiations become known. Everyone's standing as a credit or loan customer is known, and it is this general knowledge which forms the basis for the trust which secures oral personal negotiations. Creditors advertise their benevolence and debtors are proud of their credit lines. In order to keep his financial transactions secret, a Chinese must venture outside his community. This does not mean negotiating with Chinese in other cities, for word is sure to pass around. Arrangements with Filipino banks or Filipino friends (especially godparents) are more likely to preserve privacy.

In the personalistic patterns of financing and credit described here, trust, or *sìn-iõng*, and the publicity of all arrangements are clearly the cement which secures dealings between Iloilo Chinese. As with business in Western nations, confidence in management means growth potential. In Iloilo, management is synonymous with ownership, for 87 percent of the businesses are family-owned single proprietorships. Confidence in management translates into community reputation of the individual Chinese owners. The Chinese recite, *"Seng-lí ke sī tsòe hia-è lâng,"* "All business operates through just one man." By any analysis, the owner's skills and his reputation for trustworthiness are the primary factors creating business success in the paternalistic environment of Iloilo City.

Accounting

Chinese accounting methods symbolize this centrality of trust in the individual. The personality of the older uneducated immigrant businessmen, their inflexibility in a foreign culture, their reliance on kinsmen, and their simple management techniques all created commercial enterprises dependent upon single individuals. Managers and clerical staff are rare; such posts are indirectly filled by relatives. The owner is the bookkeeper, and the books are never available for examination. To urge a partner or employer for permission to examine the books is an enormous breach of trust. The accounts are kept by the owner or main partner primarily as personal memory aids. They are much simpler than Western accounts, take less time to compile, and are more prone to error. The Chinese accounting principles as followed in Iloilo are traditional and passed from one generation to the next by explicit teaching, yet every shopkeeper improvises upon this tradition in accordance with his needs and personality. Some men still rely completely on their memories.

Since 1939, Chinese have been required to keep books in English or Spanish, or they pay a translator to prepare their books for tax auditing under the Bookkeeping Act. As a result, most businessmen keep two completely different sets of books — one in Chinese for themselves and one in English for the tax auditors. The latter is often handled by a professional bookkeeper and bears little relationship to the former in either technique or content.

The Chinese keep two, sometimes three books: the *jit-ki*, or journal; the *tsong-phō*, or ledger, and the *jip-he-phō*, or warehouse record. The journal holds daily itemized income and expenses. The ledger contains a summary of journal entries by category and an inventory of goods received, notes payable, and notes receivable. The warehouse record is a warehouse inventory and record of the movement of merchandise in the warehouse. It is a detailed supplement to the ledger.

In a typical day's entries into the journal, income entries are entered vertically across the top half of the page and expenses entered vertically on the bottom half. Each entry is dated and mentions item description, item cost, count, and total cost. At the end of a day, store receipts are counted and entered in the day's income. Daily tong (graft money) and other odd expenses will be entered also, though they will not appear in the public books.

Periodically — perhaps once a week or once a month — journal entries are reorganized into categories of income and expense and written into the ledger. Merchandise purchased is entered as income, and the amount paid is entered as expenses. Wages, household expenses, rent, tong, utilities, and loans and credits are all tabulated in the ledger.

Though the amount of goods purchased and taken into the warehouse is recorded, the amount of goods going out on sale or credit is not known until a check is run by the bookkeeper before new purchases are made or until the annual inventory is made. A textile store will purchase a thousand pesos worth of checkered cloth, enter this merchandise on the books, then periodically acquire more checkered cloth as stock visibly decreases. However, it is not likely that a check will be run to determine the amount of checkered cloth left until the annual inventory is taken (usually around Christmas to New Year's Day). The amount remaining is compared to the amount purchased for the year, and thus is computed the amount sold and consequent profit. For most shopkeepers, the measure of profit for the year is the increase in value of the inventory, plus perhaps bank savings. Profits are rarely computed exactly by the bookkeeper-owner. Owners prefer a little obfuscation because of the resulting leverage they maintain with partners, employees, and family members.

The traditional bookkeeping system is the primary one for most businesses. Some of the local branches of large national corporations rely primarily on modern bookkeeping practices because of the complexity of their enterprises or preference of their owners. I do not think these businesses also keep old-fashioned Chinese books.

Partnerships

Not all businesses in Iloilo are run solely by one man, for we have seen that 6 percent of the enterprises are family partnerships (involving more than one independent household) and 4 percent are nonfamily partnerships. The methods of cooperation in a Chinese partnership, the categories of partners, and the dynamics of these unstable enterprises are the subject of this section.

Informants claim that partnerships were more numerous in the years before the Second World War. Before the sex ratio became more equal by the big influx of women during the 1930s, "bachelor" businessmen could combine capital and live together without domestic complications.

Partnerships, generally called kong-si, or "companies," almost always lacked legal and written contracts between members. The partners verbally agreed on the requirements for capital accumulation and spending, division of profits, and the divisions to be made upon a reshuffling or dissolution of the partnership. They simply followed certain, rather loose conventions. This system meant great ease in creating capital combines, but it also made for many conflicts, misunderstandings, and unscrupulous manipulations.

Partnerships were very pragmatic affairs in which men with certain skills but little capital, undeveloped personal reputations, and small families or none at all, joined together to get started. Men on the rise avoided partnerships (see Mr. Lo's story in chapter 7) because they obscured the correlation in the community's eyes between one's personal qualities and the store's success, thus slowing the development of one's business reputation. Partnerships were primarily for beginners or men whose declining conditions needed new injections of capital or skill.

Among the Philippine Chinese, at least, partnerships are volatile organizations due to domestic matters, old-fashioned management methods, and the personalistic nature of the money handling and power structure. Consequently, although a great percentage of Iloilo's businessmen have been involved in them at some point in their lives, only about 10 percent of the businesses at any one time are partnerships.

The domestic problems which split partnerships are virtually identical to those which split joint families upon the death of the household head (see chapter 6). As soon as one or more partners bring in Chinese or Filipino wives and begin their families, inevitable inequalities put a strain on the profit-splitting agreements. No longer can partners be one unified household. Partners' wives "undermine" the partnership by adding to the complexity of the power structure and arguing over the size of their respective domestic budgets. The sheer number of individuals who become dependent on the one enterprise saps it of its capital.

Old-fashioned management practices and the informality of the partnership agreements cause them to disintegrate, too. The accounting is a one-man job, and it inevitably leads to a certain secrecy and manipulation by the bookkeeping partner(s). Many times partners split because the outsider partners lose trust in the bookkeeping of the insider partners. Because every man is usually a generalized worker in the store, assuming a part of all the duties, not infrequently partners find themselves failing to coordinate their separate actions. In one rice and corn wholesale dealership, the manager-partners include the old man Ng; his son Ng Lim; his two nephews; Mr. Chua, an ex-employee promoted to full partner; Chua's son; and Jorge Lim, an adopted son, as bookkeeper. With these seven active managers, there are invariably financial difficulties and arguments as each transacts business about the province and later discover they have overpurchased, undersold, or acquired the wrong commodities. A departure of some of the partners is anticipated. Unless the partners are functionally differentiated or unless their capital contributions are so unequal as to indicate a clear decision-making structure, such disorganization is common. Individual business failures of Iloilo Chinese are not infrequently caused by cheating or bad organization in a partnership.

Partnerships are, therefore, volatile and somewhat dangerous as well as quite useful at times. For these reasons Filipinos are rarely partners with Chinese in capital investment or actual working partnerships. Adding the ethnic difference to other liabilities poses too great a threat, and informants claim there would be even less sin-iong than usual. In a few cases in Iloilo, but more often in big cities like Manila and Cebu, Filipinos are among the incorporators of businesses and organizations, but these persons are usually either inactive stockholders or fictive board members. There are very few corporations of this sort in Iloilo.

In *The Fabric of Chinese Society*, Morton Fried (1953:138) calculates that Chinese mercantile partnerships in Ch'u City, Anhwei province, run over 25 percent of all enterprises and most of the larger shops. Fried writes that partnerships allowed merchants to minimize the nepotism which threatens management of an extended family business. When they involve combinations of kinsmen,

> partnerships are designed primarily to increase the amount of capitalization as well as to formalize and contractualize the roles of various participants in the enterprise. At the same time, use of a civil and legalistic technique of combination permits individuals to escape from the too close and smothering scrutiny of a paternalistic extended family (Fried 1953:140).

In contrast to Anhwei merchants, overseas Chinese shopkeepers in Iloilo City do not form partnerships through "civil and legalistic techniques" but generally rely on the good will of all to make the arrangement work. Also, only a minority of the partnerships in Iloilo include nonkinsmen, many of the partnerships are small, and partnerships simply do not comprise as great a proportion of the enterprises as in Anhwei. Finally, as I have suggested, partnerships in Iloilo are quite prone to disintegration by the same factors which break up extended family businesses, so they are definitely not free of nepotism as an obstacle to good management. The Chinese partnerships in Anhwei described by Fried appear to be bigger, more contractual, and more permanent than Iloilo Chinese partnerships. Whether Iloilo is characteristic of all overseas Chinese communities regarding partnerships is not known.

The conventions which govern the financial and control arrangements in Iloilo's Chinese partnerships are at least seventy to eighty years old and provide the main guidelines for community categorization of partnerships. In a kong-si, or partnership, there may be regular partners, im-hūn-sia partners, am-ko partners, im-ko partners, as well as a few other more rare roles like the chē soaⁿ thâu-ke manager. These partners may further be divided by their duties (sometimes implicit in the above classification) as tūi-lāi ("on the inside") or kia gōa-si ("running the outside affairs").

Regular partners contribute shares and labor to the enterprise and receive profits according to the proportionate size of these shares and labor. Major and minor partners can be classified, then, according to their proportionate shares of the capital. All other factors being equal, decision-making power will correlate with the percentage of shares held, which in turn usually follows the respective partners' socioeconomic ranking in the community. Rarely is a wealthy man a working partner and a decision-making equal of a poorer man. If statuses outside the enterprise or shares within the enterprise become too unbalanced, the partners generally shift into one of the following partnership types in order to preserve harmony.

The im-hūn-sia partner is the "favored percentage" partner. He is often an employee promoted to this status or a man with specific talents that a firm needs badly enough that they will admit him without his making a contribution to capital. As Fried has written for Chinese partnerships desirous of a skilled staff, "the capital outlay of some 'partner' was so small as to be a mere token investment" (1953:140). The "favored percentage" partner makes no contribution to capital but receives a percentage of profits. There usually is a significant status differential between the regular partners and the im-hūn-sia partners, and the latter are dependent on the honesty of the bookkeeping of the former in order to receive their due share. They frequently suspect that their shares border on the minimum possible. The arrangement is not very stable if the im-hūn-sia partner is on his way upward in his career.

The second type of special partnership is the im-kó, or "favored share" partner, who contributes capital and labor like a minor partner, but whose profit is calculated as a larger percentage than his shares. For example, Mr. Po and Mr. Kho formed a wholesale textile partnership and split profits evenly, even though their relative capital contributions more closely approximated 70:30, respectively. Two factors entered into this division to make it agreeable to Mr. Po, the major partner. First, he was a Chinese citizen, illiterate, with few good Filipino or Chinese connections, and could not speak Ilongo. Mr. Kho could meet all of these criteria. Also, Mr. Kho had a wife and children, which entailed a greater monthly expense than bachelor Po incurred. Much of his profits, therefore, would be consumed by his family. In return, Kho agreed not to reinvest any more of his "favored share" in the business than Po could match. In this way their relative positions would remain the same, and Po would not be penalized for his original generosity to Kho. Although in theory the giver of the favored share is the patron and the recipient his social inferior, the extenuating circumstances which force the patron to offer the im-kó usually negate these status advantages.

The distinction in roles between the tùi-lāi ("on the inside") role and the kià gôa-si ("running the outside affairs") position can be seen in the jobs of Mr. Kho and Mr. Po. Mr. Po allied himself with Mr. Kho because he needed someone competent to deal with the outside — to befriend the police, deal with Filipino politicians, travel and make purchases, talk to customers, and so on. Mr. Po in return supplied greater capital, watched the employees, kept the books, manned the cash register, did inventory, handled stock, and so on. Most of these tasks can be handled alone right on the premises. In chapter 7 we will see another case, where old Mr. Lo retired to inside work as soon as his son Juan came of age to run the outside affairs. It is the man running the outside affairs whom the Chinese occasionally utilize as license "dummy," as the Filipinos call him, to avoid nationalization laws against Chinese citizens in business.

A third type of partnership is the àm-kó, or "silent share." This partner invests capital but does not actively labor in or manage the partnership. Unlike the other types of special partners, this àm-kó partner is usually an affluent respected person with a business of his own who has put some of

his money to work in a friend's or kinsman's enterprise. He may receive
his shares in cash, have them reinvested, or benevolently give them up to
increase his stature as a patron. If he relinquishes his share to help his client,
word usually spreads through word of mouth. His deeds redounds to his
credit, so his capital is not lost. In some cases, as when a widow is investing
her husband's estate, the àm-kó partnership is a straightforward profit-making
arrangement for persons who cannot work or do not know the business.
A man may also buy an àm-kó share in another's store so he can have his
sons apprenticed there.

Similar to the àm-kó partner is the chē soa^n thâu-ke, or "inactive boss."
He contributes capital but does not labor in the business. Unlike the àm-kó,
however, the chē soa^n thâu-ke is the founder, entrepreneur, main stockholder, or heir to the business and definitely recognized as the boss, or
thau-ke. Because of other demands on his time or because of lack of interest
in the enterprise, this man turns his management function over to kinsmen
or friends as his agents. He directs his business from the "top of the moun-
tain," to literally translate his label. While this type of boss and stockholder
exists in the Philippine Chinese business community, it is rare in Iloilo City.
In the few local cases known, the chē-soa^n thâu-ke lives either in Manila or
Hongkong, managing other concerns, and leaves the Iloilo business in the
hands of proteges, kinsmen, or friends.

These, then, are the main types of partnership agreements among Philippine Chinese. It should be noticed that there are two continua, one of work
and one of capital, along which partners can be placed and where the ideal
types of im-kó, àm-kó, and so on are marked out. Because of this flexibility
of terms, disagreements arise among partners regarding responsibilities and
privileges. Relative power in the business is aligned with status differentials
inherent in most partnership arrangements, but in many cases where differentials are small, power may also be a point of contention. Were these partnerships as contractual as this discussion of their criteria makes them sound,
then Iloilo Chinese partnerships would be more efficient and successful,
like those described by Morton Fried (1953) in Anhwei province in China.
However, family and kinship matters can short-circuit these verbal contracts,
and an overreliance on personalistic trust (sin-iong) inevitably makes room
for shady dealing. Because of this, partnerships, as ubiquitous and as useful
as they are in men's careers, are notoriously short-lived.

Contracts and the Law

Overseas Chinese in the Philippines have traditionally negotiated all
business and legal matters verbally or with a minimum of paperwork. These
negotiations have been secured by community knowledge of the reputation
of the parties involved. Civil suits and even many criminal suits between

Chinese have been handled within the community by traditional methods of mediation, family responsibility, and intracommunity sanctions. Recourse to Filipino law and the courts has been extremely rare.[12] But, as I have sketched above, as the Chinese community continues in its isolation from China in the Philippine environment, its members become less exclusively located within it and less dependent upon it. The inevitable outcome is a weakening of community sanctions against wayward members or against unpopular activities. The weakening of sanctions combined with increased competitive pressures in a stagnant commercial environment has led to more recourse to Filipino law and courts.

The subject of the overseas Chinese legal system and its changes is a mammoth and untouched field and cannot be treated in depth here. Two aspects of it are applicable to this discussion of Iloilo Chinese business practices: business contracts and business court cases. In chapters 6 and 7 Chinese inheritance practices in Iloilo will also illustrate Chinese law and its changes.

The official incorporation of some Chinese businesses and their registration with the Philippine Securities and Exchange Commission have meant the formal outlining of the responsibilities and investments of the members of some businesses. Even family corporations have legally defined shares in the business apportioned among its members. In incorporated businesses, therefore, individuals have clearly defined shares and responsibilities which they can defend in a court if need be. This is a development which began only in the 1950s with the Filipino nationalization campaign against alien Chinese businesses. A Filipino corporation is allowed to have up to 40 percent alien capital and directors. Thus, incorporating in response to Filipino pressures has temporarily allowed some Chinese to continue business. But this adjustment has implied a breach in the traditional practices of verbal contracts and private bookkeeping methods. Corporations are still a very small proportion of Iloilo's firms, but their practices of legal contracts between partners, use of notary publics and lawyers, and open accounting are all influencing the unincorporated businesses.

Iloilo Chinese are beginning to employ lawyers and to wield them against one another in the Philippine courts. The owner of a rice and corn store sued the owner of a variety store because the latter's son was among a group of boys who mistook the former's son for a Filipino and roughed him up one night. The case went to court, but a settlement was reached out of court. More common are civil suits between landlords and shopkeeper-tenants. Some Chinese sublease buildings to other Chinese and make a profit on the difference between their lease and the sublease. Tenants will strive to "undermine" this sort of arrangement by breaking leases and negotiating directly with the Filipino who owns the building.

Also common are eviction suits against tenants by Chinese building owners. One Chinese in hardware was treated graciously by his landlord, a Chinese who leased half of his own hardware store to him. When the tenant's business began to surpass the landlord's, the graciousness ceased and the landlord tried to evict him. The tenant resisted in court, and the case waxed and waned for half a year before the tenant decided to move.

Chinese lawyers are few, so most businesses and organizations which retain lawyers have Filipino lawyers. These lawyers are not infrequently local political dignitaries, so a Chinese man's legal adviser doubles as his political patron. The Chinese chambers of commerce, boards of directors of schools, lineage associations, and business guilds all retain Filipino lawyers. These lawyers serve primarily as middlemen in legal affairs with the Philippine government. But contact with these lawyers has led to their increasing use by Chinese in their battles with one another. Court cases are still infrequent, sordid, and expensive — most litigation is still handled informally. Yet, the very real threat of court suits in contemporary Iloilo puts the clout back into business arrangements between Chinese.

Investing

Iloilo's Chinese are more conservative financially than other Philippine Chinese. Iloilo men are viewed as frugal to the point of miserliness. Because few are in debt, Iloilo's shopkeepers are considered wealthy. An anecdote is told among Iloilo Chinese which is in character if not factually correct. When the first all-Chinese bank opened in Iloilo City in 1968, Chinese made large deposits. All the money, it is remarked, smelled musty, as though it had been buried for a long time.

Both Chinese banks handle very large savings accounts. The bank managers allege that deposits are much larger than in other comparable Chinese communities. The savings accounts are essentially idle money: the Chinese do not know where or how to invest all their funds. In their opinion Iloilo's commercial environment is unpromising and reinvesting profits in their main lines is not productive. Many consider investing in other communities risky because the money cannot be watched. Consequently, the banks conduct a thriving business lending Iloilo savings to Chinese in other cities, who have investment opportunities and are not hesitant to engage in high financing. When investing heavily in an enterprise themselves, Iloilo Chinese use their savings or borrow from friends on the basis of their reputations. A minority borrow from banks or other institutions where collateral is required.

What was referred to earlier as the i-soá and "mutual plumping up" blends gradually on a continuum of personal loans into an investment with friends and acquaintances. Most well-to-do merchants have allocated large portions of their reserve capital for personal investments with friends both in and out of town. They function as "silent partners" whose initial investment brings them a regular annual return without any management responsibilities.

This is one way Iloilo Chinese risk out-of-town investments. The joint responsibility of a partnership with a friend or kinsman makes the risk bearable.

Iloilo Chinese in recent years have diversified their business lines in order to absorb extra money and avoid profitless overinvestment in their usual lines. This practice is, of course, widespread among the provincial Chinese, whose local markets must be approached with numerous different merchandise lines in order to turn a decent profit. Men who operate cinemas have added adjacent snack bars. A man in hardware adds motors, then he begins to forge tools himself. A man with auto parts opens a service station, or vice-versa. Sometimes diversification follows the needs of the market and not simply the skills of the entrepreneur. One successful man operates a motorcycle dealership, a cement warehouse, a shipping agency, and a distillery. While diversification has always been a method of investing for certain Chinese, it has become increasingly common in Iloilo City. Many men now have complete families with a number of adult sons and daughters, each capable of managing a different branch of the family conglomerate.

There is one exception to the stagnation of Iloilo's economic endeavors, and that is agribusiness. Sugar is the primary attraction, but a number of Chinese are also venturing into piggeries and poultry farms. They have long been involved indirectly in copra, sugar, rice, salt, and fish because of their investments in equipment, seed, or fertilizer on behalf of Filipinos. The Filipino producers in return sell the crops at a discount to the Chinese investors. But besides these indirect involvements the Chinese are becoming more interested in ownership and production themselves. A number of Chinese have confidence in their Filipino citizenship status and are willing to compete with Filipinos anew in the latter's traditional territory. They are willing to purchase land or accept liens on land in return for investments of machinery and chemicals. By this investment they not only acquire shares in the primary wealth of the province, but they also eliminate a link in the marketing and distribution scheme.

Chinese investments rarely involve Filipinos except in agribusiness with Filipino producers or landholders. There is very little casual, personal investment in Filipino business. Conversely, no Filipinos invest in Chinese firms. Filipino and Chinese partnerships do not occur and corporations with both Filipino and Chinese directors are rare outside Manila.

Manufacturing is not yet an investment possibility for Iloilo Chinese. Power costs are prohibitive because electricity is a monopoly utility. Labor unions have been troublesome in postwar years. The distribution system which brings manufactured goods from Manila into the western Visayas is efficient enough to drive out competition from local manufacturers.

It became very popular in the 1960s among both Chinese and Filipinos to invest in the burgeoning Manila stock market. But devaluation of the peso in 1968 and the floating rate in 1969 caused the stock market to slip and many Iloilo Chinese lost money. By 1972 the Chinese banks in Iloilo had attracted some of the larger investors by introducing them to the money market. The Chinese bank managers, acting as brokers, were able to offer 14.5 percent profit to their money market clients. This investment was particularly attractive because, like the personal and private investments arranged between friends, it could be negotiated simply, quietly, and with little risk.

Trucks and jeeps have become a standard and nearly obligatory investment for Iloilo businessmen since 1966. Prior to that time, provincial buses, trucks, and jeeps could load and unload cargo right in front of stores and warehouses. City ordinances in 1966 changed the flow of city traffic and prevented commercial vehicles from entering the downtown area. Faced with a hiatus in their transportation system, the Chinese began buying vehicles on a large scale for the first time. They undertook more local transportation and delivery themselves and, thus, eliminated another link in the distribution system.

Real Estate and Storefronts

Until the 1950s few Iloilo Chinese owned any land, buildings, or even their own storefronts. In prewar Iloilo a number of buildings and haciendas were owned by a few very wealthy Chinese. Most businessmen invested in land and buildings in China, partly in preparation for their retirement there. The confiscation of a great deal of their property by the Communists forced the overseas Chinese to turn their interest in real estate to their adopted country. As it grew more common in the late 1950s for Chinese to adopt Filipino citizenship, more Chinese became eligible to purchase land or own buildings. Since then many Iloilo Chinese have acquired commercial buildings and lots, residential buildings, and agricultural land.

The vast majority of Chinese shopkeepers rent their storefronts. Although the land and the building may be owned by a Filipino, subleasing arrangements are sometimes very convoluted, involving several Chinese intermediaries. In such cases very few tenants deal directly with Filipino landlords.

Acquiring a storefront requires a bid to the current tenant. The bid indicates the size of a cash "goodwill" offering, called *tiam-tui*. In 1972, goodwill payments frequently amounted to ₱10,000 (about U.S. $1,500).

Demand for good locations is high. Most storefront openings attract numerous bids. The downtown area is a small group of streets around the central market and native products market. Outside of this area, rents are low because the customer traffic is light. Thus, there is great demand for downtown locations and goodwill costs continually rise. Businesses which do not cater to walk-in customers are moving out of the downtown area because rents have risen so rapidly.

The difficulty of acquiring desirable locations for new businesses is an obstacle to store expansion and diversification. Unless a storekeeper has adequate competent family members to man his branches, he strives to locate them close to each other for ease of supervision. This is not readily possible when the storefront market is tight.

Although Chinese are buying and constructing buildings in the city, they usually do so on land owned by Filipinos. The general practice is for the Chinese to construct the building and occupy it rent-free for a specified number of years then surrender it to the landowner. Chinese are preferred as landlords by Chinese shopkeepers because rents tend to be lower and payments more flexible. Chinese rent warehouses, public halls, apartments, shops, office space, and houses to one another.

Major fires are the paramount force changing the shape and composition of Philippine cities, according to Daniel Doeppers (1971). Five fires have leveled significantly large areas of the city since the Second World War. These fires have permitted Chinese to move into building construction and ownership in the business district. The last fire, in 1966, was the largest fire in a business district in the history of the Philippines. Threat of fire has forced over 90 percent of the downtown businesses to subscribe to fire insurance with the town's Chinese insurance salesmen. Businesses without insurance find it difficult to get credit from suppliers.

Chinese who own buildings, lots, and houses usually divide the titles of ownership among their family members for tax purposes to obscure their centralized ownership. Daughters are given buildings and lots as "dowries," frequently with the understanding that they and their husbands are merely caretakers for their father. Men who have capable kinsmen in Hongkong or Taiwan will purchase real estate in these countries and so further increase their holdings without drawing much attention to their wealth.

Although ever greater numbers of Chinese invested in real estate in the late fifties and early sixties, these investments had the disadvantages of being visible, immobilizing large amounts of capital, and appreciating more slowly than other assets. Buying real estate had become something of a fad. Many Chinese who precipitously invested in it found it necessary to sell out in order to use the capital elsewhere. A number of Chinese business failures in those years can be attributed to shopkeepers sinking capital into real estate and floundering when they could not liquidate fast enough to salvage their stocks of merchandise.

Anticipation of the floating rate for the peso in 1969 spurred a rash of Chinese speculation in all forms of real estate, both within the city and extending into nearby municipalities. Families with available cash who had never ventured into land now hoped to profit from the inevitable devaluation that would follow the floating of the peso. Subdivision tracts, apartment buildings, and rice and sugar land all became attractive assets. Chinese in agribusiness who had always operated previously by leasing land or merely financing Filipino producers on the land became full-fledged *hacenderos* by buying farms outright.

The movement to investing in land has meant investment in residential lots, too. Thus, the traditional apartment-over-the-store residence pattern is giving way slowly to a more suburban pattern. Fires, fashions, and wives have all promoted this trend.

Most house-buying began after the big business district fire of 1966. A few of the leaders of the Chinese community bought houses in semi-rural Molo to the west of Iloilo City. Then the rush began, as many Chinese purchased houses in Molo or large walled family compounds on the southern edge of town.

Since 1949 and the growth locally of complete Chinese families, many families have simply physically outgrown their store residences. Frequently a family head will purchase a house and lodge part of his family there, remaining himself with his wife in his downtown store. The house is occupied by the sons and daughters and often is registered in their name.

Although wives often remain over the store with their husbands, it is frequently due to their pressure that houses are acquired. Filipino and mestizo wives customarily seek a house and lot for a sense of security and insurance for their old age. The husband, who might be a Chinese citizen, registers the house in the wife's name. Since most Filipino and mestizo wives are common-law wives with few legal rights, they are providing themselves with additional leverage vis-a-vis their husbands.[13] However, Chinese women, too, have been campaigning for houses, refrigerators, air conditioners, and the like. They have been influenced by the aspirations of the Filipinos and are also competing with each other in their traditional feminine domain.

If a Chinese family had Chinese citizenship, this once would completely rule out their buying a surburban home or other real estate, but now many aliens acquire property, too. A Chinese friend or relative who is a Filipino citizen simply registers it in his or her own name. Daughters, nephews, sons-in-law, and sometimes even trusted employees fill this role. If there is any need for a bond — and frequently today there is — then the naturalized Chinese who registered purchase of the property will give collateral to the alien who actually owns it. The collateral is usually an IOU for the cash value of the property. This is held by the alien until he can legally assume ownership of the property, usually through a child or spouse.

Consumption Patterns

A community composed almost exclusively of merchant families can be expected to have somewhat unusual patterns of spending for consumption.

The Chinese can obtain most consumer items from friends, kinsmen, and business contracts. Filipinos, of course, purchase goods as much as possible through a similar personal or family network. But because so much of the middle range of business is in Chinese hands and because virtually all Chinese are in business, the difference between Chinese and Filipino buying patterns is one of great degree. Only in a Filipino farm barrio with its homogeneous population and occupational structure does the level of consumer cooperation approach that of the urban Chinese business community.

The distribution chain for consumer goods in Iloilo has many links. As an item passes further down the chain, the proportion of profit in its rising price increases. To avoid this infinite subdivision of merchandise and increments in price, the Chinese purchase most of their family needs in bulk at "friendly discounts."

Because all Iloilo Chinese know each other, there is a general "friendly discount" for any Chinese who requests it for personal use from another Chinese store. The closer the friendship or kinship to the shopkeeper, the greater the discount, to the point that goods may be sold at cost or at a loss to close relatives and friends. A loss may be incurred as follows. A Chinese housewife who is a friend of Mr. Po's wife requests a case of baby milk at cost. Mr. Po, a wholesaler, does not handle the baby milk himself but acts as an agent for the woman by ordering the milk from his friend. Mr. Po then sells the milk at cost, but because a receipt has to be made on the sale, he ultimately pays a 1 percent city sales tax from his own pocket.

The profit motive is held in such high regard among merchants that they disbelieve one another's claims of selling at cost or at a loss. Everyone expects the other fellow to make small profit from all transactions. But one also expects great protestations of sacrifice by the seller on behalf of friends, kin, and townmates. It is through these paeans to their brotherhood that the seller gets adequate recompense for his cut in profit.

The friendly discount may be used when one's friend is travelling to Manila to visit his supplier. An order is placed with the friend for goods for personal use that can be bought from the friend's supplier. The friend adds the orders to his wholesale order and is compensated when he returns to Iloilo.

The friendly discount arrangements not infrequently extend to special Filipino friends and business contacts. Goods may move both ways in this arrangement but favors usually involve Filipinos who are not merchant themselves. Filipino employees in Chinese businesses are not extended these favors because Chinese fear being ensnared in an infinite network of employees' kin and friends. Also, the friendly discount connotes "plumping up" between peers, and the employees, of course, are not peers.

By the same token, favors granted on merchandise to impecunious Chinese are not viewed as friendly discounts, but outright philanthropy. Every storekeeper will individually prescribe his limit of generosity to each family who constantly requests credit or favors for retail purchases. Beyond this limit no family, even if they are kin, dare to press.

No "free samples" are distributed among Iloilo's Chinese, nor are there unsolicited deliveries. The initiative lies with the Chinese consumer to select his contact and make a specific request. These requests are impositions on the seller, so he strives to avoid routinizing them.

The largest portion of a Chinese business family's monthly budget is spent on food. Food costs average 30 to 40 percent of a store's net profit. Virtually all families minimize this expense by buying most items at a discount and in bulk. Rice is bought by the sack from warehouses, cooking oil by the drum, canned goods by the case. Because much social manipulation is involved, buying these is usually the duty of the male family head, for he is the representative of the family business. He usually places orders by telephone and pays cash on delivery, just as if these activities were official commercial ones. In some cases men simply sign the bills and pay weekly or monthly. There is no appeal for credit or use of postdated checks, which sour the friendly discount. There is no exchange of goods for goods either; all debts are paid in cash.

Outside of these bulk purchases of food by the men, virtually all of the household budget is spent by the women. They, too, rely heavily on friends' stores and "dealer's cost" favors. In the public market and other areas where Filipinos predominate, Chinese women customers have the same sort of *suki* (steady customer) relationships with Filipino vendors as Filipino women do. Any family member may be called upon to make purchases: if a family wishes to purchase an electric fan and a son's classmate runs an appliance store, then that son will make the purchase.

In most families, the ultimate control of family expenses lies exclusively with the father or husband. Many of these men never go shopping themselves; they purchase by phone or let another member of the family handle purchases. As a result, in most families the husband gives his wife loose rein on budgetary expenses. In cases where the wife actively shares the store work, she makes her own unsupervised withdrawals from the cash register. In most other cases, the wife is given a monthly allowance for herself, the children, and other dependents. In some rare cases the family head and wife have a joint bank account, or the wife may even have her own account. This she builds from her *kò-jin-e seng-lî*, her "private extra income." From this account she provides herself and her children with clothes, toys, school supplies, and so on.

The budget of Mr. Lo, a wholesale textile owner, will illustrate how money is spent on a daily basis. Mr. Lo and his wife live over their store on a main street. Sharing the apartment with them are two unmarried sons and a daughter, one married son, his wife, and their two children. Mr. Lo's successful wholesale store is the standard space — sixteen by thirty-five feet with a back room half that size. Behind that and also extending above the store for one and a half stories are the family quarters. Mr. Lo has one delivery truck, two private cars, eight employees, and two minor partners.

Included in the household budget are four of these employees (two maids and two cooks) and the two partners who also live in the store.

On the average, Mr. Lo retails and wholesales about ₱350 worth of merchandise daily. His daily expenses are as follows:

cost of merchandise	₱200
rent and utilities	25
auto maintenance; telephone, telegraph	10
labor	35
miscellaneous (including official fees and tong)	10
total daily expenses	₱280

Thus, Mr. Lo's income before household expenses is ₱70 a day, exclusive of maintenance of his employees and minor partners. Household food expenses per day usually approximate the following:

breakfast bread	₱ 3
chicken, purchased in bulk	2
rice, a sack per week	8
meat, fish, seafood main courses	15
market items for the evening meal	5
miscellaneous cooking supplies & fuel	3
daily total	₱ 36

This food feeds a total of nineteen family members, partners, and employees. This relatively low daily expense per capita is possible only because about half of this sum is spent on items covered by friendly discounts. Rent and utilities cost cover both the store and the apartment, so a storekeeper like Mr. Lo realizes a large saving by living over his store. Smaller families spend less but cannot as often buy in bulk, and thus per capita costs are higher.

Daily net profit for Mr. Lo is about ₱34, or ₱816 in a month of six-day weeks. From this Mr. Lo allots allowances to the family members. But he is strict about allowances and usually manages to carry over ₱400 into the next month.

Mr. Lo's family is quite typical of the older style Chinese shopkeeper family in Iloilo. Conscientious attention to minimizing the household budget and widespread use of the friendly discount mean such Chinese families can live in relative comfort at lower cost than other families could manage.

Economic Advantages of the Social Structure

This chapter has provided a look at the technoeconomic base of Iloilo Chinese merchant culture. One conclusion I would venture is that the Chinese are better businessmen than the Filipinos because of advantages in their social structure. It can also be demonstrated that Chinese cultural features relating to business success are most likely to be preserved. Thus, the merchant niche and Chinese immigrant culture are interacting in several ways.

Iloilo Chinese have both a reason and a method for preserving their ethnicity, even if it is not the same Chinese ethnicity as elsewhere. The reason is business, and the method is to organize an entire commercial ethnic group. Philippine Chinese are a very homogeneous group in terms of their Chinese origins and present commercial occupations, and Iloilo's merchants conduct ten times as much business as their proportion of the population would suggest. Their commercial networks extend throughout the province and out to other Philippine cities, integrated with their sociocultural network of patrons, kinsmen, classmates, and godparents.

Chinese preferences have combined with external pressures to create a closed ethnic community under tight rein. Until recent decades enculturation into the immigrant society was strictly controlled through the family or apprentice system. Sin-iong, or trust, served well as a Chinese's prime asset for commercial survival and advancement. The fragility of sin-iong and the futility of surviving ostracism from this closed system determined the power of community sanctions. These sanctions could bring forth community philanthropy as well as squash financial treachery or prevent the "wrong" kinds of cooperation with Filipinos. Help by groups or individuals, to groups or individuals, took many forms such as friendly discounts, school donations, partnerships, and loans. Their community resembles the closed corporate community defined by Wolf (1957) in the way it responds to outside pressures by distributing burdens and benefits. A basic difference, however, between these merchants and peasants is that instead of getting little surplus while being pressed from outside for rent, the Chinese merchants accumulate a large surplus while their very right to a position in Philippine life is questioned. Their position is defended by being successful merchants; their mercantile success is maintained by being ethnically Chinese. So, the occupation and the ethnic group have nearly become one.

Many of the mercantile practices used by Iloilo Chinese are cultural forms which developed in China and were adapted by them to colonial and immigrant situations. The banking systems, apprenticeship cycle, high reliance on sin-iong, certain forms of partnerships, loans, and, we shall see later, various types of merchant organizations, were social structural features of Chinese culture which provide a competitive advantage when doing business among Filipinos, who are without similarly developed institutions.

There is a corollary to this conclusion, namely, that Chinese cultural features which assist business are usually preserved in the immigrant community while many others are dropped as irrelevant. *Hong-tsúi* (geomancy) practices are a good example of this. Hong-tsúi beliefs are understood by most merchants and practiced by many. Geomancy, or the arrangement of objects in space for maximum good future, influences the selection of storefronts, and the placement of doors, cash safes, desks, and stoves in the store. Office desks should not face the outer door nor storefronts onto intersections, informants say, because the owner will give too much credit and go bankrupt. Ideally, stoves are to be placed so the cook faces the rising sun; cash registers and safes are well placed next to great pillars, signs of strength and security in the family and store. Such considerations are not idle talk — merchants have gone to effort and expense to conform to the suggestions of individuals familiar with the geomantic intricacies. One restaurant that opened in an intersection location where two previous owners had failed completely converted a new double door to a wall and moved their entrance around to a side street when instructed by a visiting geomancer. Further, they counteracted previous bad luck of the location by building an ornamental water fountain in the main dining room. The geomancer had advised that it be left running twenty-four hours a day to encourage money to flow in. It is significant to note that the main partners in this restaurant were barely middle-aged; clearly, traditional Chinese practices believed to be commercially useful are preserved.

To return to the theme introduced at the beginning of this chapter, what does it mean culturally to be merchants instead of farmers, hunters, or herders? Although Yehudi Cohen (1968) lists mercantilism as one of his strategies of adaptation, anthropologists have not shed a fraction of the light on merchants that they have done for hunters, herders, and fishermen. I can only make a beginning here.

First, merchants are more wealthy, more visible, more powerful, and more urban than groups engaged in other adaptive strategies. More numerous might also be added, as hunters and herders become sedentarized or extinct . Unlike many of the ethnic groups anthropologists study, merchant groups are not "wretched of the earth" in the simple sense of the term; there may be exploitation and coercion in their lives, but they can give as much as they get. A simple Marxist interpretation of ethnicity as labels imposed by socioeconomic superiors will reveal little in the study of merchants.

In merchant culture the connections between people are peculiar. Like other peoples, merchants live in a society heavily influenced by kinship and balanced cooperation. But there are also complex vein connections, as Mannheim (1957) uses the term, connecting individuals in this rather homogeneous society in a hierarchical manner and apportioning nonreciprocal rights and responsibilities. Whether the Philippine Chinese are internally divided into classes is a moot point; I think they still are not. However, the merchant life has produced some unbalanced power and prestige relationships that, when entered into for the sake of business, bear a similarity to class relationships. Examples of such relationships are the cabacillo-agent dyad, nearly feudal in some cases, and the distributor-retailer, creditor-debtor, tenant-landlord, and employer-employee pairs. These ties are called vein connections because they multiply and become smaller in scale the farther away they are from the holders of money, merchandise, and political influence. The difference between this pattern of social relationships and that found in a feudal, peasant, or class arrangement is that individual merchant mobility is fairly high and the ties are not permanent, so regular cultural differences do not develop between superordinates and subordinates. The demands for merchant life produced these hierarchical vein connections with their wide gaps in power and wealth.

There is no choice in the merchant life equivalent to the peasant's choice between subsistence and cash farming. Materials and products entering the ethnic group at a limited number of points — the importers, the manufacturers, the bankers — in order to be converted into the prizes of the game, must be passed on. So interdependence between suppliers, retailers, and clients is high.

Related to this structural feature of merchant society is its organizational complexity. The demands of business and of ethnicity both lead to this complexity, as we shall explore further in chapter 4. Voluntary organizations have proliferated to meet every need from funeral services to volleyball. Working to cut across the vein connections discussed above and reduce antisocial competition within merchandise lines are many trade guilds. Kin groups, religion groups, hobby groups, and political groups incorporate at the drop of a hat — and disappear with equal ease.

Another characteristic of merchant culture is the intangible and unstable nature of wealth. Wealth is the sole measure of social status in the community. Until recent decades, a merchant's storefront rights, stocks, outstanding credits, and bank account were the sum of a family's patrimony (today there are more houses, consumer goods, and land). The merchant's wealth was intangible because much of it was converted into rights, credits, and reputation as a wealthy, generous, and lucky man. It is not easily inherited, even when the procedure is without conflict (see chapter 5). A merchant's wealth is also unstable, but for different reasons than a farmer's or pastoralist's wealth is unstable. Wealth of a merchant is liquid, necessarily highly mobile to follow a market, and risks may be taken that could wipe it out. Also, stories are told in Iloilo of distributor or partner treachery draining a merchant's wealth before he knew it. Last, wealth may go up in smoke in the form of stocks or buildings that burn. Fire is common in Iloilo.

Last, the instrumental values and personality characteristics adaptive in a merchant strategy distinguish it from other livelihoods. This is not a subject I can explore at any length here, but evidence is accumulating that merchants are distinguishable in this regard. For example, Stephen Olsen (1972) has demonstrated in Taipei that merchant families socialize their children using different values than do other families. Merchants' children have stronger positive attitudes toward work, toward business and businessmen, toward self-reliance, toward practicality and materialism, and more negative attitudes toward government regulation and toward profit-sharing. Further, Olsen concludes that "much of the pattern of values characteristic of American businessmen is also associated in various ways with business culture as it exists in Taipei" (Olsen 1972:285), suggesting to me that certain aspects of the business enterprise create crossnatural similarities in quite different cultural settings. Edward Ryan (1961) has described similar values in Chinese merchant families in Modjokuto, Java. The Iloilo Chinese merchants' expressed values are very much in keeping with these trends. Compared to Filipino entrepreneurs, both large and small, the Chinese also struck me as more tolerant of routine and long hours, fastidious about inventory, conciliatory with customers, and impressed with entrepreneurial skills.

Support for this discussion of business values and personality comes from strange quarters: de Tocqueville (1964), though writing about American character 150 years ago, seems to have captured the crossnatural essence of the businessman. Pinpointing the claustrophobic predicament of the Philippine Chinese, and perhaps all minority merchants, de Tocqueville wrote,

. . . where men cannot enrich themselves by war, by public office, or by political confiscation, the love of wealth mainly drives them into business and manufactures. Although these pursuits often bring about great commotions and disasters, they cannot prosper without strictly regular habits and a long routine of petty uniform acts. The stronger the passion is, the more regular are these habits, and the more uniform are these acts. It may be said that it is the vehemence of their desires which makes the Americans so methodical; it perturbs their minds, but it disciplines their lives.

The remark I here apply to America may indeed be addressed to almost all our contemporaries. Variety is disappearing from the human race; the same ways of acting, thinking, and feeling are to be met with all over the world (1964:64).

The following chapters elaborate on these points characterizing merchant culture as it is possessed by the Chinese ethnic group.

1. Most Chinese artisans or owners of service businesses operate from storefronts for retail customers exactly like their merchant neighbors. Most Chinese employees in Chinese businesses are aiming for self-employment, too, though at any one time there is a small white-collar employee population. Eliminating these groups entirely still leaves a preponderance of self-employed merchants in the Chinese community.

2. According to *Economic Census Preliminary* (Iloilo Bureau of Census, 1967), there are 73 wholesale establishments in the city. According to Bureau of Commerce records (1972), modified by my own survey, over 80 wholesale operations in Iloilo are run by Chinese citizens or their representatives. Of the 230-old alien retail and wholesale businesses, over 30 are in towns and barrios elsewhere in Iloilo province.

3. This is to be distinguished from ownership of agricultural, commercial, or residential land and buildings.

4. This figure is based on my own census, aided by knowledgeable Chinese assistants. Some of these single proprietorships may be family or nonfamily partnerships that merely pose as single proprietorships for tax and legal reasons.

5. Chinese are strongly discouraged from taking up business in some provincial towns like Dumangas. This is a "company town" run by a few locally powerful Filipino families who discourage Chinese competition.

6. Literally, *hoe-chhia* means "dispatching vehicle" but it had come to mean Chinese employees who manually loaded and unloaded vehicles.

7. A man without connections is called a *lŏng pang,* "wave breaking on the pier piling." Such a person usually begins life in the Philippines with connections but loses them because of business failures or family troubles. These people are not derelicts but are simply unemployed. If they were socially undesirable, friends, relatives or a chamber of commerce would raise the money to return them to China or move them out of town.

8. Employment opportunities for Chinese citizens are technically few, and some Filipino corporations choose not to hire aliens even though the law does not affect them. If a corporation chooses to hire Chinese citizens, it finds ways to do so regardless of regulations. However, most Chinese executives in Iloilo are Filipino citizens now.

9. See March and April issues of *Iloilo Times* (1970) for a synopsis of events.

10. Chapter 5 will treat this subject of business and intermarriage in more detail.

11. The conventional way of concluding a debt agreement for between a week and a month or so is to issue a postdated check to the creditor. The check is made out for an amount which includes interest on the loan and is payable at a specified future date. It is, thus, an unofficial promissory note. Woe be to the debtor whose check bounces on the due date. Informants say almost all short-term credit in the 1960s and 1970s is handled this way.

12. Freedman (1958) writes that recourse to Chinese courts beyond the Fukienese lineage system was also extremely rare. The Chinese are still following a traditional pattern, therefore, in their overseas communities.

13. For example, the proportion of small Chinese *sari-sari* store owners whose Filipino wives have encouraged them to acquire one or several houses and lots is much higher than among men with Chinese wives.

4

ORGANIZING FOR BUSINESS AND DEFENSE

RELATIVE TO ITS POPULATION OF ABOUT 5,000-6,000, the organizational complexity of Iloilo's Chinese community is great. Only Davao and Cebu are equally complex provincial cities, and their populations are somewhat larger. Beyond these few cities and Manila, most Philippine provincial Chinese enclaves have only a rudimentary structure. They usually have a chamber of commerce, a school, a Cantonese club, a few economic guilds, and perhaps a cemetery. On Panay island, Kalibo and Roxas City have these few basic community organizations, but they still recognize Iloilo City as the area's Chinese cultural center.

Most Chinese associations in the Philippines serve several purposes, though perhaps not the apparent ones or the alleged ones. Also, several unrelated associations may serve the same purpose. Most associations remain officially quite autonomous from one another, but because of their overlapping personnel, complex interrelationships between them can be traced. Further, there are basic rifts within a Chinese society like Iloilo's which bring some associations into active competition or antagonism.

Although I will not elaborate their origins here, it is important to understand the history of these associations. They are based on models of South Chinese organizations, but they are the creation of immigrants and are responses to the political and economic environment of the host country. The pattern of immigration and the needs of immigrants have both shaped the associations. Some association names, goals, and principles of operation are quite like their Ch'ing Dynasty or Republican Chinese counterparts. But the cutoff from China, and the constant changes in the Philippine environment and in the Chinese who compose the community work to complete a process of "speciation" of these organizations from their predecessors distant in time and space.

In the Spanish era, overseas Chinese were required by the government to ⬥ form a certain number of internal and externally oriented organizations (Wickberg 1965). Much of community life in that time hinged on these associations and on the direct import of South Chinese *tongs* and clubs.

Later, in the American era, the growth of Chinese nationalism and the pressures from Filipino nationalism both stimulated more organization. Philippine Chinese developed a highly self-sufficient government and society within the wider Filipino nation.

The basic tasks of this government and society are three: charitable or social, business, and defense. Charitable and social functions include maintaining schools, temples, and cemeteries; facilitating immigration; adjudicating intracommunity conflicts; housing and employing the needy Chinese; and providing emergency assistance to themselves (and occasionally to the Filipinos). Business functions include disseminating market information, raising capital and extending credit, group purchasing or boycotting, and job placement, among others. The defense function involves both public relations with a latently hostile Filipino public and organized bargaining power and legal services when confronting Filipino legislative bodies, officials, or organized labor.

In Manila or other Southeast Asian primate cities with their large Chinese communities, it is possible to separate the myriad organizations functionally into internally and externally oriented, and into charitable/social, business, or defense-oriented. In provincial cities like Iloilo the functional specialization of each Chinese association is lower and their functional overlap greater. It is useful analytically to categorize the various functions of Iloilo's associations, but the associations themselves cannot be neatly classified by function.

Defense in various ways from the Filipinos has always been a task of Iloilo's Chinese organizations. However, the relations between Chinese and Filipinos have grown more strained in recent decades. In the second chapter I cited some causes and examples of this growing friction.

The points of strain between the Chinese and the Filipinos cluster around cultural and political issues as well as economic ones. Economically, the disproportionate hold of the Chinese on urban Iloilo business rankles the Filipino nationalist and consumer alike. Economic ills such as unfair labor treatment, hoarding of commodities, and rising prices seem to Filipinos to stem from the Chinese because in Iloilo City the Chinese appear to be the entire business community. Culturally, the Filipinos are repulsed by Chinese practices which are in some cases the very opposite of theirs. Strict patrilineal inheritance, patriarchy, and a lack of interest in Christianity are a few of the traits despised. The Filipinos also resent the Chinese for their ability to immigrate to the Philippines as penniless aliens and then build something out of nothing, much as the Arabs might watch Jews working agricultural miracles in the barren Negev Desert.

Filipinos strongly suspect the Chinese are unpatriotic, that their emotional, financial, and political allegiances are elsewhere. Considering their central position in the economy, Chinese alliance to another country would constitute not only a military threat but an enormous hindrance to national development. Allegiance or suspected allegiance to Communist China has for decades aggravated the strong anti-Communist sympathies of Filipinos. Finally, to create a "Catch-22," Filipinos view with suspicion a Chinese alien who gains Filipino citizenship. The suspicion is that this is a "citizenship of convenience" so that the alien may acquire land and operate more freely commercially, without in fact being any less Chinese in culture or allegiance.

On the other hand, there are many Filipino customs and attitudes which the Philippine Chinese do not like and wish to insulate their children from. But the most important defense function of Chinese associations has been to stem the flood of formal and informal harassment against Chinese by the increasingly nationalistic Filipinos. According to Chinese informants and attested in large part by the legislative record and newspapers, campaigns against the Chinese increased regularly from the founding of the Philippine Republic in 1946 until the early 1970s. Laws excluding Chinese citizens from social and economic activities are continually being written or augmented. Enforcement is irregular, admittedly, but also unpredictable and self-interested. Many Chinese who are naturalized Filipinos are haunted by the enforcement of these laws though they should be legally secure. Filipino labor activities, while primarily antimanagement, have often taken on an explicit anti-Chinese expression. A number of bureaus regularly deliver subpoenas to Chinese for alleged marriage or immigration violations. By Filipino law, of course, many Chinese have behaved illegally, but many Chinese have also been harassed without justification. Politicians, in or out of office, have pressed the Chinese hard for contributions and "protection money." In the early 1970s, the Chinese were the obvious and favorite targets of several robbery and kidnapping rings. Finally, the radical Filipino antigovernment organizations which were seeking the overthrow of corrupt government were ironically operating in the traditional way to extort "contributions and cooperation" from the Chinese.[1]

A central theme of this chapter is the fluidity and adaptability of Philippine Chinese organization. The Chinese politics in Iloilo that are detailed here characterize the early years of the 1970s before the declaration of martial law, diplomatic ties with the People's Republic of China, and the liberalization of citizenship procedures. The political behavior of the Chinese in Iloilo has, I am sure, undergone some significant modifications, true to their fluid and adaptable nature, since these momentous changes in the nation. This is well and good: my description becomes history and, thus, far less embarassing to the efforts of the Chinese to work out their lives in the Philippines today. This chapter, therefore, is a portrait of Iloilo Chinese political life under rather different conditions than those that prevail now. The portrait is accurate, though most of the names were altered for confidentiality, and constitutes the material out of which contemporary Iloilo Chinese are fashioned. The directions the Chinese are moving today are discussed in the epilog.

Chambers of Commerce

The biggest and most important defense associations in Iloilo City are the chambers of commerce, or merchant associations. Outside Manila, Iloilo is unique in having two chambers of commerce: the Federation of Filipino-Chinese Chambers of Commerce of Panay and the Chinese Chamber. These chambers are by no means limited to the commercial activities suggested by their titles. Equally important are their functions as modern-day benevolent societies and protection agencies. The chambers, in fact, are the representatives for the city's Chinese, and as such they are coordinating agencies funneling information and activities into and out of the Chinese sector. They are where the most wealthy and most powerful as well as the most prestigious men operate.

The chambers of commerce in Iloilo are the direct descendants of the Hok-kièn Hōe-Koán and Kńg-Tang Hōe-Koán (Fukienese and Cantonese clubs) of the nineteenth century. As chambers of commerce, they emerged officially in the twentieth century American era and, thus, might appear to be solely an overseas Chinese creation. But they assumed virtually the same tasks that the Hōe-Koán had assumed in the previous century. And the Hoe-Koan themselves have precedents in South China, according to Hosea B. Morse's (1932) account of Ch'ing Dynasty merchant guilds. The merchant guilds, according to Morse, were called Hōe-Koán or "clubhouses." One of their main purposes was to organize and protect their countrymen in alien provinces, perhaps as far distant as Southeast Asian cities such as Iloilo.

The outstanding difference between a South Chinese merchant guild and Iloilo's Chinese chambers of commerce is the latter's diversity of functions. Because guilds were strictly for manipulating urban business (both within and outside their own membership), they left the religious, social, and charitable projects to kin groups and other clubs. In Iloilo and other Philippine cities the chambers of commerce have accepted a much broader responsibility ever since immigrants formed them. While part of their time and money has been spent on business and political projects, part has also gone for charity, emergency, ceremony, immigration projects, schools, and so forth. Whereas the old Chinese merchant guild controlled a city by strength of sanction, the chambers are preeminent in Philippine Chinese society by breadth of function.

In the realm of business, the chambers undertake to translate into Chinese and circulate all government announcements concerning business. They retain lawyers for the preparation of tax, incorporation, and other documents. They act as clearing houses to collect the usual annual fees and business taxes from Chinese businessmen and pay them in a lump sum. They try to warn and protect individual businessmen in advance from surprise audits, visits from health inspectors, and such officials. They represent businessmen in major labor disputes. They mediate with officials concerning the size of protection payments. They lobby with local officials to rescind or decrease business fees and taxes. They mediate between Chinese in business disputes and price wars.

In social and charitable realms, the merchant associations maintain two of the four schools and the cemetery. They provide emergency aid to Chinese merchants in the case of fire or theft and to Filipinos during natural disasters like floods. In the past they provided for the return of indigents or the remains of the deceased to Chinese hometowns. They also find employment for needy immigrants, play a central ritual role in funerals and weddings, and hold holiday banquets and plays. During the many years of immigration before 1949, they mediated with the Bureau of Immigration and smoothed the entry and exit of local Chinese to and from the country.

There has been little that the chambers of commerce have not undertaken at least once as representatives of the Chinese community. Several years ago some Taiwanese fishing boats strayed into Philippine waters and were apprehended and moored in Iloilo's port. The chambers turned out to mediate between the Philippine government and the Taiwanese embassy to free the boats. Because there is no longer a Taiwanese consulate in Iloilo City, the chambers have assumed that role, too, when the need arises.

The line between the chambers' official functions and their informal activities as a group of Chinese community leaders and businessmen is necessarily vague, as I shall explain later. Except for their boycott of the Japanese in the prewar years, which was a political act as much as an economic one, there is no evidence that Iloilo's chambers have served as economic cartels. There is no official attention to organizing buying, selling, and financing among the members, with the notable exception of the several yearly charity donations the Chinese community makes to Iloilo's Red Cross, the city's Filipino poor, and others.

The members of the chambers of commerce are exclusively Chinese and Chinese mestizos, who pay monthly dues based on the offices they hold in the association. Members are businesses, but since these are almost without exception families, the household or family head of the business is the chamber member. In the cases where a business is run by a woman, she selects some male family member to represent her. Not all Chinese join the associations; in fact, as many as one quarter of the area's Chinese businesses are apathetic or even hostile toward them. To participate in the chambers is to announce one's membership in the Chinese community. Because of personal feuds or for protection of their revokable, hence vulnerable, Filipino citizenship or because they are too impecunious to be bothered, some Chinese simply do not become chamber members. As a result, they remain but marginal community members.

The backbone of the chambers is their large corps of officers who are elected annually by ballot sent in the mail to each member business. A

president, several vice-presidents, a treasurer, an English secretary, and a
Chinese secretary are elected. In addition, several public relations and liaison
officers are elected among the younger members with good Filipino contacts.
An auditor has been elected in recent years to check the bookkeeping. A
number of standing committees are formed by electing chairmen: the temple,
cemetery, and "watchdog." The "watchdog" committee assumes the responsibility of overseeing the operations of other officers; it is composed of
elderly respected men whose money and authority keep the organization
on an even keel.

The officers conduct business of the chamber in part through formal
monthly meetings and also through emergency meetings, telephone conversations, and informal contacts. They also oversee a large volume of printed
matter circulating among their members almost daily. Meetings of all members
are rarely called, and then they are usually in the form of social banquets.

The Federation of Filipino-Chinese Chambers of Commerce of Panay
has been voluntarily tied in to a nationwide network of federations headed
by the Manila organization and allied loosely to the Taiwanese embassy.
While provincial cities' chambers rarely contact one another directly, there
are frequent opportunities for meeting in Manila. The central federation
maintains a constant agenda of cultural, social, and business programs which
representatives from the provincial chambers attend.

The Chinese Chamber of Iloilo is far more isolated. While it has a large
counterpart in Manila which is the "rival" of the nationwide federation,
the parent organization has no activities on the scale of the federation's
to involve regional members like Iloilo's. The Iloilo Chamber is virtually
a regional isolate, and few cities outside Manila have sister branches. Consequently, it restricts itself solely to Iloilo matters and avoids national and
international stances which the Federation with its political backing can
assume.

Who joins which chamber? In general, one's membership is ascribed by
one's other social connections. A Chinese opening a business in the 1970s
joins the chamber that his kinsmen are in, that sponsors the high school he
went to, or that his ex-employer belongs to. There is little or no splitting
up of kinsmen between the chambers, and few cross-overs. There are,
however, a number of marriages between chambers now, which informants
say were rare a decade earlier and which indicates a softening of differences.

The rivalry between the two Iloilo merchant associations over the years
has been mentioned in chapter 2. In the last decade several truly pan-community organizations have formed in Iloilo City. Their importance waxes and
wanes with changing local sociopolitical conditions. But they are an entirely
new level of organization in town and may indicate more centralization
in the future.

The first to form was the Iloilo Chinese Educational Finance Committee,
organized in the early 1960s to raise funds to support the three Chinese

schools which, like all Philippine Chinese schools, operate at an annual loss. Because the schools offer free tuition to many needy students, yearly expenses must be carried in great part by their boards of trustees who were beginning to wince under the burdens of inflation and school population growth. Community leaders incorporated a fund to receive donations from Chinese at the occasions when they were most likely in a benevolent mood: weddings, birthdays, funerals, and baptisms, among others.

Functioning like the conspicuous consumption taxes of dynastic China, the donations are expected to be commensurate with the celebration. At a wedding, for example, the couple receives a large number of gift checks from well-wishers. Some sizeable portion of this money (rounded to a propitious number by the family for good luck) is given to the Educational Finance Fund. If invitations exceed fifty, it is an unspoken requirement to send the wedding list to the Fund, which "taxes" the couple on each banquet table and sends requests for donations to each guest. It is not uncommon to donate ₱1,000 to ₱5,000 at such occasions.

The Fund elects officers each year from among the trustees of the three Chinese schools.[2] Though they will be called upon to solicit contributions, especially during building campaigns, officers primarily serve as examples for the rest of the community. In 1972 over seventeen officers were elected, thus providing a good base for contributions from within the Fund. Receipts from the year's donations are divided proportionately among the schools according to their enrollment.

The second pan-community association to form in the 1960s was the Joint Committee, a loose confederation of the leaders from all major associations in town. Alternating between inactivity and crisis management, chameleonlike in changing its name frequently, it is growing increasingly important in its duties but is still nebulous in its structure and image to the rest of the Chinese. It has been called the Chinese Community, the Joint Committee, and may soon be incorporated as the Chinese Merchant Association of Iloilo.

The impetus for the creation of the Joint Committee, as most Chinese still refer to it, was the worsening local political environment in the early 1970s. By banding together, the Chinese gained more bargaining power with aggressive officials. Their internecine quarrels from previous decades had weakened. Younger Chinese had been pressing for more active reliance upon sympathetic Filipinos and upon their own legal rights as Filipino citizens to avoid further outside pressures.

The Joint Committee is composed of the leaders of the two main chambers, plus increased participation from the independents and younger Chinese. Its structure is novel in its formal specialization. There are committees for finance, economic planning, business and labor relations, social welfare and charity, publications and government liaison, and research. These are staffed in part by the older prestigious leaders and in part by the young Chinese with their new approaches and different contacts. There is an executive committee informally called the "Seven Wise Men" who are the representatives of the whole body, with power to call emergency meetings among themselves and make quick decisions.

The Joint Committee has proved in very concrete cases to be the strong defense agency it was created to be. The ending of the "Case of the Nine" is a good example. The Nine were some of the richest Chinese men in Iloilo. Bureau of Internal Revenue agents from Manila had been investigating them for tax evasion, and local Philippine Constabulary officials were, ironically, threatening to arrest them for graft with the Bureau of Internal Revenue. The nine businessmen had been thus challenged from both sides for several years. Soon after the resurrection of the Joint Committee a delegation of Iloilo's most influential men was sent to plead with influential Chinese friends in Manila. Because the delegation was selected from the whole community, with its diversity of local allegiances and international political stances, they were successful in contacting just the right persons to intercede for them with the Bureau of Internal Revenue (BIR) and Philippine Constabulary (PC). The BIR agents were suspended and the Iloilo PC was ordered to drop the case. By no means had harassment come to an end, but at least the Joint Committee had greatly improved the Chinese defensive posture against it.

The Joint Committee has not been incorporated yet because the leaders are still operating it on a trial basis, in the hope that it can supplant the two-chamber cleavage in the city. But because Philippine local and national political conditions are constantly in flux, the Chinese remain flexible to respond to those changes, and the Committee, thus, remains in the formative stages. When martial law was declared in September 1972, the Joint Committee reduced its visibility for a while. The Federation of Panay rose in importance within Iloilo Chinese politics. Allied to the Taiwanese embassy which in turn was allied to the traditionally anti-Communist Filipino national government, the Federation was in a favored position to act as intermediary between Filipinos and Philippine Chinese. They took their opportunity as the most appropriate organization to step forward in place of the nascent Joint Committee. Of course, important changes soon to occur in international relations with the People's Republic of China would again alter the local balance.

Specialized Business Associations

More specialized in function in Iloilo are the particular business associations which subdivide the business community in ways unlike the chambers of commerce. Business associations are smaller than chambers of commerce in all senses: their membership and treasuries are smaller and their functions are fewer.[3] They are more direct descendants of the mainland merchant guilds in their functions, but their power is much less and they, too, have diversified somewhat.

There were, in 1973, eight business associations in Iloilo City: one each for sari-sari stores, textile stores, rice and corn dealers, lumber stores, hardware stores, bakers, cigarette merchants, and restaurants. New ones come into existence and old ones fade away constantly. Some of the new ones appear as a result of external pressures from Filipinos, and others owe their existence to internal causes. If a prominent businessman dealing in pottery or bookbinding felt such an association were necessary, he would probably start one.

In general, business associations are proliferating because of external pressures. When national and local officials increase their pressure for tong (protection) payments or against alien business, marriage, and immigration practices, associations form in defense. They strive as a group to improve the public relations of their merchant line and bargain with officials or fight extortion. In this way was the Iloilo Cigarette Merchants Association created in 1971. At that time the city government imposed its own 3 percent wholesale sales tax on cigarettes. Most Iloilo Chinese cigarette dealers incorporated a club to lobby against the tax or else to lobby against enforcement of the tax or finally, failing in the first two, to devise ways to avoid the tax.

Beyond any doubt, the main reason for the creation and existence of business associations is to deal in a unified front with corrupt and legitimate government practices. Each trade has its weaknesses upon which Filipino officials work. Bakers fight a losing battle against sanitation officials; grocers are surveyed for their pricing policies; and lumber yards and restaurants have labor problems. Because of these difficulties they build treasuries of contributions and dues from members to cover the cost of legal expenses, publications among themselves, and protection money.

In the process of fulfilling this task they assume other related business tasks, too. Like chambers of commerce they inform members of government regulations, warn of inspections, alert business to deadlines, and informally keep one another abreast of local and national market information. They undertake charity projects assisting the families of members who die, who are sick, who are robbed, or whose stores are burned. They sometimes raise clubhouse buildings and rent store and warehouse space in them to other Chinese. They mediate in price wars between members and establish informal fair price levels (which, however, are broken as often as they are observed). They also help stores to deal with Filipino customers; the Chinese sari-sari stores in the province have depended in part on protection from their urban Sari-sari Store Association to increase their security in all-Filipino towns and barrios by peaceful negotiations and protection money.

Many people in the Philippines believe that Chinese business associations are price-fixing cartels and monopoly organizations, restraining free trade.

The power of Manila business associations and of guilds in other Southeast Asian countries may be great enough to permit this, but in Iloilo it is not. Contrary to popular belief, most trade associations are not mutual aid societies in the sense of pooling capital, cooperative buying and selling, making loans, and sharing business secrets. There is probably some price manipulation, but association members actively try to undersell one another at the set prices. One important reason for the existence of the associations is to form a sense of community among otherwise vigorous competitors.

Indicative of Iloilo associations' inability to become truly cohesive organizations is the following story involving the Sari-sari Store Association, the richest, largest, oldest, and strongest of all business associations in town. A few years ago a Cantonese salesman to their stores refused to pay his dues to the association, and the officers declared a boycott on him. The vast majority of the sari-sari stores continued as usual, and the boycott failed. This is not the picture of a tightly run monopolistic cartel that some writers have created.

Business associations are exclusively for Chinese and Chinese mestizos, but not all merchants in a particular line join them. The Sari-sari Store Association has about 150 members, and the smallest, the cigarette merchants, has fewer than twenty. Membership in an association entails little except moderate monthly dues and occasional contributions, plus good-natured compliance with policy decisions. Like the chambers of commerce, a few association leaders make decisions, do the work, and handle the money.

Leaders in business associations are elected in a group of about six to twelve by mail ballot and subsequently apportion the offices among themselves. Men with money and connections are preferred as leaders because they will set the example as contributors to club coffers. There is a president, a public relations man, and a treasurer, as main working officers. The executive group meets monthly over dinner and on emergency occasions. The whole body of the association may never come together, relying instead upon the judgement of the leaders and their frequent newsletters. In the business associations, unlike the larger chambers of commerce, it is easier for a college-educated, Philippine-born Chinese to achieve leadership over the older, wealthier men of prestige. The associations are expressly and rather narrowly problem-oriented, and the younger men are recognized more often for such specific tasks as befriending the city commissioners, bargaining with radical students, and so on.

Treasuries are built of dues and contributions. Contributions come from members at ritually appropriate times such as a daughter's wedding, baptisms, and funerals. Because tong demands have been high in recent decades, association coffers have constantly been virtually empty, and frequent campaigns for funds must raise the requisite cash. Since associations have proliferated, too, many men whose business diversity makes them members of several associations are less inclined to maintain their former levels of generosity. Association bookkeeping is usually simpler than that of individual businesses, and most leaders expect complete trust from members in the discretionary handling of club money. In recent years the younger Chinese have felt emboldened to press for more explicit accounting, but these practices change by generation, not by year.

All business associations in Iloilo are organized for the dominant majority of Chinese society, the self-employed businessmen. There are no artisans' guilds and no labor unions because the persons who would form these have for the most part been moving from artisan and employee status into shopkeeper status. The former two positions are seen as merely steps on the way to the latter position, and no one tries any more to institutionalize himself in some intermediate position.[4] Historically, too, in Iloilo and other Chinese communities throughout the Philippines the artisans and laborers were parts of a tightly organized "household" of an independent businessman.

Political Clubs and Family Associations

For internal government of overseas Chinese society in Iloilo there have been more associations that are internally oriented, the political clubs and family associations. Both are actually twentieth century overseas Chinese creations, although each has functional equivalents in China which have served as models.

The political clubs in Iloilo have been the Kuomintang Cultural Association and the Anti-Communist League. They have developed from the anti-imperial, pro-Republican "reading clubs" of the early twentieth century and were closely allied with the Nationalist Chinese consulate in Iloilo until it closed in the late 1930s. Since then they have replaced the consulate and assisted the Federation of Panay as liaison with the Taiwanese embassy in Manila until 1975, when the embassy was withdrawn. Since the Communist victory in 1949, the political clubs have become less visible, smaller in membership and treasury, and less active except as supporters of positions initiated in Manila. Their members are drawn primarily from the older men in the Federation of Panay and from the supporters of the Sun Yat Sen School, where the clubs have their offices.

Not specifically a political organization, the Cantonese Club has been very active politically in its long history in Iloilo. Being countrymen of Sun Yat Sen and originating in the province where the Republic of China was born, the Cantonese have been a driving nationalistic force in Iloilo throughout the twentieth century. As a 10 percent minority dialect group of the Chinese in Iloilo, the Cantonese made of their club a composite chamber of commerce, family association, and political club, with many social and charitable functions. They were responsible for fanning Kuomintang enthusiasm in prewar years and for establishing the Sun Yat Sen School as well. When the

Federation of Panay was founded in 1954, as openly pro-KMT, the Cantonese willingly joined and their own club diminished in political and economic function. By the 1970s its operations were similar to a small Fukienese family association.

Iloilo's Fukienese family associations, six of which are formally organized and active, have been primarily internally oriented, but they have developed more externally oriented functions than they used to have. Their formal responsibilities are few, but informally they are involved in many business and defense matters. Unlike the chambers of commerce, the family associations' defensive posture is primarily vis-a-vis other Chinese, not Filipinos. They play an important role in clashes among their members and between clubs.

The family associations include as their members all adult males in Iloilo province who are twenty-one years or older and carry the appropriate surname. Most large associations like the Ong, Tan, Uy, and Chua-Gua clubs also have some members-at-large from Kalibo, Roxas City, and Bacolod. Sometimes, if a Cantonese has the same surname and shows interest, he is sought for membership. The Tan Family Association, for example, has ten Cantonese members. A man is a member as long as he desires to be counted and after he has paid a nominal registration fee. He has no dues, few duties, and only a few, mainly social, meetings to attend. His primary task is completing the officer ballot mailed once a year.

Like the leaders of chambers of commerce and business associations, the leaders (ti si) of family associations are elected in a group of about twenty and apportion the duties among themselves. Besides a president, vice-presidents, and English and Chinese secretaries, there are the usual public relations officers, honorary boards of trustees (kam sī hōe), and a "food chairman," jokingly referred to as the most important officer. The food chairman organizes the banquets served at monthly executive meetings. Some clubs also have quartermasters to care for the building and equipment, an "employment introductions" officer to help with job placement, and charity officers to screen requests for help. Not only do they run the club, the officers also contribute by far the most to the treasury.

Iloilo family associations maintain contact with their headquarters and family shrines in Manila by sending delegations of officers several times a year to participate in ceremonies there. During their own rites, Iloilo invites Manila representatives to attend. No Iloilo association produces its own regular newsletter or yearbook, but it is included in the regional sections of the materials produced by Manila headquarters. Delegations of officers also travel to Manila and other cities to solicit funds for building campaigns. Informants say Manila does not make financial requests of them, but Iloilo clubs are constantly entertaining fund-raising delegations from other cities and smaller communities who are trying to start or continue a club.

Officially, family associations may be defined as quasi-religious and patriotic clubs of sibmates, responsible for maintenance and worship of ancestors. A good overview of Philippine Chinese sibs and their operation can be found in the monographs by J. Amyot (1960) and G. Weightman (1960). A few points of comparison and contrast with these overviews will be drawn for Iloilo's sibs and family associations.

There is no evidence of family associations in Iloilo in the nineteenth century. All the local association branches were founded in the 1920s or later – as late as the 1960s. The precedent for family associations is the sib organization of South China, well analyzed by M. Freedman (1958). The impetus for founding associations in the Philippines, if Iloilo is typical, is the development of political consciousness and cultural pride that accompanied the Republican revolution in China in the early twentieth century. By their nature the family associations were culturally chauvinistic and pro-Republic. There is every reason to believe that like the political clubs in Iloilo, the family associations were encouraged in part by representatives of the Chinese Republic, for whom the associations would serve as sources of contributions and political support. All of Iloilo's associations were prompted into formal organizations by family association headquarters in Manila, which in turn were allied with and probably stimulated by the Chinese embassy there.

In discussing the family associations in Iloilo, it is necessary to draw distinctions between the sib (tzu, or clan, as it is sometimes called) in South China and the sib in the Philippines. It is possible also to distinguish between the Philippine Chinese sib as a kinship group and the Philippine Chinese family association as a different entity, more formal and more limited.

According to M. Freedman's (1958) fine overview of South Chinese lineage organizations, the lineage was a unilineal descent group identified by surname and usually localized in a village where a shrine with the ancestral records was maintained. Its members were, of course, predominantly farmers, and its leaders were mostly hereditary though there was some flexibility in selection. The major wealth of the corporate group was land.

Whereas in China lineages were virtually coterminous with villages, in the Philippines the village association (tông hiong hōe) became separate from the lineage organization (sī tsong chhin hōe). The lineage associations recruited members based upon surname, regardless of village origin, in order that the associations would have greater treasuries and political effectiveness. Thus, the traceable relation between members was replaced by putative descent from the semilegendary ancient ancestors. Some lineage associations like the Tan Family or the Ang Family Association actually include persons of five or six different surnames. Weightman (1960) calls these phratry associations because such conglomerates are justified by putative descent from a single ancestor.[5] In effect, small surname groups participate in a mutually beneficial fiction in order to improve their protection.

There is evidence that family associations were created in the Philippines from mainland antecedents; some informants remember very similar organizations in the cities of Fukien and Kwangtung with similar names and broad membership. What are immigrant organizations in the Philippines were most likely urban aid organizations in China for rural migrants to the cities.

Village lineage groups in China have become nonlocalized, putative descent groups in cities like Manila or Iloilo. Their leadership has changed, too, from primarily hereditary succession in lineage councils to oligarchical competition among leading businessmen. Furthermore, lineages lost a land base as their wealth and very *raison d' etre* and partially replaced it overseas with buildings or clubhouses and treasuries of liquid assets, congruent with their merchant profession.

There is sib consciousness and sib activity in the Philippines even where there is no relevant family association, and thus we come to a distinction between sibs and family associations. A sense of kinship and of origin from a particular town in Fukien still unites lineages of Philippine Chinese, even though they do not have a family association in their area. For example, in Iloilo the persons named Sy are numerous and are very wealthy and powerful. But there is no Sy Family Association as there is in Manila and Cebu. Nevertheless at a funeral, birthday, or wedding of a Sy, the primary guests, organizers, and contributors will be persons named Sy. Funeral programs will always mention a "Sy Family Association" as participant in order to give blanket credit to sib members for their help, but the sib members themselves acknowledge that there is no association, no officers or treasury, and no formal recognition from Manila. In chapter 2 it was demonstrated that some lineages, that of the Sy being one of them, recruited their Iloilo members from only a few places in Fukien. It is in part because of their narrow geographic origin, as well as their large number, that persons are conscious of their Sy lineage. This is also true of the Go families and the Po families in Iloilo. Those of the Sy lineage are still proscribed from marrying one another, as well as from marrying persons named Ty, with whom the Sy family had been feuding in Chin-kang County, Fukien. There is also a recognized distinction between the "front bay" and "back bay" Sy, also based upon proximity and marriage patterns in Chin-kang. In Iloilo, degrees of knowledge of and social contact with Sy members still correspond quite well to this "front bay, back bay" distinction.

The official, formal family associations are very much rooted in this recognition of lineage membership among lineage members. To it the associations add a treasury, a council of officers, and diverse charitable and recreational activities to keep the sentiment alive. The associations should be viewed, therefore, as formal extensions of the sib itself, neither identical to it nor independent of it. With the imminent disappearance of the immigrant generations in Iloilo, however, the family associations will most likely diminish also, for the sense of sib membership grows weaker with time. Family associations are not likely to continue as an important manifestation of the sib because the Catholic Church, men's clubs, the chambers of commerce, and the courts are assuming many traditional functions and new programs have not been created to merit their continuance. If they do not disappear entirely, the family associations will remain as one kind of small men's club among many.

Nevertheless, Iloilo's Fukienese family associations have performed important charitable, defense, and social functions. They have little to do with business per se. Their treasuries are filled by admission fees from members, by dues from officers, by donations from members during weddings and funerals, and by income from use of the clubhouse buildings for ceremonies, stores, or warehouses. This money is then dispersed as emergency donations to members, other Chinese, and periodically to Filipinos to improve public relations. Some is awarded as scholarships to good students whose parents are members. Some money is spent for banquets or for hosting delegations from Manila or other family association branches. Some money is spent for legal fees or "lobbying" in conflicts with the government, individual Filipinos, or Chinese from other sibs. In recent years some associations have begun athletic teams and other more visible public relations projects. Incoming members from other cities are welcome, and young men sometimes find jobs through family associations. Medical bills for indigent members are paid. The proper spring and autumn ancestor worship rites and the ancestor's birthday are celebrated by ceremonies and banquets. An altar is maintained in the clubhouse for members to consult for fortune-telling or simply for meditation.

The main family association activities which are of concern here are business and defense. Officially, business interests are laid aside in family association activities. But an association composed exclusively of businessmen inevitably becomes unofficially involved in its members' commercial interests. This usually functions in the following way. Once, a member of the largest family association in Iloilo approached the officers in executive session and requested a loan for expansion of his business. The officers gave him to understand that they refused not on the grounds of the quality of his collateral but to avoid an awkward club precedent. The would-be debtor subsequently approached individual officers of the club on a personal basis and got his loan. However, clubs through their officers have stood as guarantors for a member's outside credit arrangements or used their own information channels to investigate a business venture that a member wished to invest in. Informally, too, a great deal of Chinese business news is circulated.

More structured has been the family association's role in defense, both from Filipinos and from other Chinese. Among Chinese, the clubs serve as mediators in personal and family disputes. For example, one family named Ong may default on a debt to another person named Ong. If the latter cannot get satisfaction, his next step will be to seek leaders of his and his debtor's family association to intercede for him. Family pride motivates him to keep the case away from "outsiders," that is, anyone not named Ong. The association leaders will mediate in the dispute, though they cannot really arbitrate. Their authority derives from their social prestige, not from concrete institutional powers. In the vast majority of cases, this mediation is enough to settle disputes. When it is not, the injured party either considers himself the loser or, more often recently, goes to the Filipino court.

Brothers may challenge one another in inheritance cases through the mediation of family associations, or an Uy who is injured personally or professionally by a Lim may ask his family association to act as his counsel and present the grievance to the Lim Family Association. The two associations will represent their members to one another and also apply pressure to the two parties to come to an agreement. Representation may involve only some informal chats, or it may involve retaining lawyers and threats of suits. According to several informants who are active in different Iloilo family associations today, the associations have been the primary organizations for protecting the "little man" from bullying by members of more numerous and more powerful sibs.

Finally, family associations can serve as defense from Filipinos, and once again business interests intrude. Against individual Filipinos, there have been cases in Iloilo of family associations representing members (behind the scenes) in Filipino court suits. More frequent, however, is the association's task of entertaining and placating local officials, retaining lawyers to defend members in criminal or business suits from the government, and paying protection money. Similarly, they work to protect individuals from official attacks on their traditional marriage practices or on questionable immigration procedures.

The Music Club and the Catholic Women's Association

Two more associations should be mentioned because they are strong and active, though not involved in economic or defense functions directly. The Music Association, or the Golden Orchid Gentlemen's Society, is actually concerned with appreciation of ancient Southern Chinese classical music (Lâm Im) and not with secret societies, underground politics, vice operations, and goon squads, as has been the case in other overseas Chinese communities. My evidence for this is that I sought and heard vivid gossip about much of Iloilo Chinese history, but the music club was never implicated. The Iloilo Music Club is the postwar creation of a middle class merchant community and serves in an almost identical way with family associations as a shrine of Chinese cultural tradition, complete with altar and ancestors.

The club's approximately fifty members are mostly older men, some of whom play music but many of whom know little about it, They gather monthly and sometimes weekly in their clubhouse for dinner, drinks, music, and conversation. Several times a year they host delegations from other cities' music clubs and send their own small orchestras in return.

The music club is far less diversified in its formal functions than are family associations, having no real charitable, business, or juridical duties. Nevertheless, it is an important fraternal club because it has a large proportion of the wealthiest and most powerful men in town. A clubmate of such men can have advantages in developing contacts for business purposes, as I shall discuss in the next section; thus, even a music club can provide the setting for a number of economic, social, and political activities.

Unique among the Chinese community's organizations is the Catholic Women's Association, a women's auxiliary to the Cursillos, a laymen's religious fraternity at Santa Maria Catholic Church. The Cursillo movement itself was very active in the 1950s and early 1960s, recruiting both Chinese and Filipinos, but it has grown less active in recent years due to enervating personal factionalism which plagued its earlier years. The Catholic Women's Association, however, is thriving. It is the only Chinese association in town which is open to women, and it is today composed exclusively of Chinese and Chinese mestiza women. Its leadership ranks are filled with the wives of all the powerful men of the city. Ostensibly it exists to sponsor charities and fund drives for church coffers. Consequently, the amount of money it raises and handles is sometimes quite large. But in a broader sense the association has become the stage for a visible but cautious display of feminine power; it has also become the community's representative to the church itself. The Catholic Women's Association assists in the arrangements of funerals and in some weddings, acts as de facto trustees for the Santa Maria School, which some of their children attend, and represents the pious core of the Chinese community, which, except for mestizos, is still only rather nominally Catholic. The Catholic Women's Association's leaders and main donors are not all Catholic, either. This oddity merely serves to demonstrate that the club is primarily a woman's club, not a Catholic club. A number of the members of its board of trustees are actually practicing or nominal Buddhists and elder wives of important men selected for their power and wealth. Nevertheless, within club ranks are to be found most of the Chinese and mestiza Catholic women of above-average social status.

The Organizations and Their Interrelations

The chambers of commerce, the business clubs, the family associations the political club, the music club, and the Catholic Women's Association are the main defense and economic associations of the Iloilo Chinese community.

These associations, which are the biggest, richest, and most powerful, are multifunctional and almost all can claim to be involved in economic and defense activities.

An overview of the hierarchy and interrelationship of the city's Chinese associations as the Chinese perceive them is presented in the diagram on the following page. The Chinese themselves don't draw such diagrams; the construction is mine, but my informants acknowledged its structure. From a glance, one can see how abundant groups are, which group's members join or contribute to which organizations, and how the community contains certain distinct horizontal splits.

There are peculiarities to Iloilo's organizational structure. Most notable is the presence of two competing chambers of commerce and of the four schools with their quite different organizational affiliations. More important than these peculiarities, however, is the vast number of similarities with overseas Chinese communities throughout the world. The types of clubs, their ostensible and their actual duties, the behavior of their leaders and rank and file (to be discussed further below), and their segmentary structure illustrate very closely the ideal type or model of overseas Chinese community structure created by Lawrence Crissman (1967). Such striking similarities are possible because nearly all overseas Chinese are immigrants or descendants of immigrants from a relatively small portion of the South China coast, moving for the most part within the last hundred years into urban, commercial settings dominated by a few colonial powers. There are also many similarities, Crissman notes, between the structure overseas Chinese created to govern and protect themselves and the structure employed in Chinese cities. In both places, the many affiliations of rural migrants are reorganized into a flexible defensive and administrative structure for businessmen living at the pleasure of an ambivalent but potentially very repressive national government. Iloilo's Chinese, though Chinese in other Philippine cities may consider them quaint, are very much a part of the larger Chinese phenomenon.

This segmentary organization that Crissman has so well modeled and which Iloilo typifies may be not only the key to urban Chinese merchants' survival overseas but may also be a key to their rapid expansion and success there. Marshall Sahlins (1961) has proposed that segmentary lineage organizations in East Africa are very well adapted for predatory expansion of Tiv and Nuer into others' habitats. The segmentary structure may well have played an analogous role for the Chinese, facilitating expansion into the commercial life of overseas countries, using buying power, credit, and business skills instead of the East Africans' spears.

The diagram, therefore, conforms well to the ideal type. It excludes the full list of Chinese associations, some of which do not fit conveniently into this segmental structure because they divide the population in other ways. The family associations, for example, are omitted because they are mutually

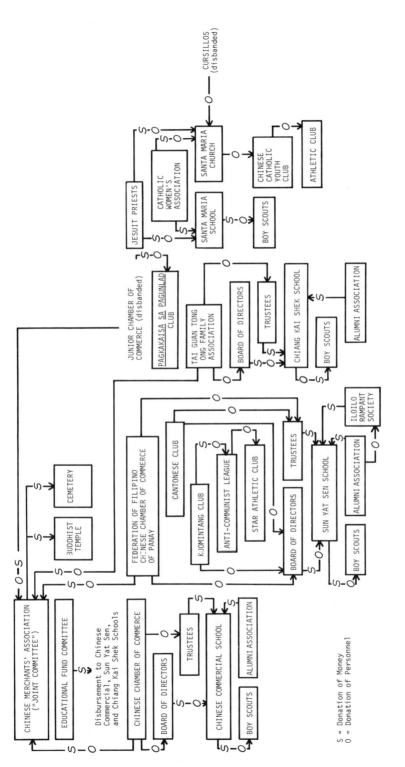

COMMUNITY STRUCTURES OF THE CHINESE OF ILIOLO CITY

S = Donation of Money
O = Donation of Personnel

exclusive and their membership crosscuts this diagram. The specific business associations, too, are omitted. They are not mutually exclusive, since a merchant can engage in several lines. They divide the community in what Karl Mannheim (1957) called "vein connections" because they follow occupation lines and pertain to the movement of economic goods and services rather than the movement of members, contributions, and political allegiances. This crosscutting and overlapping is valuable in preventing a breakdown in communication and cooperation between the more discrete segments.

Several organizations are omitted from the diagram because they are not involved in business and defense. The Iloilo Poetry Club is largely defunct as most of its talented members have died of old age; it is unable to interest or educate young people adequately in the language to recruit club replacements. The Chinese YMCA is an ethnic affiliate to Iloilo's Filipino YMCA and primarily organizes basketball teams to compete with Filipinos and among themselves. The Christian Gospel Center is a tightly knit Protestant group of approximately forty-five men and women who hold Sunday services and weekly Bible meetings at their own church building in the business district.

The diagram includes two organizations which have ceased to be or are yet to be active in business and defense. The Junior Chamber of Commerce, made up of younger, slightly more acculturated businessmen seeking new ways of accommodating to the Filipinos, was disbanded late in the 1960s and its best and brightest incorporated into the leadership of the pan-community Joint Committee. The Pagkakaisa sa Pagunlad, Inc., a branch of the Manila organization involved in civil rights and accommodation to Filipinos, is represented by a handful of leading businessmen's college-educated sons, but it has yet to go public in Iloilo behind any particular issue.

Present in other provincial cities of Bacolod, Davao, Cebu, but not in Iloilo are the Chinese Masons, or Liȯk Lim Hōe, a fraternal and charitable group. Some cities like Cebu also have Sy, Go, and other family associations and, occasionally, branches of the many organizations which have their headquarters in Manila: physical culture clubs, dried fish sellers' associations, and hometown associations, to name a few.

There are also what I shall call latent groups which have no formal or continual presence in the community. These latent groups seem to appear from the air in specific situations of need, perform a task, and disappear again. The Po, Sy, and Go family associations fall into this category. The Iloilo Rampant Association — a Sun Yat Sen School alumni fund-raising group — and several sports organizations are also in this category. Their names crop up in intracommunity newsletters (especially in funeral announcements) and in news items in pan-Philippine Chinese newspapers.

What appears to be happening is this. A community leader named Go or Po, for example, takes on the responsibility of continually reviving a defunct club or nonexistent club's name in order to aid in the formalities of recognizing a Go or Po who is deceased, celebrating a birthday, or organizing a means for community charity. Similarly, to get publicity in the Chinese newspapers or to add formality to an ad hoc delegation representing the community in another town, a group will create a name for itself, like the Iloilo Chinese Chess Club, to lend prestige to their activities. After the event the organization disappears as fast as it appeared, but its name will always be available on demand.

Principles of Leadership and Organization

To describe the structure of the community by its component associations as I have done above contributes perhaps to a mistaken notion of overseas Chinese organizing principles. Filipinos have expressed to me a degree of awe toward what they perceive as monolithic, machinelike Chinese "clannishness." In this section the actual operation of the associations, the behavior of their leaders, and their internal tension of cooperation and competition will be examined. By this discussion I hope to reevaluate the usual propositions of Chinese airtight organization and clannish unity.

The Chinese organizational principles which are in effect in Iloilo very likely also apply in Manila and in provincial cities of Iloilo's size. The difference in size of the cities and the Chinese enclaves in them is of less importance than their qualitative similarities. To begin with, Philippine Chinese in urban areas are quite similar in region of origin in China, in class composition, and in the sociopolitical setting in which they live in the Philippines. Across the nation they participate in the economy in the same way, living primarily in the cities as commercial brokers and shopkeepers. In general they are literate, connected to one another by the Philippine Chinese press. These similarities cause them to see their problems in the same way and make organizing fairly easy. The main difference among Philippine Chinese is their degree of association with Filipinos and their participation in Filipino culture and national identity. Though different degrees of assimilation make different kinds of Chinese, they also contribute to the power of Chinese associations in a Philippine political setting, as I shall show.

Chinese organizational wizardry is nearly legendary among most students and citizens of Southeast Asia. Such legends obscure the humble truth that Chinese organizations can also be puffery, camouflage – and very fragile. Some of Iloilo's Chinese organizations are virtually empty titles; others are temporary or irregularly revived as are the informal (or "latent") associations mentioned in the preceding section. This constant creation, deactivation, and retirement of voluntary organizations, each usually incorporated and registered with the Securities and Exchange Commission, should not be construed as proof of Chinese success at carrying out in unison certain actions toward agreed-upon goals. The intense personalism and paternalism in Iloilo's Chinese organizations can, in fact, cause them to grind to a halt or disintegrate when disagreements arise.

Chinese organizations are most impressive not for their cleverness at managing daily business but for their plasticity in reaction to stress. The many latent and formal organizations of Iloilo are the manifestations of an adaptive ability not unlike the ability to form a callous on a foot in a boot. In reaction to new pressures from without, the community spawns a new protective agency, reactivates an ex-middleman, or regroups a dispersed team of "workhorses."

This plasticity, along with the camouflage, the puffery, and the fragility, constitutes a much more realistic portrait of Chinese voluntary associations than do the legends of Mafia-like inscrutability. In what follows, the real power of Chinese organizations — the operation of their personalistic leadership — is analyzed.

The general picture of Iloilo's community is one of great profusion and diversity of formal organizations. Yet, for the most part, the active leadership is the same in each main organization. The leaders constitute a system of interlocking directorates, like the Chinese leaders of Bangkok (Skinner 1958). Between the leaders and the rank and file there are no qualitative breaks in socioeconomic terms. But there is an important distinction in terms of activity: the leaders do all the work, the followers do nothing. Perhaps thirty household heads can be considered to be doing all the leadership of the community.

There are roughly three types of leaders, distinguished by their activity. The "trustee" gives his money but not his time; the "president" donates both his time and money; and the men my informants called the "workhorses," such as the public relations officer or secretary, donate mostly their time. Some presidents or trustees are also the community brokers to outsiders, that is, to non-Chinese. Yet, often the brokers are not the actual powers but are persons with specific contacts or public images who are pressed into service by the leaders. Other "workhorses" shoulder most of the nonfinancial and daily burden of keeping organizations going.

The leaders of Philippine Chinese voluntary associations are actually elected patrons, like the *capitans Chinas* of the *gremios Chinos* in Spanish times (Wickberg 1965). The core group of leaders becomes the association itself, just as a business is identified with a family. The rank and file become the clients of this core of patrons. This mode of operations is similar to that of the land-based village tzu of Fukien and Kwangtung. Ordinary members are rarely called on to be a part of anything and are rather hostile to encroachment on their freedom of action or their purses.

Leaders make decisions on their own initiative because their constitutional functions are vague. They operate in an atmosphere of trust because there are few records, especially regarding financial matters, though more are coming into use. It is expected that they will in turn obtain some personal advantages from their office through contacts with people and money, though the line between scandal and acceptable privilege is vague and a constant subject of talk. There is little delegation of authority, line-and-staff structure, or direct referenda by which the leadership involves the rest of the members.

Recruitment of leaders to Chinese organizations is based on the way the community has established its social and economic divisions. In South China, according to Freedman (1958), social differentiation was strong and based on wealth, education, and gentry status. Relying on his own careful definitions of class, Frank Lynch (1965) has suggested that social classes are developing among the Philippine Chinese, too. On a pan-Philippine level or in Manila, such distinctions may be materializing. But in Iloilo and probably within other provincial Chinese groups, class distinctions are not visible nor important to an explanation of local events nor perceived by the Chinese themselves.

The Iloilo Chinese society is divided in many ways, but class is not one of them. There are no traditional Chinese gentry groups — landownership in the Philippines is a recent phenomenon and has not replaced commerce as a primary means of support. Social mobility, meaning mobility in relative social rank, is very great. The crucial and almost the sole determinant of social ranking is wealth, not necessarily inherited wealth. Self-made wealth is preferred because it reflects more directly the character of the individual. Secondary determinants of social ranking are age and length of residence in the community. Because the vast majority of Chinese are self-employed merchant families and the descendants of penniless immigrants, there is nothing that one family acquired that was not potentially available to another family. Young employees are viewed as the rich businessmen of the future, and old employees as ex-apprentices who bungled their chance of wealth. Movement through the social ranks is a "hydromatic shift," with no noticeable jumps. One informant described the socially mobile man as "the blob": he grows and shrinks with his fortunes but never changes his form.

A man need not advertise his wealth to establish his social rank. In a hostile environment that would be unwise because it provokes jealous resentment among Filipinos, and the Chinese say this. In Iloilo, perhaps even more than other less conservative towns, ostentatious consumption is a matter to be kept within the Chinese community. A man may be wealthy, but few Filipinos will know it while practically every Chinese will. The grapevine is active, and because of it most businessmen can reliably gauge one another's yearly profit, bank account, overhead, inventory value, and such matters.

Yet, there has always been ostentation within the community. As I have mentioned in chapter 3 concerning investment, ostentation is becoming more visible and widespread in recent years. Houses, autos, appliances, and furniture have become lavish. Festivities of all kinds — weddings, birthdays, holidays — are occasions for preparing expensive banquets in fancy hotels or private homes. Funerals have become more elaborate and involve more people. Donations to Chinese charities, as a form of competition in indicating wealth, have also grown.

It is a moot point whether such ostentation advertises ranking or creates it. In one sense a man's social ranking is secure just by having achieved commercial success with his reputation intact. Other men will respect him for his achievement as a reflection of his character and his judgement. Yet ostentation and philanthropy are also areas of vigorous competition for ranking. Perhaps we should visualize political ranking as being distinct from social ranking. In the social ranking, the criterion is how much money a merchant has made. In political ranking, the crucial criterion is how much he spends in the accepted ways. This ranking distinguishes the ambitious and community-minded donors from the successful, thus respectable, but miserly men. To make donations for schools, family associations, the Buddhist temple, or a Filipino-oriented charity is a way of voting oneself power. Other Chinese know that once awarded the laurel of leadership, such a donor will keep the community coffers filled, if only by his personal example.

Men of substance are often under pressure to give in proportion to their social status. Chambers of commerce, business associations, schools, and temples, especially, are in constant need of money, and their upkeep is viewed as obligatory, like a tax. The most common method of self-taxation is illustrated by the example of Bacolod City's Tai Tung High School Building Fund in the middle 1960s. Trustees and alumni were approached by men who were setting the example and were assessed a fixed amount based on their worth. The innovation on the part of the delegation was to refuse to accept anything less, thus excluding the hopeful benefactor completely from token gifts. Opposition to this sort of levy relaxed with time as competition between donors set in, and the fund was completed.

From the top ranks of the social and political hierarchy are picked those Chinese capable of spending money and those capable of winning respect for their personal authority.[6] These people are the trustees and the president, respectively. They replace the elite of the South Chinese tzu or lineage. The middlemen whom they utilize are analogous to the mainland government scholars of the lineage, who were expected to know how to approach the outside – the Chinese imperial government or the Filipinos, as the case might be. Unlike the South Chinese tzu, however, there is no qualitative difference between the president, trustees, middleman, and the regular membership of the Philippine Chinese voluntary associations. Their occupational homogeneity assures this: every man is a merchant.

The principles of trust and reputation that have been so important in business activities underlie most of the power and authority wielded in community organizations as well. Trust in business and in politics obviates the need for constitutions, referenda, contracts, auditing, collateral, and other legal matters which might provide recourse outside the strictly personal, familistic, paternal bonds that many businesses and clubs work within. Respect for an organization president is, thus, a function of who he is rather than of the office he holds; the office is the man, just as the business is the man.

How do the leaders influence the community, and how does it influence them? Again, there is an equivalence between business life and political life. The sanctions which encourage fair play in more purely economic activities also operate in the community's multifunctional associations. These sanctions are public opinion, boycotts, the consulate (in the past), and in the last resort, the Filipino judicial system.

Public opinion is the most powerful sanction and an omnipresent force. Public opinion works because the Chinese community's population has been small (relative to Manila and other primate cities) and of similar occupations. The entire population shares the basic goal of making good business and staying in harmony with, yet distinct from, the dominant host society. In a personalistic business community, as Iloilo's has been, a personal reputation is a man's lifeline to credit, suppliers, and customers. Merchants are mutually dependent, hence susceptible to opinion, because they owe their reputations to their community-mates, with whom they share their sociocultural life as well as buy and sell, borrow and lend.

Leaders, consequently, are chosen for their high reputations, gained through business, which give them a freedom of action that may be useful to other men. As for the leaders' strength of negative sanction, it arises not from any punishment they are entitled to mete out but as a byproduct of the system of interlocking directorates, which knits the city's Chinese organizations. If, for example, Tan, a baker, becomes delinquent to a creditor or offends the values of an organization, he has little escape from their bad feeling, their talk, their failure to cooperate. The man or men whose displeasure he provoked would be the same men in the chamber of commerce, the Tan Family Association, the Bakers Association, the Music Association, and the board of trustees of the school his children attend. Mr. Tan has either to come to terms and return to the fold, or he must leave town or move into Filipino society, both of which are risks to his livelihood.

Control by public opinion is not perfect and is sometimes completely ineffective. The case of the Sari-sari Store Association's boycott mentioned earlier is one example of this ineffectiveness. The So brothers' feud is another case in point. The So brothers (a pseudonym) were the wealthy heirs of the founder of Iloilo's So Family Association. Unlike their father, who had lived an exemplary life as Chinese community benefactor, the sons were profligates, adopting the worst traits of Western and Filipino ways of life and neglecting their lumber business. When the elder So died, a fierce argument over control of the property developed because the father had passed all control to his eldest son, who refused to divulge his holdings or divide them with his brothers. The case ultimately came before the officers of the So Family Association of Iloilo, where a compromise was sought for the good of the family image. The eldest son was urged to divulge his holdings to his brothers. Instead, he left town, claiming to be broke. His brothers liquidated what little remained and followed after him. The family and its feud became something of an embarrassment to the So Family Association, and since the family has ignominiously left the city, they are no longer discussed openly.

To avoid the embarrassment of ineffective sanctions as in the So family feud, community leaders concentrate on benevolent actions as patrons for their constituents and are very careful when trying to control them directly. The Chinese expect their leaders to interfere in the life of the community as little as possible until there is a crisis, when leaders are expected to mobilize and do as much as possible.

A one-on-one showdown of personal power between leaders and deviants from community norms is uncharacteristic but can be very aggressive. An unpopular Chinese who lived by extortion of other Chinese had contacts in the Filipino mass media of Iloilo City. He wielded his insider's knowledge and threatened to make reports to radio broadcasters if individual Chinese didn't pay him. Leaders of the community, through their younger intermediaries, threatened the man with physical harm, and he subsequently ceased his extortion.

Club leaders do not officially elicit the vote from their constituents on specific issues. Instead, they are connected to the community grapevine or learn of problems directly from the petitioners.

Reputations of even the highest-ranking Chinese are exposed and on trial in leadership positions. If one should make questionable use of community funds or work at cross-purposes to public sentiment, he can be driven quickly from office, not so much by angry "masses" as by pressure from the other community patrons.

At the beginning of this section I mentioned that different degrees of assimilation to Filipino culture make different kinds of Chinese and also contribute to the strength of Chinese associations. The way Chinese leaders partake of Filipino culture and associate with Filipinos is crucial to understand if we want to know how some men become leaders and how they serve their constituents.

The Chinese who serve as middlemen to the Filipinos are not always the same persons as the leaders themselves. Some of the leaders during the era of American rule and Chinese nationalism have had poor contact with the society outside the Chinese enclave; they understood little of Filipino customs and languages. They were raised to positions of leadership within the Chinese society specifically because they were wealthy Chinese, worthy of emulation, not because they were agents to the outside.

There are two quite distinct ideal types of political middlemen either within or working for the community's leadership. The first type is the ethnically Chinese man with specific Filipino contacts that he can activate when called upon to do so by Chinese. For example, a Filipino who was a fellow resister with a Chinese during the Japanese Occupation might now have risen to become municipal judge or senator. The Chinese, meanwhile, made his fortune in business. Because of their common history during the war, the Filipino judge and the Chinese merchant acknowledge a lifelong relationship of mutual debt which each occasionally draws upon. This first type of Chinese middleman with his particular friends has often been elected community leader. His polar opposite – the generalized Chinese middleman – has only recently come into his own.

The generalized middlemen are more marginally Chinese, younger, occasionally mestizos, with college educations and fluency in the Ilongo dialect and English. They have Filipino mah jong partners, drinking cronies, and perhaps Filipina wives. They join the local Lions Club and Catholic Cursillos in more than just name. They have a more generalized compatibility with Filipinos and are the type of men usually elected as public relations officers or "workhorses." They are asked to step forward in routine dealings with Filipino officialdom, Filipino student organizations, unions, and the patrolmen on the beat. Not their few highly placed allies but their familiarity with all Filipino society make them most valuable to the Chinese.

In recent decades these ethnically marginal men have begun to seek higher office themselves on the unspoken platform that specific talents and not simply money and respectability were needed in Chinese voluntary organizations' leaders. But the transition to such a leadership meets opposition from the old guard, not surprisingly, and has its own drawbacks, too. A look at the tasks of middlemen will help to clarify this.

In a word, the power of the Philippine Chinese to survive politically and culturally has been their liquid assets: they can move quickly in the commercial world, from one commercial activity to another, from one town to another. For some crises, too, money has meant protection. Thus, useable wealth within the community has lent authority to the possessor, not only in his own life but throughout the community due to his ability to step forward and bail it out of difficult situations. Wealth, therefore, leads both to internal power and to external contacts. It leads to external contacts for several reasons. Socially and politically important Filipinos have always found wealthy Chinese helpful as backers because of their liquid assets: Filipino politicians need campaign support and Filipino landholders find their own wealth not liquid enough. Also, it is the wealthy Chinese as leaders of the community who have shouldered the responsibility of collecting and presenting Chinese funds – whether it be taxes, charity, or protection funds – to outsiders. By adding to the required amount a little extra of his own, the leader can improve his position with the outsiders and may ultimately exploit that position for his own wealth and security in business. Wealth can lead to contacts which can, therefore, lead back to further wealth.

Underlying the contemporary tension between these old-style leaders and their challengers is the latter's attempt to reverse the equation somewhat. Instead of wealth in the Chinese commercial world leading to internal power and hence to external contacts, the challengers are attempting to gain internal power and subsequent commercial wealth from their marginal position as contacts to the outside. They are attempting to build up their position as valuable middlemen into status as community patrons. In recent years they have had a measure of success as various external crises have arisen that demonstrated their worth. (Examples are the "riot" in chapter 2 and the political pressures discussed at the beginning of this chapter.)

When and if the older political formula will be supplanted by the new one and its proponents is still uncertain because the new formula embodies weaknesses of its own. One of the most serious of these weaknesses is that the newer style leaders are often so fully involved in Filipino society that their political stock (and hence usefulness) can plummet due to circumstances completely external to the Chinese community. Their active participation in Filipino politics, for example, can bring them internal power only as long as their political factions are ascendent. Should their Filipino allies be removed from office, not only will their usefulness to the Chinese community cease; they may actually become a hazard as the incoming administration zeroes in on its political opponents. I witnessed such a reversal of political fortunes for a number of young Chinese merchants after the 1971 mayoral elections in Iloilo City.

Having one foot in both camps is a dangerous stance when neither foot is braced by personal wealth. In past times of political shuffles in Filipino society, old-style Chinese leaders could often survive the change with connections intact because they represented the taps to much liquid wealth. New Filipino administrations quickly found it beneficial to reestablish good relations with such men. Each side behaved most pragmatically. But for the newer style of Chinese middlemen, often without the wealth yet to make amends, their genuine political partisanships and friendships in the wider society could be their downfall. Further, until their bicultural ways of life are accepted as good and proper, they cannot fulfill the old Chinese leaders' function of community exemplars. Approaching them is awkward for the more ethnically Chinese who wish to seek favors through their outside contacts. In short, the new middleman is not yet the perfect patron within the Chinese enclave that his ethnic predecessors were. Both styles of brokerage may coexist for a long time to come.

Intercommunity Sanctions

George Weightman (1960) pondered but did not answer the question of how communal sanctions are maintained in a nonlocalized, segmented

Chinese "state within a state" like that of the Philippines. The first steps of an answer to this question can be made by examining the connections of Iloilo's organizations with other Chinese communities, especially Manila.

A central principle of supralocal politics among Philippine businessmen is that it never strays far from the realm of business. An example of this interrelation of business and politics is the Federation of Filipino-Chinese Chambers of Commerce in Manila. Like its provincial counterpart in Iloilo, the federation is multifunctional, performing defense and economic tasks. It has been the primary link of the Philippine Chinese to the Chinese Republic and to the Philippine executive branch of government, maintained through personal ties. It prepares and distributes to the provinces a great deal of printed matter such as business directories, translations of government publications, and explanations of business regulations. Its leaders act personally as brokers for complaints from provincial Chinese and for solicitations of help or contributions. Not coincidentally, these men are also the leading businessmen of the city and nation, the major buyers and sellers of the goods in which Iloilo's Chinese merchants deal.

When the Iloilo Cua-Chua family wishes to raise money for a clubhouse, for example, they approach the Chuas and Cuas of Manila for contributions. These men in Manila are business patrons of Iloilo Chinese. Exclusive distributorships, loans, long-term credit, even patronage as a godparent may flow from these men to Iloilo businessmen. By contributing to Iloilo's Cua-Chua clubhouse, the Chinese in Manila will be elected members of its honorary board of trustees and can be counted on in the future as middlemen in commercial or political ventures by individuals who are their contacts at Iloilo's clubhouse. Furthermore, the Iloilo men who do business with these larger operators and enlist them as club patrons subsequently become patrons themselves, to whom Iloilo's Cua-Chua family or other kin and business allies can go for business or political action.

Data and money flow mainly out of Manila, and solicitors of favors flow into Manila. I learned of no cases in the early 1970s in which Manila men came to the provincial cities in search of funds or political support. Only the most perfunctory official reports flow from the provinces to Manila. Soliciting contributions is in fact reciprocal at times, I was told, but because their leadership and wealth are greater, the Manila organizations spend more money in the provinces in absolute terms than provincial organizations spend in Manila.

Pressure to organize also flows from Manila. Sometimes an important Manila entrepreneur will visit similar towns and raise an organization, money, and some enthusiasm where before there was none. The Liok Lim Hōe, or Chinese Masons Temple which was recently organized in Bacolod (and does not exist in Iloilo) is a good example of influence from above. A Chinese

Mason from Manila with important business contacts in Bacolod urged the community to start the club, and he set an example by giving a contribution. The club exists today, with its small membership, as a reinforcement of social and commercial contacts between Manila and Bacolod Chinese Masons.

The principles of Philippine Chinese government within the community are also the bases for relations between communities. Both intercommunity and intracommunity organizations are based on paternalistic leadership by an elected core of businessmen socioeconomically similar to their constituents. Leaders' authority is based on respect for their wealth and connections and not directly on specific sanctions provided by their office. Business connections between Chinese frequently lead to political alliances, and vice versa, just as business success leads to authority.

In brief, there is no qualitative difference between the operations of supralocal organizations and local ones. They are both paternalistic, personalistic networks of "connections," often overlapping commercial networks and operating under the guise of normal clubs.

The power in personal connections usually works to bring the smaller, less wealthy, or less well-connected provincial Chinese enclaves into line with Manila. In the early 1950s, for example, after the Communist takeover in China and during the Hukbalahap uprising in the Philippines, Kuomintang supporters in Manila with the backing of the Republican Chinese embassy began supplying information to the Philippine Constabulary so that they might arrest and deport Chinese Communist sympathizers. The campaign was carried to Iloilo City, among others, where local Kuomintang supporters were encouraged to take up the cause. Several schoolteachers in Chinese Commercial School were arrested and some community leaders opposed to the Kuomintang were intimidated. In this case the power of the Manila Chinese leaders arose from their connection to the Philippine Constabulary, which they used in part for their own needs in Manila and provincial cities.

The exercise of control occasionally works in the opposite direction: from the provinces to Manila. In 1971 when the Iloilo Wu Family Association was campaigning for funds for a new club building, the national economy had been quite unsteady and other Chinese Wu Family associations were slow to contribute. The directors of Iloilo's club threatened their Manila headquarters that as stockholders in Manila's Wu Family Temple Corporation they would withdraw their capital to use in Iloilo. This threat brought out the money which, supplemented by a bank loan, eventually raised the Iloilo club's new building.

Even though the sanctions between Iloilo and Manila may be the same as within Iloilo and just as powerful when put into effect, they are less employed in aggressively negative ways. Blackballing, boycotting, and vetoing are rarely used. Except for the Federation of Filipino-Chinese Chambers of Commerce of Panay, the family associations, and the schools, Iloilo's associations have only the most tenuous of official obligations to Manila's organizations and even less to those of other cities. Personal networks of leaders form the only important supralocal ties. Just as within the community, the "mandate" for Chinese voluntary associations is in effect an atmosphere of maximum trust, sometimes indistinguishable from apathy, on the part of the members toward the leaders.

The same type of personal network that connects Manila to the provinces also binds provincial cities. Most of Iloilo's provincial business in other islands of the region is transacted in Bacolod City in Negros Occidental province and Cebu City in Cebu province. Associations in these cities are almost constantly approaching one another for contributions; I have, however, no evidence of any other forms of exchange except traveling teams of players of chess, badminton, or ancient music. Typically, contacts between these provincial cities are often made by men who do business together, or are school chums, *compadres,* or otherwise allied. Generally speaking, such relations are more equal than paternal, none of the cities claiming hegemony over the region. As a result, the connections between the regional associations are fewer and involve less money and less force than the connections of each to Manila.

On the other hand, smaller provincial Chinese communities which are further down the line commercially and politically from Manila than are Iloilo, Cebu, or Davao will turn to these latter cities as patrons to their small associations. Contributions from Iloilo have more impact in the smaller communities; business connections are also close and hierarchical. Should the smaller Chinese settlements like those in Jolo, Dumaguete, and Samar need defense from local political pressures, for example, they can approach Iloilo or Cebu as middlemen because these cities have more numerous and more powerful contacts to resolve the problems.

This channeling of organizational activity between the provincial cities and the smaller towns is reinforced by historical patterns of migration and by kinship ties as well as by business relations. Daniel Doeppers (1971) has discussed the "parent-bazaar" pattern whereby provincial towns are "colonized" by a few central businesses and families in the larger cities.[7] The organizational ties of these small town Chinese associations inevitably flow back along the old routes of migration, the kinship ties, and the commercial distribution chains to their "parent-bazaars" in Iloilo or other large provincial cities.

1. For a discussion in more depth of Chinese and Filipino relations in the Philippines, see recent works by Stanley Eitzen (1968), Gerald McBeath (1975), and numerous publications by Pagkakaisa sa Pagunlad, Inc., such as McCarthy (1974).

2. Santa Maria is supported independently by the Catholic Church, which covers its debts due to insufficient tuition receipts.

3. Historically the Federation of Panay was created to be an administrative confederation of all the city's specific business associations.

4. See, however, Tan's (1972) discussion of active unions in the 1930s.

5. Cf. Weightman's (1960) and Amyot's (1960) dissertations for complete lists of Philippine Chinese sib and phratry organizations.

6. A man never campaigns for office. He operates from a feeling of *noblesse oblige*. It is assumed he will accept the office if offered it.

7. See also chapter 3 for discussion of Iloilo City's connections to the provinces.

Chinese motifs combine with Spanish tomb architecture in
Iloilo's Chinese cemetery. *Chung ming,* or the Feast of the
Ancestors, has been re-dated to correspond with the
Filipino Catholic All Saints' Day; Chinese flock to the
cemetery to sweep the tombs, make offerings, and socialize.

The Iloilo Chinese Classical Southern Music Society holds
regular lively dinner parties with music. The musicians are
dedicated amateurs, and the members are drawn from all
factions in the town.

The lyrics to the ancient songs are displayed behind the young female singer. She is a mestiza, the daughter of one of the musicians, and is serious about her music.

The cultural centers of the Chinese community are its
schools, which serve as convention halls, banquet rooms,
and ceremonial chambers, and which produce cultural
shows such as this pageant on the occasion of the school's
sixtieth anniversary. The evening's program was predominantly traditional and contemporary Chinese material, but
included some Filipino songs and dances.

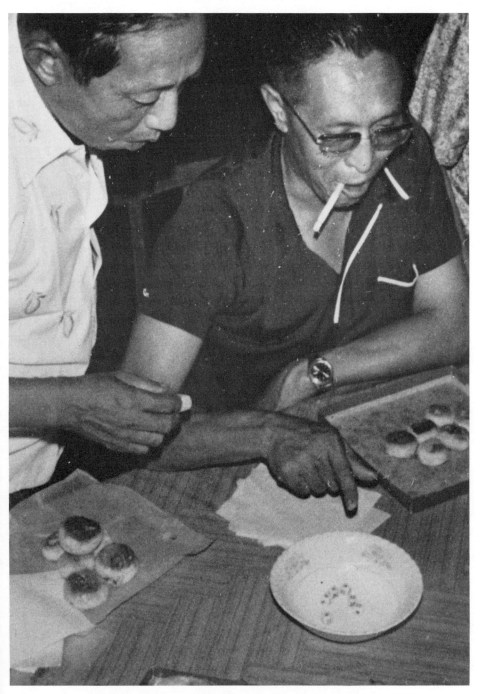

Moon Festival, marking the establishment of the Ming Dynasty in Chinese history, is still celebrated in Chinese homes and by lineage mates at the family association clubhouses. Sweet, rich mooncakes are won by the throw of dice, signalling good luck.

The Chinese style engagement remains far more elaborate
and binding to the families than its Filipino equivalent.
Weddings are almost always held as Catholic Masses.
Inset: Banquets, or *lao liat,* punctuate nearly every holiday
or ceremony. Involving as many as 100 tables, they are
held in restaurants, association halls, or the schools. Dozens
of Filipinos are usually included on the guest list.

Though a generation gap is pronounced, proper form of respect for the elders continues. Here a successful merchant's sons and grandchildren celebrate his seventieth birthday—on his sixty-ninth birthday: the end of a decade is traditionally an inauspicious time.

Top: The sons of a successful grain merchant and historically important liaison to Filipino authorities honor his birthday with a feast and photo display at his suburban compound. *Bottom:* An Iloilo merchant family of three generations celebrates the Easter holidays at their rural farm estate, a rare possession among Chinese until acquisition of Filipino citizenship became common recently.

The Iloilo Chinese temple contains the altars to Kuan Im and Tia Kong. Merchants and their families still attend for private prayers and divinatory advice in business and family matters.

The death of an important Chinese is the occasion of a
large eclectic ceremony extolling Chinese culture and
commercial and community spirit. The horse-drawn hearse
is accompanied by an honor guard of Chinese boy scouts
and local dignitaries.

Top: Charitable contributions to Filipinos, in this case
the Red Cross, are opportunities to improve local Chinese
public relations and to approach a temporary unity
among themselves. *Bottom:* This main business avenue in
downtown Iloilo City has a concentration of textile
merchants. The Chinese families—or parts of them—reside
in the apartments above.

5

BUILDING A FAMILY

UNTIL THE 1930s, LIFE IN THE PHILIPPINES for most immigrants meant either bachelorhood or forced separation from a wife in China. Household groups were mostly male relatives and coworkers. If a Chinese should take a common-law Filipino wife, he would either dwell in her home area or strike off on his own.

From the 1930s until the Communist victory in 1949, a large number of Chinese women arrived in the Philippines. These were the wives and potential wives of immigrants already in the Philippines. For the first time Chinese families formed overseas in fairly large numbers. Nuclear families and extended patriarchal households both became more common. More often a wife was acquired within one's own Philippine town, and inevitably this brought about involvement of a husband with his in-laws.

At the same time marriage to Filipinas did not appreciably decrease even though more Chinese women were available. Young Chinese influenced by the Philippine surroundings found Filipinas easier to know and simpler to marry. However, this stable intermarriage rate will not cause the Chinese to become racially extinct. The number of pure Chinese increases every generation. Mestizo women usually marry back into the community, and this also helps to sustain a large predominantly Chinese population.

In recent decades, some Chinese women have married Filipinos and mestizos. There seems to be no tendency for Chinese to marry Filipinos from financially successful families. The problems of money management owing to different cultural norms may be the reason for this.

Families are generally large and composite, to the point where they are breaking down into various smaller parts or are splitting residence between a house and the store. The big family ideal is finally attainable, but it appears to be only a temporary trend. Patrilocality is still most common, but other types of postmarital residence are not decreasing. Nevertheless, patrilocal residence appears to be one of the keys for keeping a Chinese family within the Chinese community because only the old families which have maintained patrilocality have survived.

Before examining the overseas Chinese family as an economic unit in the next chapter, let us now look more closely at the recent history of the family in the light of immigration patterns and interaction with Filipinos in Iloilo City.

Immigration

The centuries-old Chinese immigration pattern slowly changed throughout the American era in the Philippines. Movement to and from China occurred more frequently, and more Chinese women came to the Philippines. Commuting to China became more frequent because transportation was faster and relatively cheaper and because political turmoil in Fukien required more attention from its overseas citizens. More women came to the Philippines precisely to avoid this turmoil. Iloilo's Chinese community had grown enough in size and amenities to provide a modicum of Chinese environment for wives and families.

For many Chinese men before the war, their stay in the Philippines meant a bachelor's life. That is, men returned to China to marry after making progress in their merchant careers, but left their growing families in China. Sometimes they took Filipinas as common-law wives in addition to their China wives. Informants claim that the China families "understood" this arrangement as long as proper priority was given to the China family. A man who took a Filipina wife before he had married in China was considered reprobate. No China family would accept him as a son-in-law if they knew he already had a Filipina wife.

Table 4 outlines the marriage pattern for two samples of Iloilo Chinese men, both living and deceased. The first column presents Chinese citizens registered with the Bureau of Immigration. The other three columns show Chinese from sixty-four families regardless of citizenship. These men are separated into immigrant generations without regard to their actual year of immigration. A great variety of marriage situations occurs among the Chinese citizens and the early immigrant generations. The possibility of having families in two countries and the ability to move them about make for great variety as each man adjusts to sociopolitical exigencies as he sees them. About 85 percent of the first immigrant generation married in China, but only 30 percent brought their wives to the Philippines. Another 25 percent took a second spouse in the Philippines. Only 15 percent of the men married in the Philippines.[1] In the succeeding immigrant generations, proportionately more marriages took place exclusively in the Philippines. By the third immigrant generation, 95 percent of the marriages have been in the Philippines, and the variety of marriage arrangements has decreased.

Table 4

Marriage Pattern for Male Chinese Citizens and Ethnic
Chinese Men, Iloilo City, 1972

Marriage Patterns	Percent of Chinese Citizens*	Percent of Ethnic Chinese by Immigrant Generation		
		1st gen.	2d. gen.	3d. gen.
Married Chinese in China; brought her to the Philippines	8.5%	29.6%	14.6%	— —
Married Chinese in China; she stayed there	15.2	29.6	14.6	1.5
Married Chinese in China; remarried in the Philippines[+]	15.2	25.1	11.9	2.2
Married Chinese in Philippines only	23.3	6.1	40.1	59.6
Married Filipina only[‡]	24.0	9.1	17.1	36.2
Widowers or insufficient data[∮]	14.3	— —	2.1	— —
N	539	131	244	140
Percent	100.5	99.5	100.4	99.5

*Gathered from alien certificates of registration in the Bureau of Immigration, Iloilo office, 1972.

+Remarried either a Filipino or Chinese wife.

‡For Chinese citizens, the figure represents an estimate based on men claiming marriage to Filipinas, men admitting common-law wives, and one-half of the men claiming to be single but most likely also having wives.

∮Widower Chinese citizens do not identify their former wives in their alien certificates of registration.

Between 15 and 30 percent of the aliens and first generation immigrants never did have spouses with them in the Philippines. Of the others who later brought their spouses or acquired a second one overseas, many did so only after many years of residence overseas.

In any case, not until the third immigrant generation have Philippine Chinese begun a simpler pattern of marriage predominantly in the host country. Most of these third generation marriages have taken place since the Second World War, when Communism brought an end to movement to and from China. The marriage pool became restricted to the population of the Philippines – the Filipinos and the overseas Chinese.

In the years of migration to and from China, the vagaries of overseas life produced a wide range in the age of marriage for the Philippine Chinese. Some young immigrants were pressured into marrying before they left for their apprentice duty in the Philippines. Their hometown families hoped to bind them to their obligations in Fukien, so they would be sure to return. Other men were able to complete their adjustment period in the Philippines rapidly enough to return to pick a wife at the still youthful age of twenty-five or thirty. Other men struggled along, delayed by business failures, wars, or alliances with Filipinas, and did not marry a Chinese woman until well into middle age. More than 10 percent of the older Chinese men (around seventy years of age) in Iloilo married when they were over forty years old. There has been a tendency for each later group of Chinese men to marry in a narrower age bracket: the wide range in ages at marriage diminished in the postwar marriages because the marriage pool was limited to the Philippines. Most men in postwar years have married between the ages of twenty-two to thirty-four.

Chinese women were not involved in such irregular migration patterns, but they remained quite sedentary either in China or the Philippines and waited for husbands to come to them. Thus, their age at marriage has remained more stable at the eighteen-to-thirty-year age bracket. They average about five years younger than their husbands. However, there is a rather consistent 20 percent or more among the older half of the women who married before age seventeen. These latter were the girl brides of the young men who married hurriedly before venturing overseas. In postwar years this type of marriage disappeared.

The radical shift from marrying and starting families in China to marrying and raising families in the Philippines occurred rather abruptly in the years just preceding the Second World War. In the 1920s and 1930s most Chinese citizens returned to China for brides, usually leaving them behind while they returned to their merchant careers in Iloilo and elsewhere. The total isolation during the Japanese Occupation was followed directly by stringent immigration restrictions in postwar independent Philippines, which was soon followed in turn by the 1949 Communist victory. Each of these events greatly inhibited travel to China in search of wives. On the other hand, many Chinese and mestiza girls born in the growing Iloilo Chinese society came of age and compensated for the dearth of brides from China. Immigration records for Iloilo Chinese show that of the eighty-seven women who are Chinese citizens and married before 1942, 59 percent married in China. Only 6 percent of the 125 alien women who married after 1942 were married in China.

Prewar diversity in marriage was not restricted to the location and race of a man's wife but included the number of spouses. I was able to roughly determine the extent of polygyny or multiple wives from my sample of sixty-eight genealogies, which encompassed the lives of 493 men. Such a survey underrepresents the degree of polygyny because my informants were understandably embarrassed to discuss the subject. In any case, at least 16 percent of the Philippine Chinese men had more than one spouse simultaneously at some point in their lives. Most common (as high as 19 percent of immigrants or their sons) was to have a wife in China and a Filipina wife. Not infrequently the China wife would later be called to join her husband, in which case the Filipina wife "separated." This meant she left the household with her mestizo children but remained a part of the man's family, claiming some financial and inheritance rights from him. A man who had a Chinese wife in each country (around 3 percent of the sample) usually married the second in the Philippines when he abandoned all plans for regaining contact with the Chinese wife after 1949. There were 4 to 7 percent of the men who had more than one wife in one or both countries. Having several wives in China accompanied financial success. To have multiple wives, usually Filipinas, in the Philippines, had no such connotation.

To summarize, as immigration diminished, the range of polygyny, places of marriage, and age at marriage narrowed. Beginning about 1942 with the isolation of the Philippines, marriage began to take place almost exclusively within the country. Polygyny diminished because men could not maintain two residences and two families. The choice of marriage partner was restricted to Filipinos, to Chinese already in the Philippines, and to mestizos. Age at marriage narrowed to twenty-five to thirty years of age for men and twenty to twenty-five years for women.

In-marriage, Incest, and Intermarriage

As long as an overseas man's home and legitimate family were located in China, his marital alliances with Filipinas could be tolerated. A merchant often needed the companionship, assistance, protection, and connections which a Filipina wife would provide. When marriage between Philippine Chinese became common in the 1930s and after, the whole complexion of marital life changed. Not only were spouses together throughout the marriage, thus putting a damper on the sojourner's form of polygyny, but frequently the spouse's parents were in the Philippines, too. Thus, a number of affinal kinsmen were present to monitor a man's conduct after marriage.

In Fukien and Kwangtung provinces, the tradition of surname exogamy usually meant that daughters were betrothed to men in villages other than one's own. Most communities had only a few surname groups in coresidence. Iloilo City's Chinese society is much more heterogeneous than those native villages were, having dozens of surnames. Also, it is socially distant from other large Chinese enclaves. When marriage among the Philippine Chinese became common, a majority of these marriages occurred within the community. In a city the size of Manila, with a Chinese population of over 100,000, the effects of community endogamy are not so noticeable. But in a Chinese community the size of Iloilo's, endogamy has produced a complex web of family interrelationships, even though it has only been common for about 30 years.

Iloilo's Chinese men who marry in the Philippines usually select local wives or settle in the home community of their wives. In a sample of 184 Iloilo Chinese men 86 percent found their wives in Iloilo City. All of these marriages have taken place in the twentieth century, and most have involved men alive in 1972. Men who married women from other towns did so primarily in Manila, Bacolod, and small towns on Panay island. To date, about one-half of Iloilo Chinese men's marriages in the Philippines have been with Filipinas. Regardless of the race of the wife, the vast majority of marriages have taken place within the city.

When young Chinese men do marry into other communities, Manila and Bacolod are the most common destinations. Manila is attractive; first, because it has a much bigger Chinese community, and second, because it is economically much more vigorous than Iloilo. Bacolod is attractive because it is also economically vigorous and close to Iloilo. Historically, it has been colonized by many Chinese from Iloilo, so in a way it is an extension of Iloilo Chinese society.

About one-third of the married Chinese and mestizo women from Iloilo have married into other communities in the last thirty years. Well over one-half of these marriages were into Bacolod or Manila families. It appears that this percentage may be growing to 40 percent or more, while only 14 percent of the men marry women from other cities. Parents greatly desire daughters to "marry up" into better Chinese society, which both Bacolod and Manila offer. Most men, however, must return with their wives to Iloilo to work in their father's businesses.

Another reason why more women marry out of town is the intermarriage rate of the men. About 25 percent of the men are marrying Filipinos and only 10 percent of the women are, yet the sex ratio is approaching equality. Thus, 15 percent of the women must find Chinese husbands from other towns like Manila where the preference is stronger for Chinese brides.

A test was run to see just how interrelated the Chinese families of Iloilo were after years of a decidedly nonrandom immigration pattern and about thirty years of marriage primarily within the community. The number of links to other Iloilo Chinese business families was computed in a sample of sixty-seven business families (10 to 15 percent of the city's Chinese). Consanguineal links were calculated only to the distance of four intervening kinsmen (ego to father's cousin's son, for example). Affinal links were also calculated to four intervening kinsmen, but allowing only one affinal link – either at the beginning (ego's wife's relatives) or at the end (ego's kinsman's spouse). A kin connection to one or more members of a nuclear family counted as only one connection.

In spite of the limitations on the test which make the kin web appear thinner than it impressed me while living in Iloilo, the results are significant. In 67 families there were 120 consanguineal links and 60 affinal links to other Chinese businesses in town. The average number of stores to which each store in town is related is 2.7.[2] If more distant consanguineal relatives or kinsmen related through several affinal links were counted, this average would be even higher.

Opportunities for Iloilo business families to form marriage alliances (and thus perhaps business alliances) are numerous. These alliances are made in consideration of the Philippine context; that is, marriage alliances like those between surname groups in their Chinese hometowns have ceased to exist. One notable exception to this has been a number of Yu and Yap families who persisted in intermarrying in Iloilo in the first and sometimes the second immigrant generation. These two groups were members of large neighbor sibs in Chin-kang County, Fukien province. Yu and Yap families resided together in Janiuay, Iloilo province, as well as in the city, and specialized in textiles and native products. Informants claim that large wealthy families of Go and Sy who intermarry in Cebu also had an old Chin-kang County alliance. Any other traditional alliances between Iloilo Chinese surnames have long since disappeared.

Incest and Marriage Restrictions

Although traditional marriage alliances have faded, the taboos against sib endogamy are still strong. In towns like Iloilo the older Chinese still despise this practice as "incest." The son of Mr. Gan, a construction company owner, wished to marry a Miss Tiu. Although this is a different surname, the two names are allied under the same ancestor and belong to the same family association. To add to the marginality of the "incest," both sweethearts were children of Filipina mothers. Two years of struggle ensued before the fathers reluctantly permitted the marriage.

"Old country" animosities between feuding sibs have lived on among the Philippine Chinese immigrants. As a result, children of these immigrants are proscribed from marrying children of their enemies. One of my assistants has been secretly engaged to a girl whose father opposes his courtship on the grounds that the boy's Ong sib and the father's Ang sib were bitter enemies in Fukien in the early twentieth century. Other surnames forbidden to each other are Sy and Ty. Such animosities mean nothing to the young engaged couples, of course, and the taboos will die with the older generation.

Marriages between Cantonese and Fukienese are rare. Most Cantonese immigrants married Cantonese women in China and/or Filipinas in Iloilo. The number of pure Cantonese women in the Philippines has been extremely small: the sex ratio for Cantonese in 1972 was 350:100 (Bureau of Immigration). These few women are much sought after by Cantonese men. In recent decades a Cantonese man has occasionally taken a Fukienese wife. Most of these marriages are between Philippine-born and Philippine-educated Chinese for whom the regional difference is much less important or obvious than for their parents.

Cantonese-Fukienese marriages often hit troubled water precisely because of the older generation. Even though not every new family lives in a patrilocal extended family household, in-laws are omnipresent in an interrelated merchant enclave like Iloilo. A Cantonese neighbor of my assistant married a Fukienese girl from Manila and brought her to live with him and his parents in their Iloilo store. Her treatment at the hands of the mother-in-law, who objected to her Fukienese background, was so poor that her relatives appealed to the town's president of her family association. He separated her from her in-laws and returned her to Manila.

Regional differences even within Fukien province have been recognized and have influenced marriage considerations. The feeling exists among the older immigrant generation, who still participate in the younger generations' marriage negotiations, that the background of a potential mate and his personality are more transparent if he is from their county. In the past, immigrants from Chin-kang County were very hesitant to ally themselves in marriage with natives of the Amoy City area, who are believed to be shrewd and a bit unstable.

When the older generation objects to the race, background, surname group, or language group of the younger generation's sweethearts and fiancees, an increasingly common response has been for the young couple to elope. Although marriages are no longer arranged, formal marriage negotiations are still practiced and the involvement of the elders is extensive and crucial. Because parents' standards frequently differ from their sons' and daughters', youth can often prevail only by running away. In many cases the parents can be convinced to accept the fait accompli. However, sometimes the rift is dramatic. When the daughter of Mr. Pe, a rice and corn dealer, eloped with a Filipino, he went into formal mourning, wearing black and burning the personal possessions of his daughter as though she were dead.

Elopements are great family embarrassments. One shoe store family has had all five of its mestizo sons and daughters eloping with Chinese lovers. After the first two elopements, families who were being courted by the other three youths became something less than warm to their suits because of their family's reputation. Not surprisingly, this precipitated the last three elopements. Because elopements are embarrassing, families often hurry to cover them by formal recognition of the engagement, moving through the motions of marriage negotiations and celebrating with a large wedding banquet. For example, Mr. Lam is a middle-aged textile merchant of comfortable means. When his daughter eloped with the son of a small grocery store-keeper, he recovered his family's honor by throwing the biggest wedding banquet in the history of the town.

Intermarriage with Filipinos

Chinese marriage to Filipinos is perceived as a threat to the existence of the Chinese community by racial dilution and acculturation, but such inter-marriage has always occurred. Let us first examine the extent of intermarriage and then look at some effects on overseas Chinese society.

In the years of migration to and from China, a Chinese immigrant often founded a mestizo family even if he already had a Chinese family at home. Most merchants working in provincial areas married Filipinas for protection, help in the business, and companionship. To estimate the intermarriage rate in the years before the Second World War, I have examined the older generations (first and second ascending generations before a middle-aged informant). In my sample of 68 genealogies, 132 men are represented.

It appears that before the Second World War, about 24 percent of the recent immigrants married pure Filipino wives. Very few (3 percent) married mestizo women. There are two factors which may account for this. First, marriage to a mestiza constituted a legitimate Chinese marriage because she had a Chinese father. She could not serve simply as a second wife. Also, the number of mestiza women of marriageable age was minute relative to the number of marriageable immigrant men.

Let us turn now to the intermarriage patterns in 1972 of middle-aged Philippine Chinese, 315 of whom are represented in my surveys. This sample of men is not independent of that for the older men, since it is drawn from the same genealogies. Nevertheless, changes from one generation to the next can be examined. There seems to be little change: about 25 percent of the pure Chinese men still marry pure Filipino wives. The increase in the number of Chinese women in the Philippines was not reflected in increased proportions of marriage to them. There is an increase in marriage to mestiza women from 3 percent in the previous generations to over 10 percent in this group of men. About 10 percent of these middle-aged men are mestizos of one degree or another, and most mestizos (60 percent) have married pure Filipinas; only 18 percent of the mestizos married pure Chinese women.

The intermarriage pattern for men marrying after 1960 again shows little change from previous generations. My survey of 214 younger men found about one-fourth of the pure Chinese men to be still marrying pure Filipino wives. Marriage to mestizo women is at the same level as in the previous generation (12 percent). Fewer mestizo men are marrying pure Chinese women than in the previous generation (12 percent compared to 18 percent).

To summarize, the extent of marriage of Chinese men to Filipino women has remained constant throughout the twentieth century at about 25 percent. Marriage by Chinese men to mestizo women has leveled off at about 12 percent. The proportion of mestizo men who are able to marry pure Chinese wives is dropping. It appears that new immigrants have married Filipinas as frequently as have third generation Philippine Chinese. Also, marriages to Filipinas occur as often in postwar years as previously. The male intermarriage pattern, thus, seems to be very stable.

The intermarriage pattern revealed in the sixty-eight genealogies of Chinese and mestiza women is not stable.[3] To begin with, women in the first and second ascending generations above today's middle-aged women were virtually all pure Chinese and virtually all married pure Chinese men. Most married in China before immigration. If they married in the Philippines, their kinsmen never offered them any alternative to marrying a pure Chinese. Very few contemporary members of Iloilo's Chinese society have female ancestors who intermarried.

The contemporary middle-aged women who married in the late 1930s to early 1950s rarely intermarried either. Of sixty-nine pure Chinese women, only one married anyone but a pure Chinese man. Of thirty mestiza women, about 40 percent also married pure Chinese men. It is interesting to note that almost all of the other mestizas married Filipinos. Only one of thirty mestiza women married a mestizo husband. Unlike the Indonesian Peranaken Chinese or the nineteenth-century Chinese mestizos in the Philippines, there is no longer any pattern of mestizos seeking mestizas in marriage.

There are more marriages with mestizos and Filipinos in the generation of women who married since the early 1950s. About 10 percent of the pure Chinese women married mestizos and Filipinos, and about 50 percent of mestiza women did, too. So, there are more intermarriages by pure Chinese women now, but conversely, more mestiza women married mestizos and Chinese. That is, more women of mixed parentage marry back into the Chinese group than did their elders. More mestizas than in the previous decades (48 percent compared to 40 percent) married pure Chinese husbands.

To summarize, Chinese women have begun to marry Filipino and mestizo men only in recent decades, and the rate has reached about 10 percent. But the proportion of mestizo women who marry back into the Chinese community (counting mestizo husbands) has increased from 43 percent to 72 percent.

The history of Chinese women in the Philippines has been short, and their intermarriage rates are still lower than those of Chinese men, but they have changed more abruptly. When the men have intermarried, it has been mostly with Filipinas; when the women have intermarried, it has been primarily with mestizos. Both men and women have "married out" in the sense that their spouse has less Chinese blood than themselves, but the men have married out much more frequently than have the women.

One of the main reasons intermarriage has not increased much in recent decades (except among the women, who heretofore *never* intermarried) is that the sex ratio is becoming more balanced. It is simply easier for a Chinese to find another eligible Chinese.

Yet, marriage with Filipinas continues in defiance of overseas Chinese society's values. The reasons the men give for this behavior are as follows. First, Iloilo Chinese parents are extremely conservative about the social life and dating habits of their daughters. Remaining almost cloistered, the girls tend to be shy and old-fashioned. The young men, running the stores and moving freely about town, tend to be more open, more "Filipino." Because they cannot date Chinese girls in the Western sense, they date Filipinas secretly. If they wish to approach a Chinese girl, they must do so seriously, initiating formal responsibilities by both their own and the girls' families. A formal courtship is viewed as onerously boring and expensive by the young men. Filipinas, on the other hand, are more available, are attracted to the Chinese youths' wealth, and are less expensive to marry because many Chinese formalities can be dispensed with.

Many young Chinese date Filipino girls. The young man, however, ultimately enters into a formal courtship of a Chinese woman, if he is thoughtful of his responsibilities to his parents, his sisters (their fate in marriage may hinge on his), and the family store. His fiancee's parents will investigate his background — he must have been careful to cover his alliances with Filipinas. The choice of spouse, for many young men, then, hinges on supporting the double standard or opposing it. In general, men choose Filipinas because of personal interests and familiarity, or they choose Chinese women because that is what is expected.

Attachment to the Catholic Church appears to be almost irrelevant for pure Chinese males in selecting Filipina spouses over Chinese ones. Few pure Chinese men are even nominally Catholic, as defined by attending Mass at Santa Maria Church, Iloilo's Chinese Catholic church. Mestizo men are more often Catholic converts, owing to the influence of their Filipino mothers. The data show that more mestizos marry Filipinas, but this can be attributed to their general upbringing rather than to their religious affiliation in particular. In the future there will undoubtedly be a greater percentage of pure Chinese Catholic converts, which will increase their compatibility with Filipinos and may consequently increase their intermarriage rate.

Chinese girls cannot date Filipino boys at all. Engagements of girls who did date Filipinos have been broken when the prospective groom's family learned of it. Mothers have threatened to kill themselves if their daughters dated Filipinos.[4] This tension not infrequently leads to elopements in order for young men and women to break the control their elders still exercise over courtship and marriage.

Marriage and Business

Philippine Chinese fears of racial extinction through intermarriage with Filipinos are unfounded. Six out of ten Chinese men and nine out of ten Chinese women marry pure Chinese spouses. With average families of 5.7 children, their numbers will in fact multiply rather than dwindle.

However, an expanding population is not a buttress against cultural integration with Filipinos and loss of uniqueness. The pure Chinese who marry each other resemble their ancestors less each decade and the Filipinos .more. Let us make some observations concerning marriage to Filipinos and integration as they reflect on the topic of the Chinese family business.

The significance of marriage to a Filipina has changed since the Second World War. Most men who married Filipinas in the years of migration did so simply as a practical matter and had no intention of cutting off involvement in the Chinese community. Men who marry Filipinas today are announcing or confirming their dissociation from the Chinese community because choice of a Filipina represents a conscious preference now that Chinese women are much more numerous in the marriage pool.

Marrying a Filipina in previous years had its practical advantages, as I have mentioned. But there were difficulties, too. A man with a Filipina wife could not find work as an employee of another Chinese. As a married employee he surely would not be allowed to live in the store and be a part of the merchant "family," but he would live elsewhere with his wife. Employers feared that such a man, being apart from the influence of Chinese merchants and under the influence of his Filipino wife and relatives, might plot against his employer as well as clamor for higher wages and special benefits as a family man.[5] Independent businessmen who married Filipinas found their credit line cut 20 to 60 percent until they could prove themselves capable of money management in spite of their dependents.

Businessmen with Filipino wives could and did recover from their initial opprobrium and rise in the ranks of the Chinese community. A survey of the leadership of some of the main organizations in Iloilo revealed the following percentages of leaders with Filipino wives:

Federation of Filipino-Chinese Chambers of Commerce of Panay	17%	of	35 men
Chinese Chamber of Commerce	0%	of	14
Education Fund Committee	15%	of	19
Chinese Commercial High School Board of Trustees	20%	of	25
Ang (Five-Family) Association	37%	of	8
Tan (Yu Uy Tong) Family Association	20%	of	5
Chua-Gua Family Association	7%	of	13
Average	16%	of	119 men

Men with Filipino wives are moderately well represented among the leaders of the Chinese in Iloilo in the 1970s; then, 16 percent of the leaders have Filipino wives whereas 24 percent of all men marry Filipinas.

In spite of the stable intermarriage rate, there are harsh economic realities recognized by both Chinese and Filipinos which have kept the intermarriage rate from growing. Difficulties stem from differences in the control of money in Filipino and Chinese families. Secondary problems stem from the fact that almost all Chinese are merchants and from the assumption by Filipinos that most Chinese are rich.

Basically speaking, in Filipino families the wife controls the money, whereas in Chinese merchant families the husband does. In an opinion survey I conducted in four Iloilo neighborhoods, Filipinos asserted that by far the worst trait of the Chinese is "the control of the purse strings by the husband."[6]

The Chinese in turn oppose the marriage of their daughters to Filipinos for two economic reasons. First, wealthy Filipino men desire to marry Filipinas; thus, any Filipino who courts a Chinese woman is assumed to be a fortune hunter. Second, unlike the Filipino woman, the Chinese wife does not bring her share of the family fortunes to her marriage. Her Filipino husband may encourage her to sue for her inheritance rights by Filipino law. Also, the two spouses expect each other to manage the family finances. Such marriages are characterized as frightfully incapable in money management.

The Chinese oppose marriage of their sons to Filipino women for almost the opposite reasons. Both marriage partners expect to control the money. If the wife's family has any wealth, she brings her share to the marriage and expects to control it. Similarly, she will make demands on her husband that are not typically Chinese: she will try to care for relatives on her side of the family, and she will strive to invest merchant capital in land. The Chinese husband, on the other hand, strenuously avoids involvement with his in-laws and prefers to tie his capital into inventory. Finally, because residence after marriage is still frequently patrilocal, the wife too may have her share of in-law problems. Father and son will still have joint responsibility in the business, so the Filipino wife is liable to be at the mercy of her Chinese mother-in-law.

Such economic obstacles regarding the family business and money management which hinder intermarriage are of central concern to both Chinese and Filipinos. It is possible that this is the central block to the intermarriage of Chinese with more well-to-do Filipinos, who also have family wealth and are concerned about managing it.

Marriage Patterns of Mestizos

The intermarriage of mestizo men and women deserves note. Do mestizos "marry in" and thus presumably remain within Chinese society? The analysis in this chapter concluded that most Chinese men who intermarried married Filipinas and most Chinese women who intermarried married mestizos, which leads to the impression that mestizo men are marrying back into Chinese society and mestizo women are not. This would be a wrong conclusion. The social pressure upon women to marry Chinese husbands is great, and their contact with Filipino men is very slight. Marriage to mestizos is as big a social change as Chinese women are permitted at this time. Men are under fewer restrictions. This explains the difference in intermarriage between the sexes from the point of view of the pure Chinese.

From the point of view of the mestizos, the opposite trend prevails: most mestizo women do marry into Chinese society, and most mestizo men do marry out. According to the 68 genealogies analyzed earlier, 18 percent of the 524 men and 32 percent of the 238 women were Filipino-Chinese mestizos. If the men married all the mestizas available, 15 percent of the male population could marry mestizas. As it is, 13.5 percent of the Chinese men's wives in recent generations have been mestizas. Chinese men are, therefore, marrying almost all available mestizas in the community.

Of the marriages of Chinese women, 18 percent could be to mestizos. In fact, less than 9 percent of the women marry mestizos. Women (or their parents), therefore, still prefer pure Chinese husbands. As a result, there are a number of mestizo men who cannot compete with Chinese men for Chinese brides. Remember, too, that most mestiza women are also marrying Chinese husbands. Excluded in this way from many mestiza and Chinese brides, mestizo men have been predominantly marrying out of the Chinese community.

Household Composition

Dividing an immigrant's time and family between two nations has naturally produced unusual postmarital residence patterns and household composition. The Second World War and postwar developments in the Philippines and China have further modified these patterns. Postmarital residence and household composition have clearly not settled into consistent forms yet, because immigrant life and overseas Chinese merchant culture have been adjusting rapidly to internal factors and to the Philippine environment.

For most overseas Chinese in towns like Iloilo in the early American era, there were no family units per se but storekeeping households of young and old men — some kinsmen, some not. Men who married Filipinas are the main exception to this pattern. The latter fall into two categories in household composition: either they became Filipino composite family groups with a Chinese head, or the husband and wife remained quite aloof with their children and avoided Filipino kinsmen.

When women came into the community in sizeable numbers in the 1930s and families formed, Chinese households became more varied. One of the more unusual household types, common in the early years, was the store-keeping household of unrelated partners with their families. Partners attempted to apportion apartments and decision-making power in line with their respective seniority and business shares. But these households were unstable, having been formed unintentionally as a result of bachelor partners taking wives. These men usually eventually dissolved the household and often the partnership.

In the years before the Second World War, most Chinese men maintained residences in both China and Iloilo, and so their families were split, too. A man and his wife would be separated as heads of the Iloilo and China households, respectively. Each would have some of the children. In addition, as head of the overseas store, the husband might also take in lineage and town-mates, and some of his and his wife's kinsmen. Only men who were self-employed could afford socially and financially to build a Chinese family in the Philippines. One who was not self-employed usually became a part of some other relative's family.

By 1950 when migration had ceased, household composition had divided into two types. First, many immigrants had acquired Filipino or Chinese wives and had started nuclear family households where before there had been a community of bachelors and separated husbands. Second, through the last years of immigration before and just after the Second World War, men who had already begun families acquired households of greater familial complexity. Paternal and maternal kinsmen moved in with nuclear families. Or two brothers established a joint household after their marriages. Or a man's married sons moved into a newly built, traditional-style family compound with him and his unmarried children.

From my survey of sixty-two Chinese and Chinese-Filipino household histories in Iloilo, acquired from men of many different ages, I surmise that about half of the households in 1950 were orthodox nuclear families. Another 22 percent were nuclear families with one or more extra members, usually people from the household head's lineage. The second most common household type was the stem family; that is, a couple and one married son or daughter who was to take over the store after them. Only 5 percent of all informants were living in a household other than a family unit of some kind.

Most of the families in 1950 lived over their stores in the downtown business district. This restricted somewhat the size and complexity of their households. Very few Iloilo Chinese lived in houses or suburban compounds in the years before 1950.

The last twenty years have seen a beginning of house buying and more family compounds. Bigger and more complex households are possible when the storefront apartments are not the sole residences. Because immigration has ceased, many more complete families have grown up in one town, married in town, and settled in the same town. My sixty-two family histories reveal that by 1972 nuclear and "augmented" nuclear families decreased by about one-third (from 75 to 53 percent), with a proportionate increase (from 18 to 26 percent) in stem and extended household types. Split households occur now that a storekeeper buys a house and assigns part of his family to live in it while another part lives with him in the store. Additional patrilineal kinsmen have become less frequent housemates, but in-laws have become more frequent.

Miscellaneous household groups are common now, as they were before the 1930s. This apparent anachronism is actually a variation on the split household type. Comparing households in 1950 with those in 1972, we see that few additional kinsmen live with nuclear families today. As families grew, they moved out and settled on their own. They have been subsequently entreated to help raise or house members of other people's burgeoning families. So it happens that two bachelor brothers will take charge of their school-age nephews, or a grandmother will raise some of her grandchildren.

The Chinese community has a more varied household composition today than twenty years ago. Also, families have tended to increase in complexity. Comparing the same households in 1950 and 1972, we find that 58 percent have not changed much in complexity and that 18 percent have simplified (though perhaps only by splitting to occupy two residences simultaneously). By forming family compounds or by merging with another family or by taking in married sons and daughters, 24 percent increased in complexity.

Jacques Amyot (1960) demonstrated in his study of the Chinese of Manila that territorially based sib communities in China had been replaced in the Philippines by a generalized "familism," a Chinese *Familiengefuhlte* in which the extended family, the family compound, and spiritual closeness if not physical proximity are idealized. The trend in household composition in Iloilo demonstrates that some overseas Chinese still hold to this big family ideal. Greater wealth, the end of migration, and greater confidence in their status in the Philippines have impelled the Chinese to change their household composition and encouraged some toward composite family groupings.

Ricardo M. Zarco (1966) found in his study of Manila's old Chinese ghetto that family groups were very stable even in an urban setting. It is not correct, he asserted, to assume that large families will necessarily disintegrate into independent nuclear units in the city. Nevertheless, the storekeeper life and immigration patterns have indeed been factors working against composite family groupings in the past. Today in Philippine cities like Iloilo and Manila the composite family ideal has finally become generally attainable. Its renaissance, however, may also be its swan song in the Philippines. That is, the social changes which have allowed the last of the China-born immigrants to realize their ideal are making different demands on the Philippine-born younger generations of Chinese. So it is likely that in the near future the present trend toward household complexity will abate or even reverse.

Postmarital Residence

Postmarital residence of the overseas Chinese has undergone great changes in the Philippines. The mobility of immigrant life, the adoption of urban merchant life, and the sweeping historical changes all engendered these departures from traditional practices.

In the cycle of establishing a business and then a family in the Philippines, residence after marriage changed almost within a single generation. If a Chinese immigrant was the first in his family to come to the Philippines and brought his wife to join him, his residence was inevitably neolocal. Men who brought their Chinese wives into an already established family business complex came the closest to the patrilocal ideal. Men who married Filipinas could choose to settle in the place of their wife's kinsmen or to reside in a different town. Now that communities of Chinese families are well established and marriages take place primarily within town, the possibilities of uxorilocality and patrilocality in that town both exist, but neolocality continues, too. Uxorilocality is present even among pure Chinese marriages. Marriage to a woman from a larger, economically more robust city often draws the Iloilo husband away to the other city.

My survey of family histories found that postmarital residence changed strikingly after the first generation of immigrant predecessors of contemporary Iloilo Chinese arrived in the Philippines. The first generation was 75 percent uxorilocal, whereas the generation of their sons was 59 percent patrilocal, as the family settled into a business and a town and began to draw other kinsmen from China. Once this patrilocal pattern was set, it remained the predominant one. As we have seen, most marriages occur within the community, and it is possible for sons to bring their wives into a composite family grouping with the older generations. When they marry women from out of town, most men bring their wives to Iloilo. Businesses are usually transmitted patrilineally, so wives join their husbands' enterprises.

Even though patrilocality dominates, uxorilocality and neolocality continue as optional residence choices. By the third generation after the immigrants uxorilocality is holding at about one-fourth of marriages. In the early generations uxorilocality was mainly due to marriages to Filipinas. Now, a desire for social mobility may prompt husbands of pure Chinese women to move to the communities of their wives. Neolocality remains common as Chinese couples in recent decades have left the towns of their parents to open branches in new towns, to follow a corporate job, or simply to become independent.

If we compare the trend in postmarital residence over the decades to the trend by immigrant generation, the patterns are about the same. In the early American era uxorilocal residence predominated (60 percent). By the Second World War patrilocal residence became the most popular (53 percent), followed closely by uxorilocal residence (37 percent) because of the surge in marriage to Filipinas during the Second World War. After the war, patrilocality picked up again (65 percent) and neolocality kept growing to 11 percent or more today.

It is interesting to discover that the older "established" Chinese families, with a history in Iloilo dating from the turn of the century, are the most purely patrilocal. Rather than the newer immigrants adhering to patrilocal tradition and the older immigrants being influenced by the Philippine environment, the reverse seems to be the case. This is in part due to the nature of the older Chinese families who survived to be a part of Iloilo Chinese society. Generally speaking, they have followed Chinese traditions and achieved the familistic ideal best, and that is the reason why they still exist. The Chinese families with briefer histories in Iloilo are still "weeding themselves out." Those who fail in business leave town, branches of the family marry out, and others become indistinguishable from Filipino society. If Chinese society in the Philippines continues to exist as a recognizable ethnic group, it may remain solidly patrilocal as a means of preserving itself.

1. "Mail order" brides from China, procured solely through traditional intermediaries by correspondence and sent to the Philippines to join their husbands, were another type of Chinese wife, but they were not common.

2. According to A. Wolfe (1970), the density index $= 100L/ \left[n(n\text{-}1)/2\right]$ where $L =$ the number of links $= 2.7 \times 500$ and $N =$ the number of family units $= 500$. The density index for interrelatedness at the limit of four intervening kinsmen is about 1 percent. Should the present marriage pattern continue for another thirty years, the density index will increase geometrically.

3. The women in this sample are all consanguineal relatives of the men in the preceding discussion. No affinally related women arc counted so that there will be no duplication of marriage data from the previous discussion.

4. Elopements have indeed been known to provoke maternal suicide in Iloilo.

5. Employees who married Chinese women provided almost as much difficulty by raising similar requests.

6. Upperclassmen in the College of Social Work at Central Philippine University conducted 116 interviews in four neighborhoods of widely varying socioeconomic levels. The results of this study have been published (Omohundro 1975).

6

THE FAMILY AND BUSINESS

IN THIS CHAPTER WE SHALL EXPLORE the operation of the typical Chinese shopkeeping families which predominate in Philippine cities like Iloilo. In these families there are complex webs of relationship between the economic aspect and the kinship and ceremonial aspects. The shape, the development, and the functioning of merchant families are both causes and effects of the shape and development of Chinese businesses.

The Chinese merchants themselves recognize almost an identity of family and business in their epigram *"Seng-li ke si tsoe hia-ê lang,"* or "Businesses are entirely of one man." In conversation among themselves, Chinese merchants habitually equate the business name, the name of the firm's founder or present head, and the business family as a group. "Yap Tico," for example, is the name of a wealthy turn-of-the-century Philippine Chinese in shipping and export, who operated in Iloilo. His name is also used as another name for his business firm, for the sons who later managed it, and for the whole family which has descended from him.

The interaction of the social and economic themes in Chinese family businesses will be analyzed in three respects: division of labor and control, transmission of the business by inheritance, and recruitment and alliances. These three principles of family business will then be illustrated by the history of Mr. Lo and Friendship Dry Goods Store in chapter 7.

Division of Labor and Control

For the personnel who work in a Chinese family business, there are three concentric circles of decision-making and earning power. These circles are found equally in a small tinshop or a large Manila-based corporation. In the inner circle are the members of the family of the owner, who either founded the business or inherited it. A line-and-staff diagram of the business usually follows extended family lines: the family head is the apex of the diagram, followed by his wife and sons, his sons-in-law and daughters, his grandchildren, and collateral or more distant kinsmen.

While the family members may go to their separate nuclear family sub-urban houses at the end of a day, during working hours the extended family may still be a localized, cooperating entity. In chapter 5 we saw that the extended family household is a minority household arrangement in Iloilo. But in a store or factory where kinsmen gather to work, the extended family productive unit is more common. This finding concurs with the current reappraisal of the Chinese *chia*, or economic family. In the words of Myron Cohen (1970:24), "the 'family' or 'economic family' might continue to exist as a unit in the face of both physical and economic disengagement of its members." Cohen (1970:36) has observed that an estate-owning group like the Chinese chia has had a great variety of domestic forms. Its adaptability is a main reason for its survival in new environments, such as Southeast Asia.

In the second circle and closed from the inner circle are the Chinese employees: the trusted managers or accountants, the salesmen, the poor relatives taken in as dependents, and the nonkin minor partners. These are salaried personnel for the most part. Minor partners with stock in the company have in the past been dependent upon the good will of the family, who keep the books and determine everyone's shares.

In the outer circle are the Filipino employees and the new Chinese recruits to the business. In small family enterprises some of these persons may be so allied with the family as to be virtually a part of it, but they never come into the inner circle unless they marry into it. Not infrequently, Filipino employees have been admitted to the trusted second circle, but none penetrate the inner circle. And it is of course there where the money is held, where the decisions are made, where all responsibility lies, where the company is transmitted to the next generation, and where the profit accumulates.

The family business is organized in the best corporate tradition of strict hierarchy and sometimes also line-and-staff management. Sons are apportioned profit (or allowances) and responsibilities according to their birth order as often as according to their ability. Income and expenses are monitored carefully by the family head, who is the father, his widow, or the eldest son. The family head keeps his private books, and only he or she consults them.

Responsibilities and decision-making are closely related to kinship position within the family, but it frequently occurs that business acumen does not correlate with a person's kin status. The most common area for this clash to occur is between sons or brother-partners. Ideally, a son gets priority over a daughter, the older over the younger, and the married over the single, but families have difficulties when this does not accord with business ability. Some families give preference to business skills at the expense of kin position. While they have efficiently divided the labor, they have saddled themselves with roles that do not correspond with their family roles. If the family develops tension as a result, the business will inevitably suffer. Conversely, if a family adheres to kin status over business talent, the effects of the decision may be felt more immediately in the store, yet there will at least be a congruence of family and business that may sustain the group as a working team.

When a business family is fortunate to have its members' kin status and business ability coinciding, harmony and success in one realm feed back to the other. Management in such businesses is competitively superior. Most businesses with enough family members require that all handling of goods, money, collection of bills, banking, and sometimes even deliveries be supervised by a family member. In shopkeeping families, with or without Filipino sales clerks, a member of the family virtually always handles the money at the cash register. Family members must also oversee all warehouse operations. When there are many Filipino employees, the family head is their acknowledged boss, but the tasks of employee relations and supervision are usually surrendered to a son, a mestizo relative, or some other younger family member who, because of his background, might be more capable of dealing with Filipinos. If the wife or mother is a Filipina, she is often given this task.

Some large family corporations model their management structure after American corporations, but many medium and small Chinese businesses do not have a well-defined division of labor. All family members may be seen acting as sales clerks, cashiers, janitors, purchasers, secretaries, public relations officers, and representatives for the family at business association meetings. The most clearly defined roles are in families which are diversified into several lines, the management of each being wholly apportioned to one or a few family members. A diversified family never collectively manages all business lines. The sons, sons-in-law, or cousins who operate branches of the business report directly to the family head and do not expect counseling from their counterparts in other branches.

The main theme of management in a Chinese family business is the one-way flow of trust which is required for internal cooperation. The business and the family both function in the same patriarchal scheme of power and duties. The family head at the apex of this scheme is by definition the business leader. Financial dealings, contracts, bookkeeping, and general policies are almost exclusively his to make and even to keep secret. Business secrets, such as recipes, formulas, or safe box combinations, often are kept only in his head. The other members of the family business are expected as proper coworkers to offer complete trust to this family head to carry out his duties in the best way and to the advantage of all. This attitude of trust is sanctioned by the fact that the business is the patrimony in which the others are destined to share if they remain on good terms with its present holder.

The patriarch or family head, on his part, does not delegate ultimate authority or bestow complete trust on any subordinate. From his point of view, the business has been mortgaged on his reputation. As the representative of the family, whose social reputation as well as commercial future depends upon his conduct of the business, he senses that his personal career will redound to their glory or ignominy. From his point of view, again, his seniority, family status, and experience have all earned him the right to shoulder such an exclusive responsibility. Thus, it so frequently happens that a proprietor and family head will personally oversee sales clerks, the cash register, customers, or unloading of stock. No other family members with less at stake could be expected to perform a job more conscientiously or expertly than he.

This one-way flow of trust and the reliance upon only the inner circle of family members for major tasks inherently limit businesses. A business which wishes to expand is limited by its family size. If the owner has not enough time or sons to personally manage other shops, warehouses, or factories, then expansion is unlikely. Even though money or goods might be forthcoming to supply the prospective new branch, the project is usually scrapped if there is no competent family member to oversee it.

Growth is limited in a family business for other reasons, too. If a family plans to venture into a new line — perhaps adding a distillery to their tobacco dealership — new skills may be difficult to acquire. A family member must have the crucial skills, otherwise the business is at the mercy of its employees. But it is not easy to acquire skills outside of one's own merchant family. Chinese merchants are disinclined to accept as apprentice some family member of a merchant who may become their competitor. The most common ways to acquire new skills are to apprentice a family member to a friend in another city, to marry into the right business, or to form a partnership with someone who has experience.

Because the continuance of the family head and of the business are identical, acquiring the capital for a new venture hinges on the status of the man more than the soundness of the venture. Potential creditors and nonparticipating partners are investing in the family head as much as his new venture, and market research is really beside the point. Those who have money and reputation, of course, can get more capital and, thus, can diversify. But the complement to this principle is that a man with an equally good idea but less social capital is likely to be without backers.

There are social consequences within the family from expansion, diversification, and the accompanying redistribution of control and labor. Adding a branch and promoting a son, opening out of town and transferring a cousin, expanding and recalling a married daughter and her husband to help—each of these developments entails readjustments in the social family. Sons may become independent in status or, more clearly, in competition with one another. The extended family may further extend, the household composition alter. The status of wives and sisters will improve if they are needed in more responsible positions. In the same way, if a family reduces its commercial enterprises or suffers setbacks, the sons will be demoted, household complexity may reduce, women will become more dependent, and family members may separate to seek their livelihood independently.

The role of women in family businesses is still changing as the social position of Chinese women continues to change. In Iloilo, women were never cloistered and always played some part in running the store. However, many were *pak-kha* (had bound feet), illiterate, and not as well versed in Filipino customs and language as were their husbands and brothers. If their husbands were successful, wives generally were expected to turn their attention to the hearth or community social matters.

Since the Second World War the number of Philippine-born, Philippine-educated women has burgeoned. Their family status and their role in the business have been augmented. They are assuming additional, formerly masculine responsibilities in the store; they are also pressing for and winning the freedom to start their own businesses, or *kŏ-jîn-ê seng-li* (sidelines) to augment the family income or their private allowances.

Chinese or Filipina wives and Chinese or mestiza sisters, whether married or single, have all thus improved their lot. One of the most vivid examples of women's greater freedom is the employment of young unmarried Chinese women in the Philippine-Chinese banking corporations. Unmarried daughters have always been the most restricted and dependent members of their families, rarely going out unescorted and completely dependent financially on their parents. Their sole means of employment has been assisting the family in the store.[1] Two new Chinese banks and a potential third have hired dozens of young women, mostly daughters of respected business families. Women have been leaping at this opportunity: they can dress well, meet eligible bachelor sons of other businessmen, and make an income which they can largely control.

The major impetus to change the status of Chinese women in the business world has been the influence of Filipino social organization. Filipino women are very heavily represented in business and take a major role in handling family financial matters. They own property, even when they are married. They have many legal rights in marriage and inheritance law. They have mobility in public and extensive decision-making influence with their husbands. For these reasons many Philippine-educated Chinese women view their own status as comparatively too restricted, and their Philippine-educated husbands have been inclined to accept a more egalitarian relationship.

Although Filipino women have played an active role in business and financial matters, those who married Chinese did not always share in such freedom. Filipino wives of Chinese who worked in the province or in certain labor-intensive lines like noodle or shoe factories usually exercised the most power. Their skills in handling customers and labor and maintaining good public relations with their Filipino community earned them their powers. When men in urban areas and in less labor-intensive lines married Filipinas, they restricted their wives much more in the Chinese style. The wife perhaps helped in the store, but the husband was the representative of the business and the sole comptroller of the purse and books.

There are, I think, two reasons why Chinese men have curtailed their Filipino wives: in-laws and public opinion. A Chinese who married a Filipina found himself appointed the person most likely to aid her dependent relatives. Among Filipinos the wife's bilateral relatives are cared for as much or more than the husband's, but the Chinese viewed this practice as not only onerous but infinitely expandable. Overseas Chinese can afford to be more generous toward their own kinfolk because the kinfolk are limited to those who immigrated. But to acquire a Filipino wife meant a marriage alliance to an enormous file of cousins, nephews, and compadres. The only way a Chinese merchant could survive was to carefully restrict his contact with his in-laws and to limit the financial freedom of his wife lest she dispense money herself. Similarly, Filipino wives make a greater demand on their husbands to spend for consumer items, houses, and land. Many a small merchant has learned too late that all his liquid capital has been invested in houses and land by his Filipino wife and is unavailable to save his store in a temporary tight spot.

Public opinion in urban merchant society is another reason for controlling one's Filipino wife. In an enclave the size of Iloilo's, the opinion of fellow merchants is one of a storekeeper's most valuable assets. Should his family and business be run in a non-Chinese manner, a man's own credentials as a Chinese suffer, and he slides in other men's eyes from the "in-group" to the "suspect"category. Perhaps justifiably, other merchants will suspect that the man's wife constitutes a money leak and a risk, and they will balk at offering him credit or loans.

There are no reliable materials to show the commercial role of women in the past, but I did learn the state of matters in 1972. Two informants rated the commercial roles of women in 118 businesses. The women rated were of all ages. More than 50 percent of the sisters, wives, and mothers were in active management or office positions. The Filipinas and mestizas are slightly more active than the pure Chinese women, but they are also slightly younger. About 30 percent of all women beyond school age have little or nothing to do with their families' businesses.

In addition to their roles in their family businesses, some women also engage in various sideline businesses; 8 percent of the Chinese women and 4.5 percent of the Filipinas and mestizas were, thus, making extra income for themselves and their children. Their sidelines were usually designed to appeal to other women within the Chinese merchant enclave. They raised duck eggs, baked, or sold jewelry or dress cloth. A few were less characteristically involved as insurance agents or beauty shop proprietors. Chinese men are adamantly opposed to their wives and daughters working for salaries as employees of others. Such a situation reflects poorly on the family's wealth and the women's domesticity. It is strongly felt that only people who have to should work as others' employees. The young women in the banks, being the main exceptions, are not primarily working for a salary but for a husband and some family freedom.

As the number of Chinese wives in Iloilo increased in the last thirty years, so has the number of Chinese widows, who often outlive their older husbands by many years. Many of the widows have assumed active control over their husbands' enterprises and over their grown sons, and they have managed to keep the extended family's operations knitted together. The number of these business "matriarchs" in Iloilo City is still growing and undoubtedly improves the image of women as businessmen.

The greater responsibilities and freedom of women in Chinese business reflect a shift away from patriarchy toward bilaterality of power and inheritance. A third development concerns bilateral alliances with kinsmen. Because Chinese now find their spouses within the Philippines and usually within their own locality, in-laws have become important in a man's circle of kin, if only because they are living in the same town. Alliance by marriage to a local Chinese family often leads to alliance in business, and this alliance indirectly improves the position of the wife. Attention to good relations with one's affines or even financial debt to them usually induces a husband to turn over some of the control and the money of joint ventures to his wife. While Filipinos often have business alliances with affines and wives as managers, these are new developments among the Chinese merchants. These alliances with in-laws will be discussed in a later section.

Transmission of the Business

A very common saying among overseas Chinese merchants is *"Bô sán-tāi láng ho giah,"* "No third generation stays rich."[2] With many vivid local examples they will explain how the personalities of each generation change and lead inexorably to business collapse. There is first the pioneer: the immigrant who graduated from a pushcart to a successful entrepreneur with many sidelines. His story is one of pluck and struggle. His sons are the consolidators, taking on the business as a partnership and assuming the many community leadership roles to which their father's success entitles them. They are less flexible and courageous. They are followed in turn by their profligate sons who are more interested in politics, gambling, and Filipinas than is healthy for the business. Bad decisions and quarrelling among themselves rend the business so the patrimony is scattered and lost.

This story is so often told, not only in Iloilo Chinese circles but around the world, that its reality as a myth transcends its reality as a description of a business' growth and collapse. Note that the story allows each generation to lay the blame for collapse on the personality failings of the subsequent generations. This theme of family ascent and descent is the central one around which Francis Hsu (1948:10) organizes his *Under the Ancestors' Shadow,* while he explores the psychology of family relationships.

There is a great deal of truth to this Chinese myth as it applies to business-men but the theme is as much demographic as psychological. Two simple facts are crucial: Chinese families grow rapidly and all male progeny are ex-pected to share in the family wealth. A business must therefore grow at such a rate as to support a geometrically growing family. A successful merchant may pass the store he founded to his three sons, for example. They may prosper, too, with good management. But when they pass their expanded business on to their sons (ignoring for a moment the sums they give as dow-ries to their daughters), there are likely to be ten or more beneficiaries. Even assuming again that the business has been successful enough to support the ten sons, it is unlikely that these cousins can make a workable partner-ship. The business is divided so that it is manageable by families, and the process may repeat itself with the smaller shares.

There are other reasons for the decline of an overseas Chinese business family by the third generation. One of the main ones is the acculturation of the third generation to Filipino life. Even if the third or later generations are pure Chinese, they are usually Philippine-born and -educated, naturalized citizens with different interests than their ancestors, with the freedom to move from commerce into the professions, politics, or even to emigrate to America, as the Filipinos do. This movement may present new and greater risks to store capital or remove the most talented heirs.

The three generation myth exists because there is some truth to it, due to demographic and cultural as well as psychological factors. On the other hand, there are success stories in Iloilo City describing families which are at least three generations deep. Still, there are difficulties for every family in maintaining successful businesses and wealth from one generation to the next. The training of sons and daughters and the Philippine Chinese inherit-ance practices illustrate the weaknesses and strengths of the Chinese in transmitting their businesses to the next generation.

Business Training

Children in a shopkeeper's family get involved in the store operations almost from the time they start school. As children, they learn to operate the adding machine and the abacus and to write the character script used in accounting. As they grow older, they are expected to fill any role that is needed, from janitor to sales clerk and cashier. They will accompany their father to Manila on purchasing trips and learn about credit and suppliers. As members of the family they will be expected to oversee employees, help at inventory time, load and unload stock, and so eventually participate directly in every aspect of shopkeeping.

Unlike the immigrant apprentices of past years, children of contemporary shopkeeping families begin their careers in "the front" of the store, relating to Filipino customers, salesmen, and employees. Their China-born predecessors had to learn the language and culture of the Filipinos before they were of much help, but storekeepers' sons and daughters by the 1970s are better versed in Filipino ways than their parents. As a result their parents place them in the positions where they will most often deal with Filipinos and improve the family's public relations.

The eldest son is often placed as official representative of the family business long before he really does assume leadership. Because of his fluency in the Filipino dialect, his understanding of Filipino behavior, and his education, the eldest son while still in his twenties may assume the task of dealing with the Filipino government. He is asked to act as intermediary for his father and file papers, pay fees and gratuities, develop good contacts with the local police, and even assume the official ownership of the business. If he is a naturalized citizen, his father may need him to stand as "dummy" to avoid the Retail Trade Nationalization or the Rice and Corn Nationalization laws. The son will also be assigned to serve as representative to the many Chinese business associations of which his father is member. He will be sent in his father's stead to Filipino clubs that have pressed his father to join. In all of these activities, sons relay information and decisions for their fathers and are not very independent. Yet they are gaining experience in public relations, government relations, and advertising.

Sons and daughters of the smallest petty merchant and the largest trader alike seek college educations. Filipinos and Chinese have attended college in enormous numbers in the last two decades. The most common specialization for Chinese is commerce, followed by engineering and business administration.

Sons return with these degrees to work for their fathers in the family stores. Fathers say it makes sons better businessmen who know more law and government, accounting, taxes, and economics. But status within the family does not readjust to the graduates because experience is held in greater esteem by the less-educated elders. A college-educated son is rarely, if ever, promoted above an elder brother with only a high school degree.

Daughters are also trained in business but only to the point of assisting the family rather than holding much responsibility. They are usually much more active than their mothers, knowing Filipino language and culture better. They are almost never raised to positions of responsibility over their brothers, who will inherit the management while daughters marry out of the business. Rarely is a daughter trained to take over a business; parents usually adopt a son if they bear none.

Daughters are educated to make them more attractive marriage partners, but there is also a hope that daughters (and sons not needed in business) will be able to emigrate with their nursing or engineering degrees. Once in America or Europe, their income will be high enough to remit a portion to their parents. They may also marry a native, and, by acquiring his citizenship, open an avenue of immigration for other family members.

The great majority of sons and daughters learn shopkeeping from their own family business. If their family has no business, then they may be hired out to a kinsman's family as an apprentice. Children of shopkeepers do not become employees of other shopkeepers, and only rarely will they become apprentices. As I have said, competition is vigorous in Iloilo City and merchants are loath to teach valuable skills and secrets to other merchant's sons.

The main difficulty in training sons and daughters involves keeping them dedicated to the continuation of the business, which is as important to the immigrant merchants as continuation of the patriline. Several factors work against keeping the sons in the business. First, until he is sick or senile the family head may always be the ultimate business head, though his sons be forty-year-old fathers themselves. The sons are thus maintained in a hierarchy identical to an extended family household, even though they may already reside separately. Their father may still control the money and investment decisions and may even keep the account books. He may dispense or acquire loans from persons without the sons' knowledge and so become an indispensable reservoir of business records which are preserved nowhere else but in his head. And when the father makes commercial decisions, he must be obeyed.

For most of their years of training under their fathers, sons are expected to work long hours but to accept only a small allowance and very little decision-making responsibility. They may have acquired college degrees in business administration, but these relate only peripherally to the principles and practices of their merchant fathers. There will be tension then as people with two different approaches to commerce must daily cooperate. The son may feel unchallenged and overworked in a shopkeeping career, whereas his father has made the business a symbol of his own value and of his family's status. The older man values his experience above college education and expects his sons to acquire the same experience and dedication.

Brothers undergo stress as they adjust to one another as future partners. Coordination must be created between family kin status and commercial ability. Each brother perceives flaws in the others as potential disadvantages for their future shopkeeping. Each is constantly vigilant against *toā-bók, sòe-bók* ("Big eyes here, little eyes there," or partiality) by their father for one of their number beyond his objective skills or status.

Being trained in business is inseparable from assuming one's family position and laboring in that same business. That is, one-way trust, sexual division of labor, and hierarchical family control at work in the daily life of the business are also at work in the training of its successors. Any flaws in family relations and business management may therefore reappear as flaws in business training, and all three may compound the difficulties intrinsic to overseas Chinese inheritance practices.

Inheritance

Inheritance practices share with family business training the traits of informality, secrecy, and tension. Overseas Chinese follow neither the inheritance laws of the Philippines nor of China strictly, but they have developed their own syncretization of both, appropriate to their merchant culture. At the junction of the inheritance of a business many a business family will fracture, and the eruption of many years of tension can rend their fortune into small shares or worse.

When a family business head dies, his nuclear family are the primary and usually the only beneficiaries. The married sons take over the management of all commerce and real property, and they are assigned about 50 percent of the business shares immediately. The remaining half is owned by the surviving widow of the household (there may be other widows) in a manner similar to that enjoined by Filipino law. The daughters are not frequently awarded shares in the business themselves. The business and real property are better preserved intact in the hands of only the sons and the widow (whose shares ultimately revert to the sons) by overseas Chinese convention rather than by Filipino law, through which every son and daughter would be apportioned equal shares in the family business or property.

The eldest son is expected to replace the deceased as the family and business head and is accordingly awarded a slightly greater share. This division of power and shares continues proportionately through all younger sons as business partners. Some families with particular devotion to traditional Confucian ritual also award business shares to the eldest son of the eldest son. This assures continuation of the business in the patriline and marks out that son as future leader. It also provides the eldest son with a larger share, as caretaker for his son.

It is for the sons and the widow to decide what other persons will be beneficiaries of the patrimony. Daughters, faithful employees, minor partners, common-law Filipino wives, and wives and sons in China or Hongkong are apportioned their shares or lump sums in this way. Except for partners and common-law wives or daughters, who can resort to Filipino courts, these other heirs are appointed at the discretion of the controlling sons and widow. In contemporary times, China relatives are usually awarded lump sums to avoid the difficulties of regular remittance of a percentage of profits to China. Minor partners are either kept on or bought out. Common-law Filipino wives are awarded lump sums, as are daughters (in the form of their dowries).

Daughters are occasionally offered shares in the business, especially when they are *ke-chhut* or "gone out" through marriage. This gesture is in respect of Filipino law, but daughters almost always decline the offer as a point of honor for their supposedly self-supporting husbands. When they married, if it was before their father's death, they were awarded dowries of land, houses, cash, and consumer goods commensurate with the family's status.

Their dowries occasionally equal in cash value their theoretical share in the business. If their father is poor, they may get little or nothing as dowry.

If her father has died and she is still single, a daughter is supported, along with her other minor or unmarried siblings, by the half of the patrimony that her mother manages. When the daughter marries, her mother will bear the primary cost of her dowry, but her stockholding brothers also help with expenses. If the family is not well off, her dowry may be in the form of a business share. If she does not marry, she will probably inherit her mother's supervisory capacity over her portion of the patrimony or else become a dependent of her brothers.

Filipino inheritance law is more bilateral than Chinese convention. According to it, daughters have a right to participate in all aspects of the patrimony and to own property when married. The differences in the Filipino and Chinese practices have not presented much difficulty in Iloilo City yet, but in Manila great feuds have developed in wealthy Chinese families when daughters demanded their rights by Filipino law. The problems have not risen in Iloilo, partly because patrimonies are rarely so big as to merit the notoriety of a family feud and partly because provincial Chinese are less familiar with Filipino law. In Iloilo, male dominance over women is also more accepted as properly Chinese than it is in a cosmopolitan city like Manila.

Widows rarely remarry, even if they are under forty years old. As caretakers of property, family heads, and perhaps also as businesswomen, widows create problems when they remarry businessmen. By Chinese convention the wife should own no property other than chattels, so she would lose the supervision of her deceased husband's estate to her sons or her new husband. If she were allowed to remain propertied, by appeal to Filipino law, the children born from the second marriage would also create confusion. Their status vis-a-vis their mother's and father's property, held in common and separately, could not easily be solved by precedent in overseas Chinese convention.

Chattels of the deceased businessman are usually few and are handled in a variety of ways. During funeral ceremonies, clothes and most other combustible personal effects are burned. Some sentimental items like pipes, watches, or eyeglasses are entombed with the body. Heirlooms like Spanish gold coins or jewelry are held by the widow and dispensed to her sons and daughters when she wishes, usually at weddings, baptisms, and other ceremonial occasions. Sometimes widows hold all of the husband's valuable personal effects until their own death and no distribution to the children is organized; the possessions just find their way into people's hands. Women who are about to die sometimes give away all their personal effects, but men rarely do this. If her husband survives her, a wife's effects of value go to him. If the wife was a widow, her chattels usually find their way into the hands of the daughters-in-law. They are the women in closest proximity to their mother-in-law. Daughters-in-law acquire items by virtue of their husbands' role as supervisors of the estate.

Overseas Chinese inheritance practices neither follow a written legal code nor utilize written wills, or *ui-chiok*. Each case is a rather improvisatory proceeding using both Filipino and Chinese laws as they are partially understood. After several generations in the Philippines, each town or family group establishes a convention which it is inclined to follow. But changes, especially in the direction of Filipino practices, are constantly working within the conventions. Until recent decades, adjudication internal to the overseas Chinese enclave was the only way to enforce the conventions. As Filipino customs creep into inheritance practices, more recourse to Filipino law courts occurs to supplement internal Chinese mechanisms.

Very rarely does a family head prepare any written instructions for disposal of family property at his death. Informants claim that the will sometimes exists; it is handed to a trusted friend outside the family who will act as a family mediator and executor. But very few men in Iloilo City even left explicit verbal instructions to their sons before they died. It is possible that wives are instructed, but male informants claimed this was not common.

Family heads recognize rationality and irrationality in their own reasons for not preparing a quasi-legal written will nor even discussing inheritance. They loathe to discuss the possibility of their own death, for simply to raise the possibility is believed to encourage the event. For the same reason, dependents dare not mention the subject for fear of being accused of encouraging the death. More practically, a Chinese makes no will because he wants no one to see an accurate list of the extent of his possessions and wealth. He does not arrange the disposal of the family property to his sons before he dies because his authority and their respect for him are very much intertwined with his centralized control of all resources. Informants say that if a father were to announce to all of his children their shares of the estate, he would either precipitate fighting or lose control of them because they knew their shares were decided. *"Goa beh khǹg chit-thiau lāu-ún,"* "I shall keep aside a little for my old age," fathers say. No father who is healthy and sane, regardless of his age, could tolerate dependence on his children and loss of family head status. As long as he holds the family fortune, he remains the boss.

Some powerful forces are at work against this policy of procrastination and gerontocracy. The economic nationalization laws passed in the Philippines in the last 30 or 40 years have placed a premium on Filipino citizenship, for which usually only an immigrant's sons have been eligible. In 1954, when the Retail Trade Nationalization Act was passed, most men over thirty were simply not eligible for Filipino citizenship. Since then, these men have had their children naturalized and have continued their businesses through them as "dummies." Promoting naturalized sons as titular heads of the family commercial enterprises has improved their status in those enterprises. As a result of the dummy practices, a sort of anticipatory inheritance has become common. A naturalized son, by virtue of his official position as store proprietor, becomes the heir to the store and its manager even before his father dies. In some cases this dummy arrangement makes only a figurehead of the son, and the elderly father remains in complete control in the background. But in many cases the father and sons tentatively accept the fait accompli without pushing toward logical conclusions and declaring the patrimony settled.

Men with several businesses take even more concrete steps toward apportioning their businesses by assigning naturalized sons as managers or titleholders of various stores and buildings. The understanding is that the patrimony will be reunited and reapportioned at the death of the family head. Nevertheless, precedent is set during this division and each child acquires experience in the area he or she has been assigned. To try to change this precedent after their father's death usually precipitates trouble; the status quo is defended as the most efficient use of skills and the least threat to profit.

When a family head dies, there are few sanctions except moral authority in the family and in the Chinese enclave to enforce proper management and apportioning of the patrimony. The parties in a position to manage or to oversee management of the inheritance are: (1) the adult eldest son; (2) the widow; (3) a kinsman chosen by the widow to be manager; (4) the kong-chhin lâng, or mutual family friend; and (5) the family association. The latter two are simply observers and mediators.

The eldest son is in a position to take charge of the patrimony if he is seng-liên, that is, married and settled as a stable adult. A portion of profits, property, and control also remains with the widow unless she is too ill or senile to handle them. Healthy elderly mothers rarely are totally dependent on their sons. If she is capable, an active widow will strive to take her husband's place as family head, uniting her children and the patrimony beneath her through respect for her station. If she does not know the business, the mother takes a more aloof stance but is in constant contention with her sons over the management of their respective halves.

There is a special case where sons are not partners in a business but inherit it collectively. If they are busy with their own enterprises and do not wish to manage the patrimony to earn their shares, they will delegate one of their number — not always the eldest — to care for the business or phase it out. This brother-manager receives a larger share for his efforts. This share is called the phah-thiap, or bonus.

If the father dies when the children are not yet responsible adults and the widow feels she is incapable of running the business, she appoints a manager to superintend matters until her children are grown. This manager is usually a kinsman and may come from her side or her husband's side of the family. Occasionally a trusted employee is promoted to the task. Occasionally, too, the widow sells the business and invests as a silent partner in another's business or has her superintendent kinsman invest her money. The kinsman-as-superintendent or the employee-as-manager usually receives phah-thiap, too.

The transmission of a family business at the death of the family head is a dangerous occasion in two ways. Socially, the family is liable to quarrel and split, and the business will die. Spiritually, a cloud of bad luck supposedly hangs over the business. Accidents happen, sales drop, and the price of goods rises. The stronger the conviction in the community that there will be social trouble, the greater the likelihood that "bad luck" will also reign.

Some families use this belief to their advantage. Recently a group of adult brothers who were independently in business inherited their father's famous old store which was riddled with debts. The business was a burden to them, and they disputed among themselves how to manage it. Not long afterward the business burned to the ground. Because the business had not been officially transferred to the sons' names it ceased to exist, and so its debts also disappeared. Some Chinese claim the fire was intentional, but others attribute the fire to the usual "bad luck" attendant on a family head's death.

When difficulties arise within the family over apportioning shares and control of the estate, two sources of moral authority may be called in to mediate: the mutual family friend and the family association. Sometimes these constitute but one person, when a mutual family friend is selected from the leadership of the family association.

The kong-chhin lâng is a respected elderly man who was a close friend or kinsman of the deceased. He agrees to mediate when invited if he feels that all parties to the dispute will heed his advice; otherwise, he may refuse lest his own pride be injured. A widow and her children may invite a mediator for property's sake even if they do not quarrel. If they do quarrel, they do not always invite mediators. No outsider can come to them and press for a settlement.

If a family seeks mediation and no one agrees to mediate or the mediator is unsuccessful, they approach their family association. The directors of the association assume the responsibility of taking testimony from all sides of the family and seeking compromises. They, too, have no real sanctions to enforce their advice except their respected positions in Chinese community leadership. Their mediation tends to be weakened by their consistent advocacy of traditional Chinese solutions to inheritance problems. If a family is culturally marginal to the community, it is liable to turn to the Philippine courts and resume its battle in terms of Filipino law. This is still uncommon in Iloilo City but is more common in Manila, Davao, Bacolod, and Cebu, where Chinese are more familiar with Filipino law.

The most common causes of quarrels over inheritance within business families are: (1) married daughters demanding shares; (2) competition between family branches; (3) daughters-in-law; (4) adopted sons and daughters; and (5) children who marry Filipinos. The cases are numerous in Iloilo where these situations have precipitated family quarrels and ultimately disintegrated family enterprises.

In most of these causes of family dissension there is a clash of Filipino custom and law with overseas Chinese conventions. As we have seen, married daughters have the right to share in their father's real property and business according to Filipino law, whereas according to Chinese convention, after receiving their dowries they are completely ke-chhut. Filipino law and custom give persons who feel aggrieved by Chinese conventions more power in disputes with the rest of the family over control of the property.

Filipino law strengthens the hand of adopted children and children who marry Filipinos and are disinherited. In both cases Filipino law does not recognize the reasons for discrimination. Adoptions in Chinese society are not publicized; officially the children are claimed as natural children, thus giving them strong legal status. Of course, the law also does not recognize intermarriage with Filipino as justification for exclusion from inheritance.

Adoption of a child ensures that there will be an heir to take over the business ("carry on the family name") after the death of a barren couple. When there are no children but adopted children, this system works very smoothly. But it is not uncommon for a couple to adopt an heir and subsequently bear their own. The status of the adopted heir may be in real jeopardy, aggravated by the fact that he is the eldest son and supposed to be the family thau-ke. The harmony could be disrupted by a power struggle between the adopted oldest son and the oldest natural son. Most adopted heirs are adequately compensated in one way or another, but when they feel they are not, they have Filipino law or the threat of Filipino law as a recourse.

Sons and daughters who marry Filipinos against the wishes of their parents (or who eloped, which adds insult to injury), are disinherited for two reasons: they have disobeyed and dishonored their parents, and they have married financial risks to the family business. These Chinese daughters, backed by Filipino husbands aware of inheritance law, are in a powerful position if they decide to contest the family's division of property. In Iloilo City, intermarriages of Chinese daughters are still few, but the Chinese openly acknowledge the inherent dangers. More common are disputes by sons whose shares in the business have been decreased or eliminated. Although they might wish to handle the quarrel at their family association, the sons know the conservative association will not support their position. The threat of or actual appeal to Filipino law is their strongest recourse.

The crises in families created by wives in polygynous unions are not amenable to resolution by Filipino law. Over 16 percent of Iloilo's Chinese immigrant males have had polygynous families. The usual situation was one wife in China and one in the Philippines. In the process of training, educating, and protecting their children, fathers often "shuffled" their progeny from these multiple unions between China and the Philippines or between two places in the Philippines. When the father dies, therefore, champions from the various family branches are present to contest division of the patrimony. Although some wives and children may be in Hongkong or China, they usually have their kinsmen or representatives in the Philippines to present their case. There may be an official Chinese wife and a Chinese concubine or a Filipino or mestizo common-law wife or perhaps all of these. Their claims on an otherwise prosperous business may crush it.

Theoretically, the officially married wife, the Chinese wife, the wife in the household, and the wife who bore the eldest son should have first priority as heiress, and all other wives receive only lump-sum gratuities. However, these roles are not always combined in the same person. Thus,each woman who can claim one of these roles may press to be the one given priority.

Because of the number of people involved and the complexity of the family relationships in extended family disputes, it is impossible to invite kong-chhin lång mediators. The situation is settled in the Chinese family association. If some of the wives are Filipinas, they may take their case to court, at extreme expense and embarrassment to all and disproportionate to the small positive outcome.

Lastly, agitation by the wives married to the brother-partners of a family business can create tensions and fracture a newly inherited business. There are two opposing tendencies in such cases. For the sake of family harmony and business success, the brothers may table all disputes during the first "dangerous" years of inheritance. But the wives, having less invested in the harmony between their affines and their husbands and concerned for the future security of their children and themselves, press on for a clear delineation of power and wealth in the family.

The tensions between the wives in an extended family business of overseas Chinese are very similar to those of wives in an extended gentry family household in China.[3] Business wives have married into a hierarchy to which they have not had a lifetime to become accustomed. Their power to create schisms has two sources. First, the vast majority of Philippine Chinese businesses are not extended or joint family businesses, and so there is no great social pressure to remain united. Second, they fight not with one another but through their husbands by undermining one another (tsǹg tsúi-tùi, "to dive beneath the water") in the eyes of their husbands.

Brother-partners can keep the family peace if they wish to by keeping separate nuclear family residences, by not employing their wives together in the business, and by incorporating to legally define the power and shares of each in the family business.

By emphasizing the difficulties in business training and inheritance practices, I have tried to provide some cultural basis for the myth of the three generations' rise and fall. Compared to their peasant ancestors, Iloilo's Chinese merchants are faced with the situation of much wealth and fewer guidelines on how to take care of it. Their difficulty is compounded by the somewhat disruptive influence of Filipino law and custom regarding inheritance. But a foreign cultural environment, wealth, and cultural changes do not always work against the Philippine Chinese, as I shall show in the following sections.

Recruitment and Alliances

Because Chinese are limited in expanding businesses and management by the extent of their "inner circle" of trusted close kinsmen, the only way to allow growth is to create a larger inner circle. This expands the diversity of talents and can lead to more wealth and security. The ways to expand this inner circle are all rooted in kinship practices and not exclusively in business practices. That is, to expand, a Chinese merchant does not simply incorporate, merge, build, hire, and so forth. He must adopt, marry, and otherwise ally himself through affinal and fictive kin ties to other Chinese merchants. In this section I shall discuss adoption practices, marriage alliances, and two types of fictive kinship: the blood brotherhood (*kiet-pai hia^n-ti*) and godparenthood (*khoe-pe-khoe-ka^n*, or compadre).

Adoption

The adoption practices of the overseas Chinese in the Philippines are based on Chinese practices but have been modified for centuries by immigrant mobility and the exigencies of living in a foreign society. There are many examples of adoption in contemporary Iloilo Chinese society, and the practice shows no signs of abating. To be childless is bad luck, bad business, and bad social form. The patriline is paramount, and every couple feels bidden to continue it. Without children the business is understaffed and rarely continues after its founder's death. To be childless and stay childless, considering the many ways of adopting heirs, is condemned by the rest of the community as selfish and peculiar.

Parents in China or the Philippine Chinese community give out a child for adoption because they are poor and their family is too large to support. Parents in China with a child of special talents whom they hoped would take profitable advantage of the Philippine environment and support them by remittances would give that child for adoption to a childless couple in the Philippines. The child would become the son and heir of his foster parents, but he would be expected to sustain financial obligations for his natal parents.

Couples adopt children for a number of reasons. They may need male heirs and business successors. They may have borne all male children, and the mother may wish to "balance the family" and acquire some female help and companionship around the house. Even single women adopt sons and daughters—usually daughters—in order to have someone to care for them in sickness and old age. It used to be, too, that daughters could be "adopted" as future wives for sons.[4]

Childless couples in China planning for their old age might adopt a son and send him to kinsmen in Southeast Asia to make his fortune in business. The son would then be expected to express his gratitude for this opportunity by sending regular remittances to support the couple.[5]

Parents who lost a child might adopt another to ease the pain of loss. Children might be shuffled about in an immigrant's polygamous family, changing countries, citizenship, and mothers through adoption procedures. Families without sufficient members with Filipino citizenship might acquire more through adoption. Finally, some families who could afford them would accept children for adoption from burdened friends and kinsmen as a humanitarian gesture.

Children could be adopted in China or in the Philippines. In China, foster parents preferred children from within the extended family or sib, but in the Philippines this has been less possible and less important. In Iloilo City, even pure Filipinos have been adopted. In most cases, the child adopted was one of the youngest of his natal family A typical example of adoption in the Philippines and within the family is as follows. Mr. Y and his two brothers were struggling entrepreneurs in fishing. Mr. Y, the oldest brother, had no children. On the other hand, his two brothers each had six or more children. So Mr. Y adopted three children. The first and eldest was a pure Filipino boy acquired through contacts by his mestizo wife. The second was the last-born boy from the second brother's family; the last adopted child, for balance, was the last-born daughter from the third brother's family.

Sometimes even the eldest son of the eldest brother might be adopted, if the family head decided it was propitious for all concerned. Mr. Tui, the salt dealer, was adopted by his childless uncle in China and brought to the Philippines because his real father, an eldest son himself, was poor and burdened with family. The uncle, however, was successful in tobacco in the Philippines. Mr. Tui, the first-born, was adopted because he was the only child in his family old enough to make the trip and help in the business when help was needed.

Filipinos are not rare as adopted children for Chinese couples. They have some advantages over Chinese children for overseas merchants because they can often be adopted complete with their birth papers and can remain Filipino citizens, which is helpful for business purposes. At times when contact with China has been difficult and no children from Chinese families have been available for adoption, couples have not hesitated to adopt Filipinos.

Chinese with wives in China who did not bear sons might recruit the mestizo sons by their common-law Filipino wives to be their official heirs. The sons were taken back to China, educated, and returned to the Philippine store almost as culturally Chinese as a pure-blooded son. Some of Iloilo's prosperous Chinese merchants are this kind of "mestizo immigrant."

The reverse form of adoption has also occurred. Mr. Tan, a textile merchant, had six daughters by his Filipino wife but no sons. His Chinese wife in China had a son whom he ordered brought into the Philippines under another name. The Filipino wife adopted the boy and gave him her Filipino citizenship. Mr. Tan got his son and a legal heir at the same time.

Adoptions have usually been made in person or by correspondence with the kinsman who donates the child and who is already well known to the recipient. But like "mail-order" brides, "mail-order adoptions" have also been obtained. The would-be foster mother would correspond with kinsmen in China who might not themselves have a child to give but would find one for her and send him or her to the Philippines. She would send money and documents, then she would go to Manila to meet the ship bringing her new foster child.

Adoptions are total and final. The child leaves his natal family and becomes in all respects the child of his foster parents. He may even be encouraged to refer to his natal parents by their names or kin terms other than "mother," "father." Children usually know they are adopted and sometimes correspond with their natal parents or send them money. Only if the foster child was adopted after about the age of ten years is he permitted to continue to visit his natural parents.

There is no prescribed relationship between the natural and foster parents of the child. When the two families are kinsmen, their social relationship after the adoption is unchanged. If the donor family is living in China, the foster parents are usually responsible for periodic remittances to them as "gratitude gifts." Donating children for adoption does not create patron-client relations but may conform to and intensify preexisting ones. The foster parents may always have been benefactors of the natal parents, and the adoption is another transaction to the advantage of each.[6]

For business and legal purposes, adoptions sometimes are of adults and the participating families are neither poor, childless, nor in a patron-client relationship. These adoptions for convenience, or "paper adoption," are made to conform either with Chinese custom or Filipino law. The adult adopted does not necessarily become a member of the household, a full heir, or a permanent family member.

For example, a Chinese merchant may be advised by temple fortune-tellers that the number of his children is extremely unlucky. Not wishing to cross Fortune when it concerns his business but quite undesirous of adding to his family, the merchant will "adopt" a friend's or kinsman's son as his own. In a ceremony of their own devising (since memories of such practices in China are very dim), the two merchants will complete the spiritual adoption. As far as the son is concerned, his life will change not a whit; the merchant fathers, however, have conformed to superstition and intensified their social bonds. These bonds may be expressed someday in a commercial transaction-- perhaps they will join in a partnership or lend one another money.

Paper adoptions may take place for legal convenience. Mr. Que had a son by his Chinese wife. He was brought to the Philippines and adopted as the son of another couple so that the son might acquire their Filipino citizenship without bureaucratic or financial hardship. In the 1950s, when this adoption occurred, Mr. Que had no desire to become a Filipino citizen himself, but he realized the future advantages for his son. This boy continued to live with Mr. Que and to learn his business. Later, when naturalization was more common among Chinese and Mr. Que had become naturalized himself, he applied to have his child's papers "rectified," and thus adopted the young man back into his own family.

In the arduous and insecure life of immigrant shopkeepers, adoption is a common, useful, and accepted way to start or balance a family. However, as I have pointed out in the preceding section, there can be serious problems, too. The most awkward and most frequent situation is the adoption of heirs to be business successors followed by the birth of one's own children. There are few cultural conventions applicable to this matter. Each family works out its own solution. With an eye toward future inheritance, adopted and natal children inevitably become jealous and competitive with one another unless their present and future status in the business is defined as concretely as in a conventional, hierarchical merchant family. For the smooth functioning of the family store, the decision must be made to honor the adoptions and take a chance on future discord, or to begin immediately to "phase out" the foster children, especially the sons, who would become heirs. If they are not satisfied with their lot, those who are phased out may return to contest the division of the patrimony when the family head dies.[7]

Sworn Brotherhoods

Blood brotherhood and blood sisterhood are other ways of extending the inner circle of kinsmen who can be called upon for business purposes. The blood brotherhood is a sworn fictive kin status between peers. The institution was imported from South China. In the Philippines the Fukienese refer to this blood brotherhood as *kiet-pài hia^n-ti.*[8] The practice, as the mainland Chinese observed it, is diminishing and is being replaced by the more informal Filipino *barkada*, or "clique" group.

The persons who entered into sworn pacts were almost always young single people who became close through coresidence, school, or work. Wartime and immigration experiences also promoted brotherhoods. In the early and unstable years of an immigrant businessman's life, when perhaps there were few kinsmen available to offer help, a man's blood brothers meant more personnel to rely on and, thus, an additional measure of security and adaptability. Later in life, the merchant's blood brotherhoods might become inactive as other types of kin and fictive kin came into prominence.

Blood brotherhoods formed in a variety of ways. The teng-ki-toa^n-lī was the alien certificate name by which many immigrants came to the Philippines ostensibly as another man's son. Sometimes young men who acquired papers that declared them brothers worked together for their patron in their early years in the Philippines. Their work together and their feigned kinship often encouraged them to ally themselves to one another by brotherhoods.

Classmates in Iloilo's Chinese schools still swear allegiance to one another in small groups in the 1970s if they are sufficiently familiar with Chinese customs. An oath may also be sworn before the altar between friends simultaneously baptized in a Catholic church or in the Buddhist temple after burning incense and making prayers. In the past a chicken was sacrificed and a dish prepared of the blood, which the sworn brothers ate. The breaking of the pact, informants claim, brings the chicken's fate to the blood brothers.

Unlike foster children, blood brothers increase a merchant's inner circle without immediately and directly involving the business. Blood brothers may scrupulously avoid commercial involvement with each other. Also, not every overseas Chinese man or woman makes brotherhood pacts. Nevertheless, many blood brothers do utilize their connection for business purposes. Loans, credit, supplies, and emergency aid flow along this link. Blood brothers may seek to betroth their children or invite one another to become Filipino-style godparents (compadre-comadre) at the baptism or marriage of their children. They may join in a partnership, market each other's manufactures, or accept each other's sons as apprentices.

The distinction between a Chinese blood brotherhood and a Filipino-style barkada among Chinese individuals is weakening through the influence of Filipino customs. The ceremony to formalize the relationship is becoming simpler and less distinctively Chinese; even the use of the term *"kiet-pài-hià^n-tī"* is diminishing relative to the term "barkada." Barkada relationships are not always ceremonially formalized nor are there special terms of address between pact-makers. Functionally, however, barkada relationships are almost the same; they are as numerous and can be as emotionally intense as a Chinese blood brotherhood.

Godparents

A godparent relationship between Philippine Chinese or between Chinese and Filipinos is another way of extending the inner circle of kinsmen. Whereas the blood brotherhood is a Chinese practice undergoing modification in the Philippines, the godparentage is a Filipino custom reworked somewhat by the immigrant Chinese.[9] It has been a common form of alliance between Iloilo Filipinos and Chinese for at least eighty years now. Among Chinese themselves, such alliances are a more recent practice. Godparentage is a relationship that assumes importance later in a man's or woman's life than the blood brotherhood because it is only formed between parents. Unlike the blood brotherhood, the creation of godparent (or *khòe-pē, khòe-kán*) relations may lead to, rather than stem from, close personal ties. A couple accepts their possible future role as family patron when they enter into a godparent relationship with the children of friends or social inferiors. The compadre relationship is always a patron-client relationship between the godfather and godchild, but the status relationship of the child's father and the godfather varies. Chinese ask Filipinos who are peers or superiors to become their compadres, and Filipinos almost always ask Chinese who are their superiors to become their compadres. Among Chinese, peers and superiors are both common as godparents.

The godparent relationship is as important for the godparents and the parents as it is for the godparents and the godchild. Either of these links may be utilized for business purposes, although in different ways. Compadres may join in a business venture on equal terms, as partners perhaps. On the other hand, my study of business biographies showed that godchildren never entered into business ventures with godparents on any but hierarchical terms, that is, as the godparents' debtors, employees, or trainees.

People are invited to become godparents at the baptisms and weddings of one's sons and daughters. The Chinese have worked a few changes in these practices to conform to their eclectic marriage and other rituals. First, among Filipinos the godparentage is basically a communion between Catholics, but among Philippine Chinese the relationship to Catholicism can become very weak. Perhaps only the godchild is a nominal Catholic; the parents and godparents may be Buddhists. Second, among Filipinos the godparents at marriage are invited to participate in the wedding, but among Chinese the godparents are selected and they take part in the elaborate engagement ceremonies two to twelve months before the wedding ceremony. Third, among Filipinos, when a man or woman is invited to be a godparent, his or her spouse automatically becomes a godparent also. There may be four or more sets of godparents in all. Among the Chinese, however, godmothers and godparents are selected separately, thus doubling the number of bonds created at the ritual. On the other hand, the Chinese usually invite fewer godparents than do Filipinos; four godmothers and four godfathers imply a large ceremony indeed for Chinese, but not for Filipinos.

Some Chinese select a pair of Chinese godparents and a pair of Filipino godparents for each child, for each of his two major *rites de passage* (baptism and marriage). In an average size family of five children, then, the parents have created ritual kinship links to as many as twenty Filipinos and twenty Chinese. Each child is the godchild of four Filipinos and four Chinese.

Filipino-style godparents differ from Chinese-style godparents in a variety of small ways, too. At birthdays, Christmas, and anniversaries of the wedding or baptism, Chinese godchildren send the Chinese godparents bottles of

Spanish brandy, eggs, candles, canned pickled pigs' feet, and pastry cakes (*ho-pià^n*), all marked in red. Godparent relationships between Filipinos or between Filipinos and Chinese do not entail these gifts. Godchildren also have specific mourning practices to observe at the death of the Chinese godparent. Full black mourning garments are worn just as by members of the immediate family, but a black armband or chest sash edged in red is added.[10]

New Developments in Affinal Relationships

Blood brotherhood and godparentage are both ways of increasing the inner circle of a merchant's kinsmen that have been common since long before the Second World War. Relations to affines, however, have not meant much until the last thirty years because of the fragmented nature of immigrant kin groups. A major postwar development in Chinese family business life is the possibility of acquiring affines for one's business inner circle. The Iloilo Chinese frequently make use of affines in business. One of the results of these in-law alliances is an improvement in the status of wives and sisters. A second result has been a definite weakening of the patrilineal, patrilocal bias so characteristically Chinese.

To repeat briefly the situation as explained in chapters 2 and 5, marriage has been virtually all within the Philippines since 1949; no longer does a man travel great distances to marry, nor does he live separated from his wife and family. Further, the majority of marriages are local marriages; community exogamy is the exception rather than the rule. The result of these trends which concerns us here is that every marriage produces a major kin link between two Philippine Chinese merchant families. Quite often kinship links become commercial links.

Filipino in-laws have always been a factor in Chinese merchant families where the wife is a Filipina. Filipino in-laws have served as employees, agricultural suppliers, and as a sort of defense to improve rapport with the local Filipino community. On the other hand, the relatives of the wife have also posed a threat to Chinese merchant husbands, who have had to develop mechanisms to avoid being their perpetual benefactors. In recent decades the relation of merchant husbands to their Filipino in-laws is broadening, as some Chinese are marrying Filipinas and mestizas of higher social position than previously. These Filipino affinal kinsmen have proved of help in legal and governmental affairs, and even occasionally as financiers and patrons of Chinese businesses. However, in Iloilo at least, there are no partnerships between Chinese and Filipino affines, nor do Chinese work as employees of Filipino affinal kinsmen.

Relations with Chinese in-laws have shown the biggest changes. Chinese affinal kinsmen today serve as one another's suppliers, distributors, partners, benefactors, employees, creditors, and so forth. When a young Chinese man begins formal courtship of a Chinese woman, the families involved always conduct intensive investigations into the background of each other. All manner of gossip, biography, and genealogical material go into these "dossiers." When an engagement occurs, the two families are so well informed as to one another's strengths and weaknesses, bank accounts and debts, that they are in a strong position to offer each other concrete commercial proposals, either immediately or some time in the future.

Besides the sheer preponderance of community endogamy (see chapter 5), the main impetus to deal with affines comes from the acculturating influence of Filipino culture. Many financial and commercial matters, from house buying and family budgets to factory management, are in the hands of Filipino wives; they turn to their side of the family (and to other women) for advice, assistance, and money. This bilateral distribution of power and activity in the host society has influenced the Chinese minority.

All sorts of business relations with affinal relatives have occurred, but some are more common or preferred than others. Affines may form partnerships, act as one another's distributors, train one another's sons, manage one another's branches, make loans of cash, stock, or facilities, and in a variety of other ways become economically allied.

Mr. Uy, for example, is a prosperous glassware merchant and leader in Iloilo community associations. He began his alliance with his affines unusually early, in the mid-1920s, when he married a woman in China whose close kinsmen formed a large industrial combine in Manila. From these affinal kinsmen he received credit and supplies to accelerate the growth of his struggling new business in Iloilo. After the war, as his three sons and two daughters began to marry, his affinal alliances began to multiply. His eldest son married a Chinese woman from a Manila industrialist family, who became Uy's glassware supplier. His wife's cousin in Manila manufactured candy and convinced Uy to become the distributing agent in Iloilo, using his glassware trucks to make deliveries. Meanwhile, Uy's oldest daughter had married a Chinese whose sister's husband (two affinal links!) operated a plastics factory. When the daughter's husband became manager of that factory, Uy became distributor for their plastic products. Lastly, in recent years, Uy's youngest daughter married a manufacturer of plumbing equipment, from whom Uy also acquired a distributorship.

Although his daughters had married out of his family, they had married right into the Manila Chinese community where Uy's wife's family was so influential. And so the relationship to their natal family in Iloilo was reinforced by myriad kinship links. Ten years ago, Uy's eldest daughter, who is a practicing medical doctor, began representing her father to his glassware suppliers in Manila and acting as the purchasing agent for his several restaurants in Iloilo.

Mr. Uy's case is unusual only in that he began making important affinal alliances almost fifty years ago and in that he has commercial alliances with so many affines concurrently. Most business histories of Iloilo Chinese do not reflect such a wealth of alliances, but many do repeat all of these kinds of examples at different times.

Marrying above one's own social rank has always been an avenue of social mobility, but it is preferable in public opinion if the bride is the person "marrying up." The woman's beauty or brains and experience merit her social advancement. Her parents and brothers may indirectly benefit from her marriage, too, but because she has married out of her family, their connections to this married wealth and social status are rather distant.

If a man marries above his social rank and financial condition, the other Chinese will suspect calculated fortune hunting on his part, at the worst, or unavoidable reliance on the wife's parents, at the least. It is even more a cause for disapproval if the young groom lives with his in-laws or becomes their partner or employee. Instead of making his wife a part of his father's business family, the husband has left them to become a part of his wife's father's business family.

Mr. Ti exemplifies typical patronage of one's in-laws. Mr. Ti, the "cracker king" of Iloilo City, made his fortune by practically monopolizing crackers baking in the city thirty years ago. Since then he has branched into many new lines — imports, rice and corn, and sugar. He married off his two beloved daughters in postwar years, one to a Mr. Uy in the shoe business and one to a Mr. Hua in a Manila corporation.

Mr. Uy's shoe business was always struggling, and because his wife was so close to Ti, he frequently visited Ti to request to cash a postdated check (in effect, to obtain a loan). Occasionally his checks even bounced on their due dates, but Ti tolerated this financial burden. When the daughter died of cancer and the elderly Ti passed away, Uy still continued to visit the sons of Ti in search of financial help, and he was usually granted it. Neither the death of the affinal link (the daughter) nor of the patron himself seems to have terminated the relationship of the family Uy with the family Ti.

The second daughter's husband, Mr. Hua, quit his job in Manila and came to live with the Ti family so that his wife could help create a "big family household" around Ti's widow. He was the object of some derision for this move: people say a married man should provide for his wife, not be salaried to his mother-in-law. Nevertheless, both Mr. Hua and Mr. Uy have prospered in their affinal arrangements, and this success in itself bolsters their self-images and their community reputation.

Alliances with affinal kinsmen are becoming just another way of extending the family business "inner circle." But because the community has depended heavily on its conformity to the Chinese patrilineal, exogamous, patrilocal tradition, merchants who have chosen to ally themselves with their in-laws have ventured knowingly onto socially insecure ground. They often become the subjects of disapproval for other Chinese. When a business deal between affines sours, fellow shopkeepers assume an I-told-you-so attitude. If the business deal succeeds, however, as many of them do, other Chinese remain discreetly silent. Among the younger Chinese, business connections between affines more often are accepted as natural because the Filipinos also form such connections. Thus, it is likely that opposition will diminish with time.

The question might be raised if Philippine Chinese marriage alliances are also calculated business alliances. Are marriages still arranged, and, now more than ever, arranged with business interests in mind? Some marriages are still arranged by parents and go-betweens, usually with a veto power remaining to the boy and the girl. However, these usually occur only for China-born immigrants who are either overage or not desirable as mates, or both. Such marriages have become rare; perhaps one or two occur annually in Iloilo's Chinese society of 5,000 to 6,000, which has dozens of marriages a year.

The vast majority of commercial cooperative alliances between affinal kinsmen in Iloilo formed after a young couple received their parents' permission to marry. Had the parents withheld permission, the couple might have eloped, so the parental right to permit or forbid a marriage does little to create alliances intentionally. It is subsequent to the elaborate investigation of each other during courtship that two families become commercially interested in each other. It may be only after many years of marital alliance and establishing rapport that the two families become involved in each other's business lines. Families do not create marital alliances for business then, but create business alliances after marriage. Because affinal kinsmen are usually peers in social rank and economic standing, they represent eligible kinsmen to utilize in widening the inner circle. The Chinese are not slow to realize a ripe opportunity, even if it involves twisting the community's views of kin relations a bit.

Economic alliances to affines have begun to change the patriarchy, patriliny, and patrilocality characteristic of shopkeeping families several decades ago. In most cases of uxorilocal residence analyzed in chapter 5, the husband had become commercially allied to his parents-in-law, either for himself or as an agent of his own business family. Under these circumstances he often moves away from his parents' family business to the town of his parents-in-law's operation or to the part of his own town where his affines' business is located.

Patriarchy in Chinese business families decreases when the new bride's family becomes a business associate or benefactor of the groom's family. The wife or daughter-in-law is not simply removed from her family to become a dependent in her husband's household. She becomes instead an active agent for her own family, from whom she is not greatly estranged because the two families themselves are closer. The daughters of Mr. Uy, the glass merchant, assumed more family power as a result of their roles as commercial links to their father.

In cooperative business ventures it is not infrequently the wife who brings skills and experience from her side of the partnership to run the new venture; in such cases she becomes actively essential to the store and her status increases even more. In her management of property and commerce and in her decision-making power relative to her husband, she becomes almost the equal of her Filipina counterparts in Filipino businesses. However, unlike the Filipinas, the Chinese wife still has to contend with sharp power differences between generations. When she is the link, actively or not, in a joint business venture, she is less dependent on her husband's parents than would otherwise be the case. But because her husband is still firmly ensconced in a family hierarchy, the wife's status can be no better than her husband's vis-a-vis the older generation.

In the final analysis, male power over women within generations can be weakened by alliances between affines. But male power over women between generations can be altered only to the degree that contemporary father-son power relations can be altered. And the father-son relations, as I have pointed out earlier, are changing only slowly.

Patrilineality of Chinese business families is altered, too, by commercial alliances with affinal kinsmen. Descent patterns have changed less than the sexual division of labor and postmarital residence, but this is predictable. H. Driver (1956) has shown that adaptive changes in social organization can proceed along a causal chain from technological changes to division of labor, postmarital residence, and finally to inheritance and descent patterns. In the case of the Philippine Chinese, the shopkeeping life and alliances with affines have led to a change in the roles and status of the women and affected the division of labor. Postmarital residence patterns have modified in the direction of increasing uxorilocality in order for men to do business with their affines. Because of these changes and because of the influence of Filipino law and custom, Chinese inheritance practices have changed toward more participation for women. Descent patterns may some day follow suit.

The changes in patrilineal inheritance practices have been influenced by the new division of labor. Daughters who become managers in their father's business often become equal to their brothers as heirs. There are several successful businesses in Iloilo City run by women who either continued as one of their fathers' branch managers after they married, or have never married and plan to carry on the family business in place of or in partnership with their brothers.

Patrilineality has been modified by the continuing minority of sons who move to live and work with their affinal kinsmen. These sons often become heirs through their wives to the branches or shares that they manage. This is not a new practice: Fei-Hsiao-tung (1939:71) described a similar practice, the *lendiugoxofen,* in peasant villages of Eastern China. One difference between the overseas and the mainland practice is that the son-in-law does not change his name to that of his wife. The business shares he inherits belong to him and his wife, not his extended family. The husband is not continuing a surname and descent line but forming a single-generation alliance simply by changing his residence and place of work.

Daughters who marry Chinese with Filipino citizenship become automatically naturalized, too, and can be very useful to Chinese-citizen natal families. Their Filipino citizenship gives wives the right to own property and engage in certain lines of business such as rice or retail sales. To avoid legal tangles, a woman's brothers and father may place their properties and business licenses in her name. For this reason many young Chinese women who marry naturalized Filipino-Chinese are given large business shares or buildings for dowries. As often as not, titular ownership means nothing in terms of control and inheritance. But sometimes the daughter and her husband are in a good position to actually assume responsibility and management of such properties. As I have pointed out earlier, control of a property at the time of division of the patrimony is sometimes tantamount to inheritance and becomes accepted as a fait accompli.

These new developments in Chinese affinal alliances and the subsequent changes in family and kinship practices are occurring throughout the Philippines, in towns smaller than Iloilo and in the larger metropolitan centers. Rather than build alliances (and extend businesses) through descent group membership, which is a vertical system of connections, Philippine Chinese have turned to building alliances by marriage, a basically horizontal system of connections. One's vertical system, the descent group, is usually somewhat decimated by its history of immigration and dispersion. On the other hand, the horizontal systems, the affinal groups, expand each generation as each merchant's children marry. At marriage, new and close potential allies are created at the very time that an established man needs to expand and a young groom to start on his own. These facts are central in explaining the great popularity of affinal alliances.

1. The one exception to this is teaching in Chinese schools, a traditional occupation for Chinese women in the city. In the last decade many young women have graduated as nurses, but many who graduate cannot or do not practice due to citizenship laws or their fathers' or husbands' objections.

2. Or *"Hó giàh bô kè san-tãi,"* "The rich never last three generations." The saying is common in China, too (see Martin Yang [1945:1321]).

3. Maurice Freedman (1958:21) notes these tensions in Southeast Chinese extended families, and Eric Wolf (1966:68) suggests that the problem of outsider wives is a universal strain on extended families.

4. The son, however, might refuse to marry the woman, and the father would have to marry her off at expense to himself. The practice was most common for wealthy merchants living in rural areas but has now ceased entirely.

5. Chen Ta (1923) quotes the old *Min Records* of Fukien: "Haiten (Chang-chou) has many junks. Some people borrow money and go beyond the seas. Sometimes people bring up children of poor families or even abandoned children in order to let them trade with barbarians overseas" (*Fukien T'ung Chih,* vol. 38, chuan 56, p. 25).

6. In the Philippines the natal parents occasionally become godparents of their own child in order to keep contact. However, godparents are usually recruited from well-to-do friends. Parents who adopt out children are often poor and, thus, do not usually qualify.

7. Foster parents might "phase out" their charges, to be sure, but the adopted child could jilt the foster parents, too. In the years of immigration a husband and wife in China often "invested" in a young man's future by adopting him and financing his journey to Southeast Asia, where he was to make his fortune and support them by remittances. The proportion of immigrants who arrived in the Philippines and promptly reneged on their promises appears to have been fairly high.

8. This blood brotherhood is to be distinguished from the formal associations like the Hung Men Hui or "Free Masons" and the musical associations, which are also called sworn brotherhoods, or *meng chu t'uan t'i.*

9. Amyot (1960) makes a passing reference to a Chinese practice of godparentage, *yi fu yi tze,* practiced in China, but Iloilo Chinese informants knew of no such practice in their home areas in Fukien and Kwangtung.

10. The red (for joy) edge surrounding the black (for misfortune) banner is claimed to contain the misfortune and prevent it from contaminating the mourners outside the agnatic group.

7

LO'S FAMILY DRY GOODS STORE: A CASE STUDY

THE LIFE HISTORY OF MR. LO and the development of his business and family in Iloilo illustrate most of the themes which I have discussed above in chapter 6. The composition of his household, the division of power and labor, the training of his children, his alliances through marriage and fictive kinship, and the problems of transmitting his successful business to his sons make Mr. Lo's life rather typical of Iloilo's Chinese merchants. His family and business are interdependent and their changes must be analyzed together. The profile of Mr. Lo's life will most likely not be repeated in the lives of his children or other younger Philippine Chinese; too many changes in China, in the Philippines, and in the Philippine Chinese community have occurred to make such continuity likely. But Mr. Lo's story provides a good picture of the Chinese merchant's life in the past fifty years.[1]

Early Beginnings

Mr. Lo was born in Chin-kang County, Fukien. He sailed to the Philippines in steerage on a steam freighter from Amoy City in 1924, when he was fifteen years old. Although he traveled with several young companions, they separated upon debarking for their separate assignments. Mr. Lo's parents, who had never been to the Philippines, apprenticed him to an unrelated townmate, Mr. Huan. Mr. Huan operated a large retail-wholesale dry goods store on the plaza of the town of Jaro, about two kilometers from Iloilo City.

Lo worked in Mr. Huan's store for six years without visiting China. Because the store was large and successful and one of several Chinese businesses on the plaza, young Lo had a number of coworkers to provide him with some semblance of family. Most of his fellow employees were kinsmen and townmates of his employer, Mr. Huan. There were one adopted son and two agnatic kinsmen (also named Huan); two young men, named Ong C. and Ong S., who were townmates of each other; and a Mr. Ang, who was a distant affinal kinsman of Mr. Lo's family. Next door in another dry goods store were two more men named Ang who were distant kinsmen of Lo's friend. A complex web of friendship, kinship, and town loyalties thus made a familiar coterie of the apprentices, employees, and employer. All but two of these men or their descendants are living and running businesses in Iloilo today (1972); most are still in textiles and dry goods and remain close to one another through nostalgia for their early years. We shall see that they are still occasionally involved in each other's business lives, too.

In 1930 Mr. Lo returned briefly to Chin-kang County. His parents arranged his marriage to a young woman named Go from a nearby village. Lo returned to his employment in Jaro almost immediately after the marriage, leaving his young (and pregnant) bride with his parents.

Returning to Mr. Huan's store a married man and experienced employee, Lo was promoted to purchasing stock, handling money, and venturing forth as salesman. His fellow workers were moving up too, some of them setting up independently, others taking new jobs in Iloilo City.

In 1934, at the age of twenty-five, Lo became his own boss. With long-term credit from Mr. Huan, he opened a little dry goods shop next door to Huan's, adding a line of sari-sari (variety store) merchandise on credit from another friend in Jaro. He had been able to raise ₱4,000 of his own to invest in his textiles. He specialized in retail sales to local Filipino families so as not to cut into the business of his wholesale patron Mr. Huan.

The business began so well that Lo could not handle it alone, so he sailed back to China a year later and fetched his wife and five-year-old son to join him. Accompanying them were two brothers of his wife to help as employees. Textiles were selling much better than general goods so Lo phased out his variety store line and concentrated on ready-made shirts, trousers, and underwear. His two brothers-in-law had no shop experience, so although they were nearly his age, they held very little responsibility, acting as salesmen and stockboys. Lo's wife watched the store for shoplifters and tended her baby but did little else; she was so frequently pregnant her first fifteen years in the Philippines that she had little time to be a businesswoman. Lo also employed several Filipinos to work as clerks to sell to the Filipino customers.

Needing additional competent assistance, Lo hired a Mr. Ong in the late 1930s to help with bookkeeping and stock purchasing. Mr. Ong was a townmate of the two Ongs who had been Lo's coworkers. He was slow but scrupulous and honest. He became a permanent fixture of the business, sharing in a certain percentage of the monthly profit and living with Lo like a kinsman, for he never acquired any family of his own. Ong eventually became Lo's only real (though minor) partner in his main business line; because Lo had already brought his family from Chin-kang and because he had his own savings and good credit from men like Huan, he never needed to take a chance on forming a partnership with other men. Later, when he became an established merchant and community man, Lo often entered into partnerships but as sidelines with friends and struggling proteges, not as a livelihood.

When the Americans entered the Second World War, they began evacuating Iloilo, so Lo made plans for a possible invasion by the Japanese. He buried his cash and American-made expensive stock, along with some canned goods he suspected would be valuable in the future.

When the Japanese arrived in Iloilo in April 1942, Lo sent his wife and his four sons and daughters with some of his Filipino employees to a small provincial town to hide. They lived there with a small circle of Chinese friends who were also from Jaro. They all relied on employees, friends, customers, and Filipino wives in the town to support and protect them.

Lo remained in his shop in Jaro, with his two brothers-in-law, several Filipino employees, and several Chinese drifters not related to him. The drifters were single men whose jobs had been eliminated by the war's confusion and whom Lo had been gracious enough to take in without the usual assurances because they had no references from family or townmates. Together they slowly sold Lo's inexpensive old stocks and created a small pants factory, making shorts from the rice sacks Lo had been farsighted enough to buy before the occupation.

When the Americans regained the Philippines in 1945, Lo's wife, children, and Filipino employees joined him, and the drifters left. Ong C., Lo's cohort during the years of apprenticeship to Huan, also joined them. Lo dug up his money and precious stocks, closed out his sack pants industry, and moved into downtown Iloilo City to expand his store and his market. His good quality dry goods and canned goods sold rapidly at high prices. Profits ran about 40 percent on his ₱15,000 inventory (approximately U.S. $7,500). During the war Lo had become good friends with several other textile merchants in town, whose wholesale business was also booming. As his suppliers, they extended large amounts of credit to him.

Business Expansion and Family Problems

As a result of such fast turnover, Lo expanded into wholesale sales himself. Whereas his old customers were retail consumers in Jaro, now he was selling dry goods to provincial Filipinos who bought for resale. It was a wide-open market; the city contained only three other dry goods wholesalers: the sons of Huan, his ex-employer, a Filipino establishment, and one of his former coworkers.

Lo's wife, who by now had borne six sons and a daughter, was pregnant with her eighth child and undertook no tasks in the store. Now that they had moved to the center of the business district, she spent most of her time socializing with her many neighbor Chinese women. Ong C. and the two brothers-in-law were still employees. Mr. Ong, the bookkeeper, was promoted to minor partner, receiving 5 percent of the net profits after store and household maintenance expenses.[2] The two eldest sons, Carlos, eighteen, and Dion, thirteen, also helped in the store between school hours. They served as sales clerks and cashiers, and helped with inventory or loading and unloading of trucks. There were also several Filipino employees, some sewing, wrapping, and loading, while others cooked, cleaned house, did the laundry, and helped Mrs. Lo with her small children.

By 1950 the two brothers of Mrs. Lo took Filipinas as common-law wives and moved away to start independently. Because of their intermarriages, they knew they could get little commercial support from Lo. Also, China had just closed its borders, and both men had wives there whom they were expected to support or retrieve. So they simply moved away without requesting help from Lo.

Lo was becoming a secure, established city merchant. However, there was only so much wholesale ready-made dry goods business that he and his several competitor-friends could acquire without infringing on each other's territory or expanding beyond their family enterprises (which was considered unmanageable and a big risk). So, Lo began to expand in different directions. For six years he and a townmate named Lo Que combined capital to purchase native products. Lo Que had already become expert at this and made his fortune. Lo Que supplied expertise and capital, and Mr. Lo assisted passively with more capital. Lo Que split the profits according to their original capital investments. When Lo Que died in 1954, altercations within his family caused his sons to break the partnership with Lo.

It seems Lo Que's younger brother had joined him as a minor partner, and Lo Que had lent him money to bring his wife from Hongkong to join them. Lo Que also pressed his younger brother to become naturalized, for his Chinese citizenship was a hazard to their business. Lo Que's younger brother spent the money on his wife's sick parents in Manila instead of fetching his wife and also refused to become a Filipino citizen. His presence in the business was a threat to Lo Que's wife and four sons, so when Lo Que died, they cut the brother off and compelled him to leave. Our Mr. Lo of Friendship Dry Goods liked the younger brother and accepted him into his household so that he might have a place to live. This is what destroyed Lo's partnership with Lo Que's sons.

At this time Ong C., the former coworker, found a partner in another wholesale dry goods house in Iloilo, so the two of them left their employers to start another textile store. Once again, the composition of Mr. Lo's business household changed. Ong C.'s new partner had been an employee in the store of Ong Pai, who was the brother of Ong S., who was our Mr. Lo's coemployee in the years of working with Mr. Huan. So not only did membership in the store households fluctuate, it seemed to shuffle among a large group of kinsmen, townsmen, blood brothers, and former coworkers. To further complicate the shuffle, when Ong C. left Mr. Lo, a Mr. Chua replaced him. Mr. Chua was an affinal kinsman of Huan Y., also one of the apprentices from the days of Huan's store. Chua was also a kinsman to storeowner Huan himself.

By 1955 Lo was the father of six sons and two daughters. His three eldest sons — Carlos, twenty-five; Dion, twenty; and Jorge, eighteen — had finished Chinese school and worked fulltime in the business. Lo would send them out as salesmen with a small truckload of dry goods to sell to the sari-sari stores in the small markets scattered about the province. His daughter Eliza, who was sixteen, still attended Chinese school and did not work in the store at all; she helped her mother with the smaller children (Juan, ten; Cristobal, eight; and Maria, six) and with the direction of their small household staff and the shopping. Willie, fourteen years old, learned the business by helping inside the store as his brothers before him had done.

Lo's business had grown to the point that all of this help was needed. Not only did he sell wholesale to Filipinos in the province, he had also developed Chinese wholesaler contacts in Bacolod, Cotabato, and Davao, who also purchased from him. The profit possible in the postwar boom years had now shrunk to about 15 percent as competition increased and the prices of his Manila suppliers rose; nevertheless, Lo had become a respected business success and community leader. He was elected to the board of trustees of his children's school, Sun Yat Sen, and acknowledged as one of the leading lights of the informal Lo Clan clique in Iloilo.

But a number of disappointments were to become his lot once he achieved such status. Lo felt convinced that his sons were pleasure-seekers, too much influenced by the Filipinos with whom they worked and played, and not dedicated enough to the rigors of store management. He held his money closely and gave them only small allowances so that they could not squander store funds. He became frightened at their desire to run the store in different ways, to change the accounting and inventory methods and the division of labor among the employees. They argued with him frequently, and among themselves as well.

In 1958 it became known that Carlos, the eldest son, had been keeping a Filipino *querida*, or mistress, for several years and had a son and a daughter by her. Lo was apoplectic with rage that his eldest son's first marriage and first children should be in secret with a Filipina. Their relations as father and son were soured for all time by this breach of faith and tradition. Carlos was threatened with disinheritance if he failed to return to Lo's store and marry properly. The stress of the situation destroyed Carlos's ties to his common-law wife, and she left him. She gave him custody of his two children because she could not support them. Carlos came back to his family with his mestizo children.

The Lo family kept the son as the first male of the third generation, but they attempted to give away the daughter. However, she ran away from her foster parents repeatedly and returned to the Lo family, so they ultimately and grudgingly accepted both children.

Carlos, drastically limited in the responsibilities to which he was assigned in the family business, pressed his father to allow him to become independent or start a branch. Because Carlos quarreled often with his brother-managers Dion and Jorge and also with Ong, the minor partner (who always sided with the father), Lo finally let him go to try his hand at business, for Carlos had married a Chinese woman and had given the impression of being sêng-liên, or "settled" again. In 1963 Carlos moved across the street from his father's dry goods store and opened a *camiseria* (shirt store) with ₱7,000 loaned by Lo. This was a very small sum to run even a retail outlet, but Carlos managed to survive by his good credit rating in Manila with importers whom he selected for himself. Carlos's suppliers were a Chinese classmate from college, two sibmates named Lo, and a blood brother (*kiet-pāi*) from Chinese high school. Because they had known him for many years, these men trusted Carlos with as much as 50 percent of his shirt stock on ninety days' credit.

Carlos's business was small, run only by him and a few Filipino employees, but he had hopes his father would release the ₱40,000 he had tentatively promised so Carlos could expand to a wholesale store, which requires much larger volume because the profit margin is small. Carlos kept assuring the old man that his shirt store was really just a branch of Friendship Dry Goods. But perhaps Lo feared the competition and the independence of his wayward son, for he never released the ₱40,000 for the shirt store.

Carlos's wife worked as a Chinese schoolteacher, so her income and his small profits could support them and their two young children. But Carlos was definitely *kiầⁿ-tò*, stumbling along, neither able to grow nor able to close because he did not have the cash to repay his debts to the Manila importers. He lost hope in his little enterprise, and, with the acceptance of his suppliers, closed down. He became a schoolteacher in another province, using his college education to repay his business debts. He rented his store space to his wife's kinsman, who opened a grocery store. But he retained the apartments over the shop for his wife and children, who remained in Iloilo while he worked out of town. Before he left, he took his younger brother Juan to Manila to meet his suppliers and become their customer, too. Juan, twenty-three, was the only naturalized son in the family and was the legal license holder of Friendship Dry Goods, so Carlos was passing his shirt store business back to Friendship through Juan. It was also his way of staying in touch with and in the good graces of his Manila suppliers, for Friendship had a high reputation among Chinese dry goods merchants all over the Philippines. Carlos was taking care to keep his reputation intact by this transfer.

In 1967 Dion, the second son, age thirty-two, also ventured on his own in the dry goods business. He married a Chinese woman from nearby Bacolod City. Feeling useless at Friendship Dry Goods around so many partners, employees, and brothers, Dion moved to Bacolod to set up a dry goods branch. He used his father-in-law, a naturalized Filipino citizen, as the "dummy" licensee. He opened a small shop with this man, with his wife also helping occasionally. Within three years he went nearly bankrupt. Dion did not have his father's sense of bookkeeping or judgment of character, with the result that his profits slipped away and he made bad loans and credit extensions. His partner, his father-in-law, also proved to be his downfall, for the latter had been a bankrupt shopkeeper before they merged. He would remove stock from the store for resale elsewhere and pocket the profits. Dion dejectedly returned with his wife to Friendship Dry Goods, leaving behind his stock and his debtors.

Carlos had just returned from school teaching and removing himself from debt. He was dispatched to Bacolod to extricate Dion from his debacle. Carlos closed the store, sold the stock, and dunned his brother's debtors until he had recovered a great deal of the lost capital and removed some of the smudge from the Lo family's reputation.

Unlike Carlos, Dion was still close to his father, and old Lo assisted him again, this time on the street abutting the back of Friendship Dry Goods Store. Dion operated a small wholesale dry goods distributorship to the provincial Filipino retail stores. Without the encumbrances of his father-in-law or a strange town and under the close supervision of old Lo, Dion began to turn a profit.

The third son, Jorge, in his late twenties during these events (1968 to 1970), had married a mestiza Chinese. He went away to establish another branch of Friendship Dry Goods in the town of Kalibo, Aklan province, the home of his wife. He specialized in wholesaling of imported shirts as a bulante, or traveling salesman. Because he traveled and visited Iloilo often to move stock, he maintained his wife and child in a suburban house in Iloilo City rather than in the small town of Kalibo. His wife, a nurse, stopped her hospital work to raise children. She talked Jorge into suburban life in order to stay away from the confusions and quarrels of Friendship Store and her old-fashioned parents-in-law. As a result she was fortunate enough to be an outsider in the family quarrels of the past and those yet to come.

Eliza, the eldest daughter, now twenty-nine, had married a pure Chinese man from Manila who used to travel to Iloilo on business. Her husband was originally a grocer, but he became very enthusiastic about mah jong, both as a gambler and as an investor. Soon after their marriage he began approaching the old man Lo for capital, ostensibly to expand his grocery. Carlos knew what his brother-in-law was really doing, and so he proposed instead that the two of them form a grocery partnership in Manila or Iloilo, each raising ₱60,000. In this way he could watch his father's investment and his brother-in-law, who had married old Lo's favorite child and was given more support than even Lo's own sons. This brother-in-law, Mr. Te, refused the partnership offer but accepted from Lo a large lump sum representing shares in Lo's sons' names. Te invested some of this money in mah jong parlors, and some he gambled with. He promised to remit ₱1,500 a month as loan repayment to the sons but almost immediately fell delinquent. His gambling debts mounted and his grocery, having been drained of capital, was forced into bankruptcy. When pressure from his creditors became too great, Te evacuated his family from Manila and moved into Friendship Store at the invitation of Lo. He and Eliza became virtual dependents of Lo.

Even before Eliza and her husband arrived at Friendship Dry Goods Store, the household was crowded and complex in structure. In 1969 their numbers had been lightened somewhat when Willie, now twenty-seven, and Cristobal, twenty, emigrated to Los Angeles in search of work, in spite of pleadings from Lo and his wife. Willie married a Filipina nurse there. In 1972, at the grand seventieth birthday celebration of Lo, he and Cristobal were ordered home for the event.

Juan, the fifth son, had become the most important son working in Friendship Store by virtue of his position as licensee. Socially at ease in Filipino society and at the same time on good terms with his father, he was most useful in negotiating contracts, visiting the municipal government, making friends with salesmen and local policemen, and handling important Filipino customers. Old Lo put him in active management of all day-to-day routine, although he retained control himself of the treasury and the main decisions. Lo then had more time to sit about with other older respected businessmen, who informally kept the Chinese community governed, and basked in their mutual esteem as venerated elders and benefactors.

Maria, the younger daughter, helped occasionally in the store after she graduated from Chinese school, although she had no responsibility. The store household was so large and complex that she was always needed somewhere to babysit, shop, watch customers, fold cloth, and so forth. She had no suitors yet and was simply biding her time. She made good company for the two unmarried mestiza employees who worked as sales clerks and were all that remained of the store's Filipino work force. With such a large household, coupled with requests for employment from friends and kinsmen, Lo had no need of outsiders. He hired the two mestizas from old friends who had no stores of their own and considered their daughters financial burdens.

Friendship Store was now an enormous extended family complex, not typical of Iloilo's merchants, but by no means unique, either. Within the store itself and in the apartments over the store were twenty-four people in all: Lo and his wife; Willie and his Filipino wife with two small children; Juan; Cristobal; Eliza and her husband with three small children; Maria; Carlos's two mestizo children; Mr. Lo (Lo Que's younger brother); Mr. Chua and Mr. Ong, the minor partners; two mestiza employees (who returned to their families at night); two Filipino cooks; and two Filipino maids. Facing them in the store across the street were Carlos, his wife, and two small children, with one maid. To the rear a few doors down were Dion, his wife, three small children, and a maid. If all three residences are counted, there was a total of thirty-five people in Lo's great Friendship Dry Goods Store household.

Lo's Control of Family Finances

Lo was still in control of this big family, in the sense that he was the final decision-maker and the keeper of all the money and account books. Yet he certainly was not in control of his family's behavior. To begin with, his sons pleaded with him to release their shares of the business so that they might develop Friendship Store further. Lo was a wealthy man but his sons felt that far too much of that wealth was idle in bank account, and they pleaded with him to invest it. Lo knew his sons could not cooperate well, and so he feared they would split the enterprise if he released his control. Instead he invested as much as he thought advisable in different projects on behalf of his sons. Eliza's husband's grocery had been one project; Carlos's and Dion's dry goods shops had been others. He also invested in a Manila auto parts importer who was a *kiet-pai* (blood brother) of Carlos. When Carlos returned from his school teaching, he agitated for a business again. Lo released a sum through Juan to help Carlos open a small haberdashery. The money was given to Juan as an allowance; Juan then loaned it to Carlos. For a son or for friends of his sons or for himself, Lo apportioned out investment sums of as much as ₱15,000.

Nonetheless, it was still Lo who made all decisions. From an insider's point of view, there are several reasons why Lo holds on as he does.

First, his own standing as a community leader and philanthropist hinges on his active control of family fortunes; others might suspect that after partition of the patrimony Lo's sons would not release to him the amounts of money it takes to underpin his leader status. His image and influence in Iloilo could slip, when they should be growing as he ages.

Similarly, Lo fears to have his business reputation (somewhat distinct from his civic reputation) in the hands of such a large group of quarrelsome brothers, all but one of whom (Cristobal) are struggling for control of Friendship Store. They might split up, and his capital and power base would disintegrate.

There are others who would suffer if the sons took charge. Mrs. Lo is a dedicated mah jong gambler, playing almost daily with her friends. Her sons superficially tolerate this, but she knows they would curtail her gambling if they were in power. Ong and Chua, the minor partners of Lo, know that their sinecures as Lo's old-fashioned bookkeepers and stock clerks would probably come to an end if the sons succeeded the father. They would be replaced by men with newer methods of bookkeeping and inventory about which they know nothing and are not inclined to learn.

Finally, Lo's own closest friends, mah jong partners, competitors, and former coworkers are in virtually the same position as he and support his stand to maintain the patriarchy. Their bastion of self-conscious traditionalism will be broached if one of them turns over control to his sons and retires.

For their part, the sons have become concerned for their own business reputations while Lo defends his. Other men in town have already set up their sons in large enterprises, if not effectively retired from family management. Lo's sons feel other men will suspect that their father is in complete control because his sons are incompetent. The sons claim that irreparable damage may be done to Friendship's reputation even before they take charge: other Chinese businessmen will write off the store as having failed to survive the change of generations.

As the sons, the father, the minor partners, and other household members enter into arguments over these matters, the disunified and overcrowded household fractures and Friendship Store's daily profit reflects the family disasters. When Willie and Cristobal returned from America, tension among the numerous brothers and the parents drove Juan to run away to friends in Manila, and Cristobal ran away to Bacolod City. Without Juan's important "front of the store" management, Friendship began losing money. The arrival of Eliza and her husband, who had squandered the brothers' money, also raised hackles, and Carlos in protest refused to cross the store threshold. The fighting also began to affect old Lo's health and subsequently his ability to keep in touch with his store's operations and make accurate, well-timed decisions.

Future of the Store

When old Lo dies, the sons Carlos, Dion, Willie, Jorge, Juan, and Cristobal will converge again in the household of Friendship Store to make some major decisions. There will also be Eliza and her husband and Maria to consider, unless the former are reemployed somewhere and Maria is married. Mrs. Lo will probably outlive her husband a number of years, and respect for her will probably save Friendship Store from partition for a while. Carlos will seek to integrate his small branch with the management of Friendship. Cristobal, who dislikes shopkeeping, will probably withdraw his share and leave town for Manila or Bacolod. Dion and Jorge are rather independent already and will probably let their shares of Friendship ride as silent partnerships in the store. Juan and Carlos will take active management responsibilities. Willie will try to return to America, but if he cannot, he will remain with Friendship. The brothers will swallow their disagreements for a time in respect for their mother and to pass over the "bad luck" period. Mr. Ong and Mr. Chua will not be fired, but they will lose their bookkeeping responsibilities to the brothers.

As long as Mrs. Lo survives her husband, this is the most likely future of Friendship Dry Goods. When she dies, the brothers might continue as before or split in a variety of ways, even to the point of Friendship Store ceasing to exist.

The story of Mr. Lo and Friendship Dry Goods Store has been greatly abbreviated to draw attention to a few themes: household composition, business development, and difficulties of transmission between generations. Mr. Lo's life vividly illustrates the analysis of business kin alliances and family division of labor presented in chapter 6. However, Lo is not typical of most Iloilo Chinese because his family, and consequently his difficulties, have been bigger than most. With regard to his problems, he resembles more the Manila Chinese, except that the solutions to his family problems have been less influenced by the modern, cosmopolitan options present in such big cities. That is, his daughters do not press for shares of the patrimony, nor his sons go to court.

Lo began, as all immigrants began, as an apprentice member of a storekeeping "family" whose members remained important business and social contacts all through his life. He brought his own family from China only after he was established independently. His suppliers, salesmen, coworkers, and employees almost always had some relation to Lo other than their purely commercial link. As he prospered and his household grew in consequence, Lo provided jobs, credit, loans, and partnership opportunities for many old friends, townmates, and a new son-in-law and father-in-law. As a result, he not only increased in civic stature as a respected benefactor but usually profited financially. As he prospered, he moved more toward the center of town, more toward the higher reaches of the distribution pyramid (retail to wholesale), and more into diversified, related lines (to underwear, to neighboring towns, and to more store outlets). His household in turn advanced from a nuclear family group to a stem family, to oscillating between a great patrilineal extended family with male affines and a "split" (or nonlocalized) extended family household.

Lo responded to the postwar Philippine nationalization campaign by naturalizing his son Juan and making him legal licensee. He placed almost all of his sons in the dry goods business, even if there might seem not to be room for them. But he did not employ his daughters or his wife. He had many sons and did not need to do so; besides, a merchant of means prefers not to work his womenfolk.

However, Lo eventually reached the limits of his expansion in Iloilo City, and his great network of family and store began to buckle. His profits accumulated faster than he knew how to invest them. His sons matured faster than he was prepared to accept by entrusting them with his reputation and life's work. As long as he did not redistribute power among the management of Friendship, he could not broaden its market nor ensure its security at the core, which depended solely on his personal competence. When he expanded by entrusting his kinsmen with independent management of his branches, he lost as often as he profited. When he tested their ability as a group to handle the business, they fought, both with him and among themselves.

Whatever the fates of Friendship Dry Goods Store and the sons who will inherit it, they will not be the same as Lo's. He represents the last of a type of Philippine Chinese immigrant merchant whose prime has come and is already passing. The last of his type will die in the next twenty years. Unfolding in the last twenty years has been the story of a new type of Chinese merchant, Philippine-born and educated, with a wider set of cultural options for both family and commercial life. The subsequent variety of their family structures and businesses will make their stories even less uniform than the ones to date have been.

1. For the sake of confidentiality, I have altered certain dates, places, and names in Mr. Lo's story. For the reader's ease I am using Filipino instead of Chinese first names (most Chinese have both).

2. See chapter 3 for an account of Mr. Lo's family budget.

EPILOG

SINCE I LEFT ILOILO IN 1973, some very important events have occurred in the Philippines to change the position of its resident Chinese ethnic group. Normalization of relations with the People's Republic of China, naturalization of aliens by administrative procedure, and – less dramatic but no less significant – the nationalization of Chinese schools have combined with the declaration of martial law in 1972 to produce an environment quite different from the open and frequently unsettling national and international picture of the previous decade.

The combined effect of these changes in Philippine law and international relations can only be to accelerate integration of the Chinese into Filipino political and social life. How quickly will the Chinese integrate? What aspects of their life are changing rapidly, or very little? And what will be the outcome: complete disappearance of the ethnic group and their traditions?

Throughout this book, rather than take the assimilationist perspective in studying the Philippine Chinese, I have spoken of adaptation. That is, I have examined the evolutionary adjustments of Chinese cultural and social forms to the Philippine environment, treating Filipinos and their culture as background, as part of the environment, which has itself been evolving. I have stressed preservation and continuity rather than "Filipinization" or such assimilation processes. Romer's Rule, that is, the essential conservatism of evolutionary change, appears to apply to the Philippine Chinese. The image of the melting pot, so common in past Philippine and American ethnic research, did not seem appropriate to the Chinese situation. Stressing ethnic preservation and continuity is now much more common among social scientists as they have become sensitized to the newly politicized ethnic groups they study.

When I conducted the research on which this book is based, I was fascinated with that which made the Philippine Chinese different from Filipinos. Being a student of Chinese civilization, I shared with many of my informants a sense of the glory of Chinese culture. I was happy where it was preserved, disappointed where it was lost. In writing and reflecting these last four years on the lot of the Philippine Chinese, I have come to support a more conscious and deliberate accommodation of Filipinos and Chinese. There is powerful logic in John Bennett's remarks:

> Perhaps as ethnologists we have no business celebrating ethnicity in any form; we might have in the age of cultural isolation, but that age is past, gone forever, and cultural ethnicity is now one of its lag phenomena. The new ethnicity . . . is a symptom of what is out of joint in the human mentality as human population becomes worldwide (1975:10).

In this epilog, I will draw together the evidence from Iloilo of the state of Filipino and Chinese interaction in marriage, business, politics, school, and social life. With some caution I will look at the near future of these relations and suggest several areas that need more attention, both by the players in this human drama and by the social scientists who watch them, in order to aid and understand further integration.

The declaration of martial law in September 1972, in one move, stopped the accelerating crime and extortion against the local Chinese. The Philippine Constabulary deposed and jailed the presiding mayor, a man much feared by the Chinese as their exploiter. A few Chinese whose Communist sympathies were suspected were also jailed. My language tutor was one such unfortunate, the victim of too many enemies in his own Kuomintang-oriented school. He was soon released after a Chinese delegation approached the Constabulary. All in all, the quiet that descended on Iloilo was welcomed by the Chinese merchants. The reduced likelihood of being kidnapped, robbed, extorted, or destroyed by a revolutionary mob compensated for the increased likelihood that a unified regime would take harsh action on the Chinese question. The most prominent fear was of a rightist backlash after the open expressions of interest in Maoist China by some Chinese during Nixon's historic visit to China in early 1972. The backlash came, as expected, through the actions of the Kuomintang supporters among the Chinese themselves. But as noted in chapter 2, the backlash was mild: the KMT supporters were less numerous and less powerful than they had been in the 1950s. And they were soon to be undermined entirely.

For about two years after the declaration of martial law, the Chinese adopted a typical "wait and see" attitude and made a concerted effort to establish good relations through their best Filipino-Chinese middlemen with the local ruling military government. Open demonstrations of their allegiance to the Philippines were common. For example, on New Year's Day, 1973, a large ceremony of charitable food donations to Iloilo's poor Filipinos was held in the city's public square, complete with school bands and Philippine governmental officials as guests. As part of the national effort to improve tourism, the downtown business area, predominantly Chinese, underwent a "facelifting": buildings were cleaned, streets and sidewalks rebuilt, and storefronts renovated.

In the last months of 1974, the rumors of profound changes to come received a boost. Mrs. Marcos led a trade delegation to the Peoples' Republic of China to discuss an increase in trade relations and, the Philippine Chinese anticipated, a normalization of diplomatic relations. A new Filipino-Chinese paper appeared, the *Orient News*, taking a pro-Peking stand that in earlier years would have caused the editors' expulsion. Pro-Peking papers from Hongkong were permitted into the country and sold on newstands in the cities.

In 1975 events began to occur even faster than rumors. In April, as preparation for visiting China, President Marcos published Letter of Instruction (LOI) 270, converting the legal procedure of naturalization of aliens to a far more convenient administrative one. The high expense and patient effort previously necessary for a Chinese citizen to become naturalized had, apparently in one act, been swept away. Replying to entreaties by Filipino-Chinese delegations, President Marcos further liberalized the requirements for naturalization with LOI 283, lowering the income minimum required for college age aliens just beginning socially useful careers, and LOI 292, allowing applicants to acquire Filipino first names at the time of naturalization. Further, Presidential Decree 725 allowed for the naturalization of aliens who had lost their citizenship: this was valuable to Filipino women who had legally married Chinese aliens and, thus, lost their Filipino citizenship.

The deadline for naturalization applications was extended from 15 May to 30 June, then to September. By this deadline some 20,000 applications had been received. During 1976, about 8,000 of these applications were approved. The President declared a grace period for further applications from January to March 1977, liberalized the language requirement, and lowered the application age limit to eighteen years. By the end of 1978, over 18,000 persons had been naturalized, and another 19,000 had filed applications (*Pag sa Pag Newsletter*, Nov.-Dec. 1978). The nation appeared to be making a grand effort to settle once and for all the uncertain position of its alien residents.

The impetus to settle the Chinese status had never been greater. Anticipating discussions with the Philippines, Vice Premier Teng Hsiao-ping of the People's Republic of China had addressed the United Nations in early 1975, speaking of his confidence that the Philippines "will soon open wide the door for mass naturalization" (*Far Eastern Economic Review*, 6 May 1975:40). In early June, the Marcos administration traveled to Peking to normalize Philippine-Chinese external relations, signing on 9 June a Joint Communique concerning diplomatic and trade affairs. The People's Republic encouraged the Filipino-Chinese to become participants in their host nation, and the Philippines acknowledged Taiwan as a province of the People's Republic. So each nation supported the national integrity of the other. The Communique abolished all formal Philippine diplomatic ties with the Republic of China, whose Manila embassy closed its doors for good that month. Now that the Philippines recognized only one China, and that one a Communist regime, the Philippine Chinese aliens, many holding Republic of China passports, became de facto stateless persons. The Marcos government declared it had no interest in pressuring aliens to become citizens of the People's Republic; so the only recourse for either the government or the Chinese aliens was naturalization.

The response of the Philippine Chinese to the Joint Communique was a vigorous expression of internal schism, exceeding that expressed in 1972 during Nixon's visit to China. At that time, while I was in Iloilo, student drawings of Nixon, Mao, and Chou En-lai appeared on the classroom walls of Chinese schools, and acquaintances smuggled copies of *China Reconstructs* into wedding banquets to talk excitedly with me of the reemergence of China and the new power balance in Asia. Declaration of martial law squelched those expression, but the Joint Communique brought them out again with renewed energy.

During the Marcos visit to China, Mao posters and the flag of the People's Republic were prominently displayed in some Chinese businesses in Manila. Dozens of pro-Peking organizations, one of the most prominent being the Filipino-Chinese Amity Club, under the leadership of influential Chinese businessmen, surfaced to act as host to the new Chinese embassy. The expressions of enthusiasm were more muted in Iloilo, always cautious about open political stances; Iloilo Chinese remained content to participate vicariously in the battle to be joined in Manila.

The center of the open schism in Manila was the Federation of Filipino-Chinese Chambers of Commerce, long the spokesman of Filipino-Chinese and closely allied to the Taiwanese embassy. Decades of suppression of pro-Peking factions in the Philippines were responsible for the almost gleeful outburst of allegiance by those factions following the Joint Communique. The sources of power among the Filipino-Chinese were rapidly changing, and the opportunity for revenge and a reorganization — sought for economic and personal reasons as well as doctrinal ones — was happily taken. The Federation leadership had formally stated in the press its approval of the Marcos trip, but after the Taiwanese embassy closed and reemerged as the less prominent Pacific Economic and Cultural Centre, the dominant local pro-Taiwanese faction attempted to continue as before. Factional strength had become more even, however, and the dissension and power struggle that ensued were visible far beyond the Chinese district. The pro-Peking faction attempted to fly the Chinese flag at Federation headquarters and opposed singing the Republican national anthem prior to meetings. They were also outspoken in their opposition to the "decadence" of the 1976 Miss Chinatown contest. Everyone prepared for a grand battle in the Federation convention in 1977. Sometimes supported by the Marcos administration, as in their opposition to expressions of Taiwanese nationalism, and sometimes overruled, as in their opposition to the beauty contest, the newly emboldened non-Kuomintang factions appeared to be a permanent threat to Filipino-Chinese stability. The national government repeatedly chastised all groups for threatening national security and for failing to drop old enmities in favor of a pro-Filipino stand, the only position the government considered acceptable.

The schism is certain to be reflected, but more discreetly, in Iloilo City, having a history of doctrinal and personal feuds between the local chapter of the Federation and the neutral or perhaps pro-Peking Chinese Chamber of Commerce. The excitement about impending changes in the status of the People's Republic that I saw in 1973 among Chinese Chamber members was not widespread in the community, however, and it appeared that many businessmen both young and old either found the struggle in Manila arcane or an embarrassment. Some of the enthusiasms I heard were very practical: "Perhaps naturalization will be easier now," and even more common, "Imagine: if I could sell just one cigarette to each Chinese — eight hundred million cigarettes! "

The Filipino-Chinese power struggle will continue for some time, as old and serious scores (in Iloilo as well as Manila) are settled. The Philippine government, however, has grown exasperated with the bickering expressed in the excessively polarized terms of pro-Peking and pro-Taiwan symbols. As we have seen, the government has repeatedly liberalized regulations, extended deadlines, or declared grace periods to defuse potential internal explosions and resettle the Chinese alien minority as a Filipino ethnic group. Mrs. Marcos's campaign, with the support of the Chinese community, to create a tourist attraction of Manila's Chinatown may be seen as a related effort to provide for a national ethnic pluralism, but only on terms that benefit the country as a whole (*Fookien Times Yearbook* 1974:168).

The citizenship campaign, too, is a necessary step toward integration, but not because it will make patriotic nationalists overnight of the Philippine Chinese; Iloilo Chinese who talked politics with me seemed to represent the usual range of cynics and patriots to be found among Filipinos. Gerald McBeath (1975), surveying the political attitudes among Chinese high school students in 1969, found that by a scale developed in America, the Chinese students were politically alienated. He discovered, however, that by the same scale Filipino students were also politically alienated. Calls for Chinese patriotism to the Philippines must consider the Filipino norm and not an unrealistic ideal.

The citizenship campaign is necessary because it will remove another point around which a "we-they" dichotomy between ethnic Chinese and Filipinos has materialized. This is especially true now that the China on which resident Chinese may officially rely is the People's Republic, a nation about which the Filipinos, sharing an anti-Communist history with the United States, will be slow to feel comfortable.

Occurring more quietly but nonetheless significant among the changes in recent years is Presidential Decree 176, providing for the nationalization of Chinese alien schools. In April 1973, alien schools were informed of a three-year deadline in which to bring their ownership, faculty, and curriculum into line with Filipino schools. P. D. 176 required all alien schools, most of which were Chinese, to be totally owned and operated by Filipino citizens by April 1976. Teachers were required to be Filipino citizens, and no Chinese subject other than language arts – and these were to be only optional courses – could be taught. Chinese language classes could only occupy a hundred minutes per day, and the books used could not encourage allegiance to another country or culture, as the Taiwanese texts previously had done.

Iloilo's Chinese schools made the transition without difficulty because those Chinese owners and teachers who were aliens availed themselves of nationalization by administrative decree. The curriculum, which was previously one-half Chinese subjects and language, became indistinguishable from Filipino schools except for the prominent optional Chinese language classes. P. D. 176 stipulated that knowledge of Chinese language could not be a prerequisite for admission to these schools, thus facilitating the entrance of ethnic Filipinos to these schools. But Filipinos had always been admitted to Iloilo's Chinese schools, though not in large numbers, and many Chinese children who were entering the school could not speak Chinese either. As the schools are now constituted, both Filipinos and Chinese could graduate from them without having learned any Chinese, without having been made in many subtle but cumulative ways a Chinese ethnic. Iloilo's Chinese recognize this and shake their heads, but they accept the train of events. Creation of an ethnic Chinese is becoming ever more the responsibility of the private spheres: the family, the family business, and private social groups.

Let us examine, in light of these recent changes, the course and future of Filipino and Chinese relations in business, social life, and politics.

The business world of Iloilo's Chinese is perhaps the critical area of relations with the Filipinos. Even in the early 1970s there was already abundant evidence of economic cooperation at every level or type of business except in partnership operations, which are not very popular or stable bonds even among Chinese. One might say that both parties – the Filipinos and Chinese – are simply being pragmatic and pursuing similar courses of self-interest in working together, but such a view totally overlooks the fact that what is "pragmatic" is culturally defined. The degree of cooperation shows a growing compatibility of what Chinese and Filipinos define as useful and smart.

Some statistics from a survey I conducted in 1972 of ninety-seven Iloilo Chinese merchants will illustrate the degree of relations in business with Filipinos. On the average, 20 percent of a Chinese merchant's benefactors (those that supply help such as money, advice, or connections from a superior position in the economic or social hierarchy) were ethnic Filipinos. In the course of a merchant's life, 27 to 41 percent of his coworkers (partners, salesmen, employees, and the like) have been ethnic Filipinos. Filipino benefactors and coworkers were sometimes godparents, wife's relatives, wartime or school chums, and sometimes had no social or emotional connection at all to the Chinese they worked with.

Filipinos and Chinese in Iloilo are one another's customers, employers, and financiers. Virtually no Chinese business in Iloilo except for the banquet caterers relies solely on Chinese clients. Even the Chinese traditional medicine herb store is mostly filled with Filipino customers.

The Chinese, however, remain disproportionately in the storekeeper role between Filipino protectors and Filipino employees. Until the 1970s the majority of Iloilo's Chinese shopkeepers were aliens, "locked in" as much by law as by personal preference to the merchant's role in the Philippine economy. Nationalization laws had restricted aliens and their Filipinizing but still alien children from the civil service, the professions, and the military, all alternative and promising careers to that of commerce. The recent changes in the citizenship laws may make possible a new social mobility for ethnic Chinese. And with this social mobility will come a weakening of ethnic boundaries between Chinese and Filipinos.

This book has supported the view that Chinese ethnicity owes much to the fact that almost all Chinese are merchants. Until recently, to cease to be a merchant was tantamount to leaving the ethnic group. Now, it may be possible for more young men and women to create families based on other occupations, heeding the social sanctions or emulating the models of other reference groups besides that of their fathers and mothers, the immigrant merchants. They will not be as dependent upon the Chinese social networks for career success nor need to join Chinese merchant groups for mediation to protect their livelihood. In short, the Chinese ethnic group will become less homogeneous, less closed, and less powerful over its members. Chinese in noncommercial careers would not be as vulnerable to Filipino stereotypes of Chinese merchants, and performance in their new occupations may contribute to a weakening of those stereotypes.

Acquiring Filipino citizenship has not automatically opened doors for the Chinese because there is a tacit official and folk category of "second class citizen" that places the naturalized Filipino with his alien cohorts. For example, the government has repeatedly threatened to strip naturalized citizens of their Filipino citizenship and deport them for certain crimes. For the Filipino-Chinese, deportation usually has meant a trip to Taiwan. In 1970 the Yuyitang brothers of the *Chinese Commercial Press* were deported to be jailed in Taiwan, even though they were stateless persons, having declined their Nationalist passports eight years earlier (Chaloemtiarana 1977:76). In 1973, Presidential Decree 278 symbolically equated aliens and naturalized Filipinos by requiring the registration of both at the same time for identity cards. Naturalized Chinese Filipinos, who might have been citizens for as long as twenty-seven years, were understandably insulted and anxious about the implication of the decree. The decree implies that not all citizens are the same. Filipinos are suspicious of a Chinese who acquires Filipino citizenship because the motive is presumably pecuniary rather than patriotic.

My conversations and correspondence with Chinese in Iloilo and Manila have always uncovered a palpable fear about their unstable status in the government's mind. During the unrest of 1971, after the declaration of martial law in 1972, and again after the Joint Communique of 1975, the Chinese were on edge about what steps others might take to "solve" the Chinese problem once and for all. A sense of desperation pervaded my acquaintances' unguarded moments. Filipinos feel that commercial success compensates Chinese for this anxiety (Bulatao 1974), but I strongly disagree. The Chinese in the Philippines are now family men, and their interests have grown correspondingly broader. Government ambiguity or self-contradiction in matters Chinese merely prolongs the anxiety.

If we examine intermarriage between Chinese and Filipinos, we see a constant crossing over the ethnic line each generation. For the last several generations, about one-quarter of Iloilo Chinese men have married pure Filipinas. The rate at which Chinese women marry pure Filipino men has grown from virtually 0 to about 10 percent in the last twenty years, and that figure may be growing still.

When a Chinese man marries a Filipina, he usually brings her into the commercial life with him and raises his children to be Chinese as best he can, sending them to Chinese school, teaching them the shopkeeper's life, introducing them to the Chinese community's social clubs. When a Chinese woman marries a Filipino, usually against the wishes of her family, she leaves the Chinese commercial life and follows her husband's occupation and social circles. Though she is ethnically Chinese and will impart something of that to her children, she is less likely to send them to Chinese school, teach them Chinese business, or reintroduce them into the Chinese social groups.

Thus, there is no middle culture arising among mestizos of Filipino-Chinese intermarriages. Mestizos either remain a part of the Chinese community or leave it altogether. If the intermarriage of Chinese women to Filipinos should continue to increase, the number of mestizos in Iloilo who have little to do with the Chinese will also increase.

There are still some ethnic differences which discourage intermarriage or create difficulties in crosscultural families. In chapter 5 I discussed the problem of differences in Filipino and Chinese traditions concerning the wife's economic independence or control of family finances. Different traditions concerning the role of the wife's side of the family had also been a problem until recent decades, but now that more Chinese marry Chinese whose families are in the Philippines, social or economic relations with one's in-laws are coming to resemble those of the Filipinos.

Recent liberalization in the citizenship laws reduces one obstacle to intermarriage, but in the last twenty years most intermarrying couples in Iloilo were Filipino citizens to begin with. The laws, however, do not appear to be the main obstacles to intermarriage; the low level of social intercourse between Chinese and Filipino youths is still the important obstacle.

We need to know more about what conditions today bring a Filipino and Chinese together in marriage, what if any ethnic differences pose marital problems, how the decision is made concerning the ethnic affiliation of the mestizo children, and if it is a conscious decision or imposed by circumstances.

Unless the rate of intermarriage increases significantly, the population of pure Chinese in the Philippines will not disappear. Both the Filipinos and the Chinese construe a close relationship between blood and culture, but in fact Chinese culture will change or disappear at a rate that is almost uninfluenced by racial purity. Besides, intermarriage is not the most likely way to integrate an ethnic group into a nation. What is important is the reduction of isolation and mutual suspicion between those that behave like Filipinos and those that behave like Chinese.

The social realm is one of the slowest areas of change in Filipino-Chinese relations. That is, a good deal of social interaction has always been present between Filipinos and Chinese in Iloilo since the Second World War, but that amount does not increase nor do the areas of social interaction grow at visible rates. Filipinos and Chinese share membership in the city's Rotary and Lion's clubs, they gamble at cockfights and mah jong parlors together, they attend one another's weddings and funeral ceremonies, and especially, one another's banquets. But the increase in these interactions since 1946 has been very slow; the relations are mostly very casual and primarily involve the adult males. I knew Iloilo Chinese who were close gambling partners or political allies with Filipinos, but these relationships were rare. Children and women seldom get together with their ethnic neighbors.

Chinese women and girls, who now constitute half the Philippine Chinese population, are still isolated from Filipinos. Women with bound feet can still be seen in downtown Iloilo, and these women exert a strong conservative influence over the women in the households where they live. Nevertheless, without socializing with Filipinos, the unmarried Chinese girls and wives are showing signs of resembling Filipina women, a trend caused by proximity to the Filipino culture rather than to Filipino individuals. As I illustrated in chapter 6, girls and women are refusing to be totally financially dependent upon Chinese patriarchal families and are striving to emerge from "the back of the store." Employment in Iloilo's larger Chinese corporations and commercial sidelines from the family business are both bringing Chinese women into greater public exposure and inevitably reducing their isolation from Filipinos.

Crossethnic godparentage ties are common, as we saw in chapter 6, and in some cases the bond between the elders in a *compadre-comadre* arrangement will be a close one. Just as often, however, the Chinese forgets who his godchildren are. The godparent-godchild connection is usually of less social interest to the godchild, whether Chinese or Filipino, and the social distance is even greater when the godparent is of the opposite sex. One cannot look to ritual kin relationships such as godparentage for an index of close social integration, but it would be revealing anyway if current crossethnic ties spread to a larger proportion of the Chinese population.

Separate Chinese schools have been primarily responsible for the social gap between Filipinos and Chinese. A shared childhood or youth is what makes lifelong barkadas, or buddy groups, and even though Iloilo's Chinese schools have been open to ethnic Filipinos, segregation by choice has meant few Chinese meet Filipinos on a regular basis until college age. One might argue that it is not necessary for social integration to reach the point that Chinese and Filipinos form strong personal friendships through informal contacts; a necessary prerequisite of such intimacy is an almost complete cultural and social assimilation of one group by the other, which neither the Chinese support in principle nor the Filipinos are pursuing in practice. Next to naturalization of aliens, however, an important pillar of Chinese integration is the issue of their separate school system.

To disband the Chinese schools entirely would be unfortunate. They have developed strong curricula and faculties and the students work hard to emerge quite well educated, albeit often more ethnically Chinese than when they entered. To maintain the schools as reorganized in 1976, however, would be to accept a fairly high degree of de facto segregation of Chinese from Filipino children. The issue of how much Chinese language and culture is taught in such schools is less serious to integration than the "separate but equal" issue. Resolving this problem by balancing the values of ethnic integrity and social integration will prove as difficult as it has been in the United States.

Very few Chinese in Iloilo have entered the Filipino world of law or politics. The community has relied upon those within the group whom I described in chapter 4 as bicultural brokers, or else upon special Filipino patrons in law or government. I only met one young man in all of Iloilo who had serious plans to pursue a legal and political career – but in Manila.

Until recently, citizenship problems were the main obstacle to the development of Chinese political clout similar to that wielded by Filipinos in the sugar, lumber, or mining industries. The Chinese have always been supplicants before the thrones of power. As political outsiders, but with a large stake in Philippine decisions, the Chinese have depended on the Taiwanese embassy, and they have also served as the "milking cow" of Filipino political factions, participating in politics with their sole available means: money. For example, in the 1971 Iloilo mayoral elections, the Chinese had a strong sense of which candidate was in their best interest but were under enormous pressure to support all three, to hedge their bets. Seen in this light, the generous and highly publicized Iloilo Chinese charity drives for Filipinos have been an avenue for nonpartisan political activity. The transition out of their long tradition of dependency and the weakening of the role of "milking cow" is a rough one, as we saw in chapter 4, but surely worthwhile under the new pressures for integration that prevail. I predict, and further research could confirm this, that after the present turbulence of the changing Chinese power bases, more bicultural intermediaries will emerge to aid the Chinese shift from an old-fashioned ethnic group to a modern political bloc. This is a process that Fredrik Barth (1969) observes as a common transformation in multiethnic nations.

Turning now to Iloilo Chinese participation in Filipino cultural beliefs and practices, we find several models that might help to organize the evidence. The Cultural Replacement Model postulates that as Filipino ways of thinking and behaving are acquired, Chinese ways will disappear. This model applies well to some features of Chinese life in Iloilo. For example, in dress and eating habits, the young Chinese are almost indistinguishable from Filipinos, whereas their parents, much changed themselves, still retain some Chinese touches such as wearing Chinese slippers or eating *lu kao* for breakfast. McCarthy (1973:126-42) has outlined many areas of Philippine Chinese culture that have been heavily influenced by borrowing from Filipinos: names, material possessions, etiquette, sports, games, family structure and behavior, language, values, residence patterns, and religion are some of these areas.

But an earlier study I conducted on Chinese ethnicity in San Francisco (Omohundro n.d.) suggested alternative ideas of what to look for in Iloilo. Three facets of ethnicity I called language abilities, social interaction with majority culture members, and participation in cultural beliefs and practices, each showed great variation among San Francisco's Chinese and appeared to involve different mixes of Chinese and majority culture components for each individual. Social interaction with non-Chinese fit the Replacement Model best: as contacts with non-Chinese went up, one's contacts with Chinese went down because there are only so many hours in a day. Language ability was somewhat different: the ability and interest to read and speak Chinese dropped more precipitously than the ability and interest in English grew. The implication is that there are San Francisco Chinese who aren't very fluent in either English or Chinese. Lastly, the ways individuals participated in Chinese and American beliefs and practices were the most interesting result of all: active adherence to American ways did not preclude active adherence to the Chinese. John Wayne and Bruce Lee, Chinese temples and Christianity, love of Chinese culture and American patriotism, all coexisted rather/comfortably. A Bicultural Model applied well to this aspect of ethnicity for many individuals.

Most evidence in Iloilo suggests that the Bicultural Model rather than the Replacement Model best fits the changes going on in Chinese customary beliefs and practices. The Bicultural Model specifies that the Chinese will adopt many Filipino characteristics without giving up all of the Chinese ways.

One prominent example of biculturalism is Chinese ceremonial life. In Iloilo Chinese funerals, the bereaved wear black as Filipinos do, not the traditional white. Paper flowers and white candles in the Filipino Catholic custom are everywhere during necrological services, but so are Chinese eulogistic pennants and the gifts of dress pieces which are hung on the walls. The rosary is read by the Catholic Women's Association at the home of the deceased, but ritual offerings of fruit, incense, and imitation money are also standard. Tombs in the Chinese cemetery are an eclectic blend of Spanish and Chinese motifs. And the deceased is carried to the cemetery in a Spanish horse-drawn hearse. The combination of traditions is also obvious in Chinese weddings and engagements, where the Catholic Mass is the ritual center of events, but ceremonial meals of sweet eggs and noodles and the exchange of dowry and bridewealth between families are very familiar to the China scholar.

Some Chinese – and not simply the old folk – continue to place great stock in aiding business success by horoscopy and the ancient art of geomancy. They visit the Iloilo temple of Koan-Im, the Goddess of Mercy, to throw the fortune blocks and make up their minds on family and commercial matters. But Filipino folk beliefs have also made an impact. Chinese have patronized a popular charismatic Filipino fortuneteller in a nearby town. And when one merchant was plagued with spirits in a tree behind his store, he sought the services of a Filipino *babaylan,* or spirit priest, to exorcise them. If the Chinese beliefs weaken, and they are bound to as the secular age permeates the Philippines, those beliefs will change no faster nor slower than the Filipino beliefs which for years have supplemented them.

Overall, though the Bicultural Model of change applies well now to many areas of Philippine Chinese life, I foresee the acceleration of Chinese ethnicity's retreat to the private sphere of life. This private sphere includes among its parts familial behavior, religious beliefs, value systems, and recreational, social, and aesthetic activities that can be conducted in private: in the home, the temple, or the clubhouse. Chinese security and Filipino self-respect are interrelated and depend upon reducing the perceived political and economic distinctiveness of the Chinese in the public sphere of life. The Chinese cannot benefit any more by remaining distinct in the marketplace and the political world. At the same time, the Filipinos cannot afford any measures that hold the Chinese apart.

To conclude, an understanding of Filipino attitudes toward the Chinese can provide clues to some of the obstacles – or opening doors – to further integration. Filipino attitudes toward the Chinese both influence behavior and also reflect other sociocultural problems.

In the eyes of the Filipino, the Chinese have two strikes against them. First, they are truly Oriental, heirs to an Asian culture very different from the Occidental ways influencing the Filipinos for the last four hundred years. George Weightman (1967) proposes that this feature of Filipino anti-Chinese attitudes has an element of group "self-hatred" in it. The ethnic Chinese are rejected, in other words, for representing the Oriental elements in Filipino culture and physique that prevent more complete identity with the much-admired West. Without imputing any deep psychological motives, however, one can appreciate Filipino worries about the cultural allegiance of resident Chinese to China, which until recently was seen as a political and military threat to the Philippines.

The second strike against the Chinese, ironically, reduces any real threats of a Communist fifth column, but the two strikes do not cancel one another. Namely, the Chinese are merchants, capitalists in the grand old tradition, and are placed in the relatively small urban middle class. Chinese and shop-keeper are nearly/synonymous in Iloilo City. In surveys I conducted in 1972 (Omohundro 1975) Filipinos spoke sometimes disparagingly, sometimes admiringly, of what they perceived as single-minded devotion to making money. Iloilo's urban middle class residents, whether struggling or successful, saw Chinese commercial zeal as a narrow life-style, without the nobility or grace middle class Filipinos seek. Chinese success in the commercial world means less room for a struggling Filipino middle class, but even more important, such a well-entrenched position in the economy was seen as hazardous to Philippine security as long as the patriotism of the Chinese was so much in question.

This is not the place to argue against deeply rooted, long-standing, and sometimes irrational feelings of Filipinos and Chinese toward each other's group. As mentioned earlier, group prejudices are in part symptoms of real social problems. Suffice it to say here that my surveys among Filipinos pointed strongly to the conclusion that Filipino attitudes toward the Chinese as a group seemed to bear little relationship to Filipino dealings with Chinese as individuals. This appears to have been true for a long time: witness the long history of intermarriage. Part of the problem may lie with the Ilongo's pervasive lack of knowledge of Chinese culture or Filipino-Chinese ways, except for a few items of business or family life. It appeared in 1973 that no effort was made in either Filipino or Chinese schools to reduce group antipathies, and worse: my impression is that teachers in Chinese and Fili-pino schools are, as a group, rather intolerant of ethnic differences. Weight-man (1964), Coller (1960), and Bulatao (1974) provide support for this impression. Obviously, reform in Chinese schools is necessary but only half of the needed reform. An inquiry into the content, the amount, and the tone of curriculum in Filipino schools about the nation's ethnic groups is definite-ly a first step to such reform. I cannot imagine how a multiethnic nation could succeed without joining sympathetic ethnic studies to a patriotic education. To the extent that this book about Iloilo's Chinese, which is neither flattering nor damning, provides material for such a reform, I would consider it well worthwhile.

BIBLIOGRAPHY

Alip, Eufronio. 1959. *Ten Centuries of Philippine-Chinese Relations.* Manila: Alip and Sons, Inc.

Amyot, Jacques, S.J. 1960. *The Chinese Community of Manila: A Study of Adaptation of Chinese Familism to the Philippine Environment.* Philippine Studies Program Research Series No. 2. Chicago: University of Chicago.

Barth, Fredrik. 1969. *Ethnic Group and Boundaries.* Boston: Little, Brown.

Benedict, Burton. 1968. "Family Firms and Economic Development." *Southwestern Journal of Anthropology* 24(1):1-19.

Bennett, John. ed. 1975. *The New Ethnicity: Perspectives from Ethnology.* St. Paul: West Publishing Co.

Bernstein, David. 1947. *The Philippine Story.* New York: Farrar, Strauss.

Berreman, Gerald. 1972. "Social Categories and Social Interaction in Urban India." *American Anthropologist* 74(3):567-87.

Blaker, James R. 1970. "The Chinese in the Philippines: A Study of Power and Change." Unpublished Ph. D. dissertation, Ohio State University.

Bonacich, Edna. 1973. "A Theory of Middleman Minorities." *American Sociological Review* 38(5):583-94.

Bowring, Sir John. 1859. *A Visit to the Philippine Islands.* London: Smith, Elder & Co.

Bulatao, Rodolfo A. 1974. "Ethnic Attitudes and Prejudices in Five Philippine Cities." Manila: University of the Philippines Social Research Laboratory.

Census of the Philippine Islands, 1903. 1905. U. S. Bureau of the Census. Washington, D. C.: Government Printing Office.

Chaloemtiarana, Thak. 1977. "Peking, Southeast Asia, and the Overseas Chinese." *Problems of Communism* 261(1):75-79.

Chen Ta. 1923. "Chinese Migrations, with Special Reference to Labor Conditions." *Bulletin of the U.S. Bureau of Labor Statistics* 340(July).

Chua, Antonio R. 1974. "Manila's Chinatown: A Coming Tourist Attraction." *Fookien Times Yearbook 1974.* Pp. 168-70.

Clarkson, James D. 1968. "Cultural Ecology of a Chinese Village: Cameron Highlands, Malaysia." Ph. D. dissertation, University of Chicago.

Cohen, Myron. 1970. "Developmental Process in the Chinese Domestic Group." in *Family and Kinship in Chinese Society.* Edited by Maurice Freedman. Stanford: Stanford University Press.

Cohen, Yehudi. 1968. "Culture as Adaptation." In *Man in Adaptation: The Cultural Present.* Edited by Yehudi Cohen. Chicago: Aldine. Pp. 40-60.

Coller, Richard. 1960. "A Social-psychological Perspective on the Chinese as a Minority Group in the Philippines." *Philippine Sociological Review* 8(1):47-56.

Coughlin, Richard J. 1960. *Double Identity: The Chinese in Modern Thailand.* Hongkong: Hongkong University Press.

Crissman, Lawrence. 1967. "The Segmentary Structure of Urban Overseas Chinese Communities." *Man* 2(2):185-204.

Despres, Leo A. 1975. "Ethnicity and Ethnic Group Relations in Guyana." in *The New Ethnicity: Perspectives from Ethnology.* Edited by John Bennett. St. Paul: West Publishing Co. Pp. 127-47.

De Tocqueville, Alexis. 1964. *Democracy in America.* Excerpted in *The Character of Americans.* Edited by Michael McFiffert. Homewood, Illinois: \ Dorsey Press.

Doeppers, Daniel. 1971. "Ethnicity and Class in the Structure of Philippine Cities." Ph.D. dissertation, Syracuse University.

Douglas, Carstairs. 1873. *Chinese-English Dictionary of the Vernacular or Spoken Language of Amoy.* London: Trubner & Co.

Driver, Harold. 1956. "An Integration of Functional, Evolutionary, and Historical Theory by Means of Correlations." Indiana Publications in Anthropology and Linguistics, Memoirs 12. Pp. 1-35.

Economic Census Preliminary. 1967. Iloilo Bureau of Census and Statistics. Iloilo City, Philippines.

Eitzen, D. Stanley. 1968. "Two Minorities: The Jews of Poland and the Chinese in the Philippines." *Jewish Journal of Sociology* 10 (December): 221-40.

Federation of Filipino-Chinese Chambers of Commerce Business Directory 1965. 1965. Manila.

Fei Hsiao-tung. 1939. *Peasant Life in China: A Field Study of Country Life in the Yangtze Valley.* London: Paul, Trench, Trubner & Co.

_____.1953. *China's Gentry.* Chicago: University of Chicago Press.

Freedman, Maurice. 1957. *Chinese Family and Marriage in Singapore.* London: Her Majesty's Stationery Office.

_____.1958. *Lineage Organization in Southeastern China.* London School of Economics, Monographs on Social Anthropology, no. 18. London: Athlone Press.

Fried, Morton. 1953. *The Fabric of Chinese Society: A Study of the Social Life of a Chinese County Seat.* New York: Praeger.

Golden Jubilee Anniversary Yearbook 1911-1961. 1961. Chinese Commercial High School. Iloilo City, Philippines.

Grageda, G. M. 1966. "Changes in Iloilo City." *Philippine Free Press*, 15 January.

Hsu, Francis L. K. 1948. *Under the Ancestors' Shadow.* New York: Columbia University Press.

Iloilo Times. March-April, 1970.

Jensen, Khin Khin Myint. 1956. "The Chinese in the Philippines During the American Regime 1898-1946." Ph. D. dissertation, University of Wisconsin.

Kaye, Barrington. 1960. *Upper Nankin Street, Singapore.* London: Unwin & Co.

Landon, Kenneth P. 1941. *The Chinese in Thailand.* Shanghai: n. p.

Levi-Strauss, Claude. 1963. *Structural Anthropology.* New York: Basic Books.

Liao, Schubert, ed. 1964. *Chinese Participation in Philippine Culture and Economy.* Manila: Liao.

Light, Ivan H. 1972. *Ethnic Enterprise in America.* Berkeley: University of California Press.

Lin, Yueh-hua. 1947. *The Golden Wing: A Sociological Study of Chinese Familism.* New York: Oxford University Press.

Liu, William; Rubel, Arthur J.; and Yu, Elena. 1969. "The Urban Family of Cebu: A Profile Analysis." *Journal of Marriage and the Family* 31(2):393–402.

Loney, Nicholas. 1964. *A Britisher in the Philippines, or The Letters of Nicholas Loney.* Publications of the National Library, no. 23. Manila.

Lynch, Frank. 1965. "Trends Report of Studies in Social Stratification and Social Mobility in the Philippines." *East Asian Cultural Studies* 4(1-4, March):163-91.

McBeath, Gerald. 1975. *Political Integration of the Philippine Chinese.* Berkeley: University of California Press.

McCarthy, Charles J., S.J. 1972. "Chinese Schools in the Philippines: Rationale and Record." *Solidarity* (April).

_____.1973. "The Chinese in the Philippines: The Case for Integration." in *The Filipino in the Seventies.* Edited by Vitaliano Gorospe, S. J., and Richard Deats. Quezon City: New Day Publishers.

_____. 1974. *Philippine-Chinese Profile: Essays and Studies.* Manila: Pagkakaisa sa Pagunlad.

Mannheim, Karl. 1957. *Systematic Sociology.* Edited by J. S. Eros and W. A. C. Stewart. London: Routledge and Kegan Paul.

Mitchell, J. Clyde. 1969. *Social Networks in Urban Situations.* Manchester: Manchester University Press.

_____.1974. "Perceptions of Ethnicity and Ethnic Behavior." in *Urban Ethnicity.* Edited by Abner Cohen. London: Tavistock.

Morse, Hosea. 1932. *The Gilds of China, with an Account of the Gild Merchant of Canton.* Second edition. London: Longmans, Green, and Co.

Murdock, George. 1949. *Social Structure.* New York: McMillan Co.

Nagata, Judith. 1974. "What is a Malay? Situational Selection of Ethnic Identity in a Plural Society." *American Ethnologist.* 1(2).

Nash, Manning. 1966. *Primitive and Peasant Economic Systems.* San Francisco: Chandler Publishing Co.

Newell, William H. 1962. *Treacherous River: A Study of Rural Chinese in Northern Malaysia.* Kuala Lumpur: University of Malaysia Press.

Olsen, Stephen M. 1972. "The Inculcation of Economic Values in Taipai Business Families." In *Economic Organization of Chinese Society.* Edited by William Willmott. Stanford: Stanford University Press.

Omohundro, John. n.d. (1971). "Chinese Ethnicity in San Francisco." Ph. D. Candidacy paper, University of Michigan.

———. 1975. "Social Distance in Iloilo City: A Study of Anti-Chinese Attitudes in the Philippines." *Asian Studies* 13(1):37-54.

Park, Robert. 1928. "Human Migration and the Marginal Man." *American Journal of Sociology* 33(6).

Philippine Census Survey 1967. "Report by Province: Iloilo" Bureau of Census. Manila.

Purcell, Victor. 1960. *The Chinese in Modern Malaysia.* Second edition. Singapore: D. Moore for Eastern Universities Press.

Ravenholt, Albert. 1955. "Chinese in the Philippines: An Alien Business and Middle Class." American Universities Field Staff Reports. Washington, D.C. 9 December.

Reynolds, Harriet R. 1964. "Continuity and Changes in the Chinese Family in the Ilocos Province, Philippines." Unpublished Ph. D. dissertation, Hartford Seminary Foundation.

Revnolds, Ira Hubert. 1964. "Chinese Acculturation in Ilocos: Economical, Political, Religious." Ph.D. dissertation, Hartford Seminary Foundation.

Roxas, Sixto K. III. 1968. *Iloilo: A Heritage of Greatness.* Iloilo City: The Iloilo Press and Radio Club and Bureau of Travel and Tourist Industry.

Ryan, Edward. 1961. "The Value System of a Chinese Community in Java." Ph. D. dissertation, Harvard University.

Sahlins, Marshall. 1961. "The Segmentary Lineage: An Organization of Predatory Expansion." *American Anthropologist* 63(April):322-45.

Skinner, G. William. 1957. *Chinese Society in Thailand: An Analytical History.* Ithaca: Cornell University Press.

———. 1958. *Leadership and Power in the Chinese Community of Thailand.* Ithaca: Cornell University Press.

Sun Yat Sen High School Yearbook 1953-1963. 1963. Iloilo City, Philippines.

Survey of Business Establishments in Iloilo City. 1966. Iloilo Bureau of Census and Statistics. Iloilo City, Philippines.

Tan, Antonio. 1972. *The Chinese in the Philippines, 1898-1935, A Study of Their National Awakening.* Manila: Garcia Publishing Co.

Tan-Gatue, Belen. 1955. "The Social Background of Thirty Chinese-Filipino Marriages." *Philippine Sociological Review* 3(3):3-13.

Tan, Giok-lan. 1963. *The Chinese of Sukabumi: A Study in Social and Cultural Accommodation.* Monograph Series. Ithaca: Cornell Modern Indonesia Project.

T'ien Ju-k'ang. 1955. *Chinese of Sarawak: A Study of Social Structure.* London School of Economics and Political Science, Monographs on Social Anthropology, no. 12. London.

Watson, James L. 1975. *Emigration and the Chinese Lineage: The Mans in Hong kong and London.* Berkeley: University of California Press.

Weightman, George. 1960. "The Philippine Chinese: A Cultural History of a Marginal Trading Community." Ph. D. dissertation, Cornell University.

_____.1964. "A Study of Prejudice in a Personalistic Society: An Analysis of the Attitude Survey of College Students — University of the Philippines." *Asian Studies* 2(2):87-101.

_____. 1967. "Anti-Sinicism in the Philippines." *Asian Studies* 5:220-31.

Weldon, Peter. 1974. "Indonesian and Chinese Status and Language Differences in Urban Java." *Journal of Southeast Asian Studies* 5(1).

Wertheim, Willem Fredrik. 1964. *East-West Parallels.* Chicago: Quadrangle Books.

Wickberg, Edgar. 1965. *The Chinese in Philippine Life, 1850-1898.* Yale Southeast Asia Studies, vol. 1. New Haven: Yale University Press.

Williams, Lea E. 1966. *The Future of the Overseas Chinese in Southeast Asia.*

Willmott, Donald E. 1960. *The Chinese of Semarang: A Changing Minority Community.* Ithaca: Cornell University Press.

Willmott, William E. 1967. *The Chinese in Cambodia.* Vancouver: University of British Columbia Press.

Wolf, Eric. 1957. "Closed Corporate Peasant Communities in Mesoamerica and Central Java." *Southwestern Journal of Anthropology* 13(1).

_____.1966. *Peasants.* Englewood Cliffs: Prentice-Hall.

Wolfe, Alvin. 1970. "On Structural Comparisons of Networks." *Canadian Review of Sociology and Anthropology* 7(4):226-44.

Yang, Martin. 1945. *A Chinese Village: Taitou, Shantung.* New York: Columbia University Press.

Yoshinara, Kunio. 1972. "Economic Nationalism in the Philippines." *Solidarity* 8(9).

Zarco, Ricardo. 1966. "The Chinese Family Structure." *The Chinese in the Philippines: 1570-1770.* Edited by Alfonso Felix. Manila: Solidaridad Publishing House.

Zulueta, Lazaro M. 1968. "The 'Illustrious' Inhabitants of Iloilo." *Sunday Times Magazine,* 22 December.

INDEX

Accounting practices, 68-70
Acculturation, models of, 191-92
Adaptation, as perspective for ethnic relations, 180. *See also* Chinese-Filipino interaction
Adoption, of Chinese, 23, 154, 156-59
Affinal relationships, in business, 162-67. *See also* Intermarriage, Chinese-Filipino interaction
Agribusiness, in Iloilo province, 77
Alien Registration Certificates, 8, 17-18, 22-23
Am-kô, or silent share partner, 73-74
Amoy City, 19, 20-21, 23, 26, 27, 40, 128
Amyot, Jacques, S.J., 22, 28, 101, 136
Ang-King (*Liôk Kui Tông*)Family Association, 37, 101
Anhwei, county in Fukien province, 71-72
Anticommunist sentiments and acts, among Philippine Chinese, 29-30, 33, 38-39, 99
Anticommunist League, 99
Antique province, Chinese in, 56-57
Apprentice system, 57-59, 142, 169-70
Au-piah-soa^n, or financial backer, 67. *See also* Credit arrangements
Babaylan, or spirit priest, 192
Bacolod City, Chinese in, 2, 25, 26, 37 39-40, 44, 54, 55, 108, 112, 117, 126
Balasan town, Chinese in, 10, 26
Balut, or duck eggs, business, 144
Bangros fish ponds, business, 53-54
Banks, 34, 35, 62-64, 76, 78. *See also* Exchange companies
Barkada, or buddy group, 159, 190

Barth, Fredrik, on ethnic transformations, 191
Bennett, John, on ethnicity, 182
Bicultural model of ethnic adaptation, 192
Boe-ti-tit, or unpredictable debtor, 66
Bookkeeping Act of 1921, 35, 69
Bulante, a-hen-te, or traveling salesman, 54
Bulatao, Rodolfo A., on anti-Sinicism, 193
Business: Chinese types of, 50-51, 57, 75; district city, 5; education and training in, 146-48. *See also* Partnerships
Cabacillo-agent system, 16, 62, 65, 85. *See also* Patronage
Camiseria, or shirt factory, 174
Canton City, Chinese from, 19, 33
Cantonese, 11, 23, 25, 26, 45n, 128
Cantonese Club, 16, 20, 29, 89, 99-100
Capitans Chinas, in Spanish Iloilo, 110
"Case of the Nine," extortion case, 96
Cebu City, Chinese in, 2, 5, 15, 18, 19, 25, 40, 44, 61, 71, 119
Cemetery, Chinese, as manifestation of ethnicity, 11-12, 20, 27, 31, 192
Chambers of Commerce, structure and function of, 12, 29, 92-96. *See also* Federation of Filipino-Chinese Chambers of Commerce, Joint Committee, Junior Chamber of Commerce, Guilds
Chhau-kheh, or bad credit customer. 66. *See also* Credit arrangements
Che-soa^n-thau-ke, or inactive financial backer, 72, 74. *See also* Partnerships

Chia, or economic family, 139
Chiáh-thâu-lò, or employee, 58. *See also* Apprentice system
Chiang Kai-shek, 38
Chiang Kai Shek School, in Iloilo, 20, 30
China, People's Republic, 33, 38, 42-43, 181, 183-85
China, Republic of, or Taiwan: business with, 79; as cultural model, 89, 101-2, 106, 112; deportation to, 187; education in, 20, 27, 28, 34; embassy in the Philippines, 33, 38, 183-83; influence by, 18, 38, 47, 182 ff. *See also* Kuomintang, Immigration
China Reconstructs, magazine, 184
Chinese Aircraft Construction Corporation, 30
Chinese Buddhist Temple, 12, 20
Chinese Catholic Women's Association, 37, 104-5, 192
Chinese Chamber of Commerce, 29, 33, 37, 39, 92-96, 185
Chinese Chess Club, 109
Chinese Commercial Press, newspaper, 187
Chinese Commercial School, in Iloilo, 19, 28, 29, 30, 33, 34, 37, 38, 118
Chinese Community, or Joint Committee, 95
Chinese Educational Finance Committee, 94-95
Chinese Masons Temple, 117
Chinese Merchant Association of Iloilo, 95
Chinese People's Society, Iloilo, 18
Chinese schools, Iloilo: enrollment in, 7, 19, 28; nationalization of, 185 ff.; social structure of, 12, 43, 95, 190; political aspects of, 29-30, 33, 38-39, 118. *See also* Chiang Kai Shek School, Chinese Commercial School, Santa Maria School, Sun Yat Sen School
Chinese-Filipino interaction, 17, 32, 60, 114-16, 157, 182-94; antagonisms in, 37, 47-48, 90-91, 96; economic discrimination in, 34-36, 59, 91, 143-44, 193; financial, 77, 78, 131, 187; through intermarriage, 62, 121-26, 128-33, 134, 162-63, 173
Chin-kang (Chin-ch'iang) county, 17, 23-24, 25

Christian Gospel Center, Iloilo City, 37, 108
Christianity, influence of, 12, 34, 37, 43, 105, 131
Chua Family, spatial-occupational clusters in Iloilo, 26
Chua-Gua Family Association, 20, 100, 117
Cigarette Dealers Association, Iloilo, 36, 97
Citizenship: population estimates by, 7, 9; acquisition of, 9, 35, 37, 78, 91, 183-84, 185, 187-88; dummy systems in, 151-52
"Clannishness," of Philippine Chinese, 109
Class system. *See* Social stratification
Coastwise Shipping Trade Act of 1923, 35
Cohen, Myron, on the Chinese economic family, 140
Cohen, Yehudi, on mercantilism as a strategy of adaptation, 85
Coller, Richard, on anti-Sinicism, 193
Commonwealth Constitution, 35
Communist sympathies, of Chinese, 29-30, 33, 38, 182-83, 184-85
Compadre-comadre, godparentage relationships, involving Chinese, 156 160, 190
Compadres, in Amoy, 19
Concubines, or *muîⁿ-tsai,* 23
Confederation of Chinese businessmen, 18, 19, 29
Consumption patterns, Iloilo Chinese households, 80-83
Contracts, formal and informal, 74-76
Corporations, involving Chinese, 75. *See also* Business types
Credit arrangements: from banks, 62-65; among Chinese, 39, 57, 65-68; from foreign trading houses, 26
Crissman, Lawrence, on segmentary organization of overseas Chinese, 106
Cultural Replacement model of acculturation, 191
Cursillo Movement, in Iloilo, 37, 105
Dagupan City, Chinese in, 13n
Davao City, Chinese in, 2, 5, 11, 25, 40, 44, 89, 108
Decision-making, in family business, 139-45

Division of labor: in family business, 139-45, 149; in partnerships, 70-74

Doeppers, Daniel, on urban Chinese communities, 23, 79, 119

Dumaguete City, Chinese in, 13n, 119

Economic studies, by Philippine Chinese of themselves, 3

Education, 20, 27, 28, 34, 146-48. *See also* Chinese schools

Employees: Chinese in Filipino business, 60-61, 186; Filipinos as, 61-62, 81, 186; types of, 59-62; unionization of 29, 61, 119n. *See also* Apprentice system

Ethnic group: definitions of, 3, 4-5, 12; Iloilo Chinese as, 39, 40-41, 48; maintenance of, 186-92; Philippine Chinese as, 4-13,38, 42-43, 46, 84

Exchange companies, 63

Familism, 136

Family, Chinese: average size in Iloilo, 10; business expansion of, 142, 173-74, 179; management in, 132-33, 177; residence patterns of, 10-11, 134-38, 140, 179

Family associations, or sib associations: origins of, 20, 101; as part of social structure, 12, 102-4, 106-8, 153; structure and function of, 100-3

Federation of Filipino-Chinese Chambers of Commerce, 33-34, 38, 92, 94, 96, 117, 184. *See also* Chambers of Commerce

"Filipinization" as assimilation process, 180. *See also* Nationalism; Chinese-Filipino interaction

Filipino-Chinese Amity Club, 184

Filipino-Chinese Save the Country committees, 30

Filipino-Chinese Support the Anti-Japanese Campaign Committee, 30

Fires, urban, in business districts, 79, 86

Freedman, Maurice, on South Chinese lineages, 101

Fried, Morton, on social connections in mercantile partnerships, 71-72

Friendship Dry Goods Store, history of, 169-80

Fuchow City, 19, 21, 25

Fukien: city of, 23, 30, 33, 34, 63, 102, 110, 122; counties in, 23; province in South China, 21, 125, 127, 128

Fukienese, 11, 17, 23, 127

Fukienese Club, 100

"Ghetto Era," 41-42. *See also Parian*

Go Family Association, 108

Golden Orchid Gentlemen's Society, or Music Association, 43, 104, 105

Great Depression, of 1930s, influence on Philippine Chinese, 26-27, 29

Gremios Chinos, or Chinese enclaves, in Spanish era, 110

Guilds, merchant, 12, 43, 92, 96-97. *See also* Chambers of Commerce

Hoe-chhia, or stevedores, 58

Hó-hêng, or good credit risk, 66. *See also* Credit arrangements

Hok-kièn Hoe-koań, or Fukienese Club, 92

Hong-tsuí, or geomancy, 84-85

Ho-san county, Fukien province, 20

Households, Iloilo Chinese, 10, 134-38, 139, 145, 179

Hsu, Francis, on psychology of family relationships, 145

Hukbalahap uprising, 118

Ilocos province, Chinese in, 13n

Iloilo City: Chinese demography in, 2, 5, 7-11, contemporary urban trends of, 5, 39-41; map, 9

Iloilo province: Chinese population outside Iloilo City, 10, 56-57; Chinese provincial business in, 51, 56-57

Iloilo Poetry Club, 108

Iloilo Rampant Association, 108

Ilongo, or Ilonggo, Chinese ability in, 41, 115

Ilustrado class, of Filipinos, 17, 18

Ìm-hun-sia, or favored percentage partner, 72-73. *See also* Partnerships

Ìm-kó, or favored share partner, 72-73. *See also* Partnerships

Immigration, of Chinese: to China from Philippines, 27, 34; expenses associated with, 26; involving subterfuge, 17-18; in late nineteenth century, 16; patterns of, 21-28, 43, 122-25; within Philippines, 37; to US from Philippines, 36; of women, 19, 123-25, 134

Import Business Nationalization Act of 1953, 35

Incest taboos, and marriage proscriptions, 127-28

Inheritance: dispute settlements of, 153-56; of family business, 59, 149-56, 178-79; of personal property, 150-51

Intermarriage: of Chinese with Filipinos, 129-31, 134, 137, 188; business implications of, 132-33, 154, 162-63, 173. *See also* Chinese-Filipino interaction

Investment, by Chinese, 76-78, 79-80, 124, 179-80. *See also* Family, business expansion of; Intermarriage

I-soá, or short term loan, 68, 76. *See also* Credit arrangements

Janiuay town, Iloilo province, 10, 26, 56, 127

Japanese in Iloilo: and anti-Japanese sentiments, 30; business interests of (1930s), 29; occupation by, 31-32; and political events among Chinese, 28, 30

Jaro town, Chinese in, 10-11, 15-16, 17, 26

Jensen, Khin Khin Myint, on growth of Chinese nationalistic sentiments, 34

Jesuit priests, in Iloilo, 34. *See also* Santa Maria School, Santa Maria Catholic Church

Jip-hè-pho, or warehouse record, 69. *See also* Accounting practices

Jit-kì, or accounting diary, 69. *See also* Accounting practices

Joint Committee, in Iloilo, 95-96, 108

Joint Communique, Philippines and People's Republic of China, 183

Jolo, town in Iloilo province, 119

Joint Chamber of Commerce, 108 *See also* Chambers of Commerce

Kalibo town, Chinese in, 26, 39, 55, 57, 89

Kam Si Hoe, or Board of Trustees, 100. *See also* Family associations

Ke-Long-Su island, Fukien province, 20-21, 27

Ker and Company, Ltd., 18

Khoe-pe- Khoe-kaⁿ, or Chinese godparenthood, 156, 160-62

Kià-goa-si, or frontman partner, 72, 73. *See also* Partnerships

Kiet-pai Hiaⁿ-ti, or Chinese blood brotherhoods, 156, 159-62

Kng-Tang Hoe-Koan, or Cantonese Club, 92

Koan-Im, or Goddess of Mercy, 12, 192

Ko-jin-e seng-li, or side-line business, 82, 143. *See also* Family, management in

Kong-chhin lang, or mutual family friend, mediator, 152, 153, 155

Kong-si, or company partnership, 70. *See also* Partnerships; Business, types of

Kuomintang, Iloilo branch, 20, 29, 31, 33, 38, 99, 118

Kuomintang Cultural Association, 99

Kwangtung province, South China, 23, 24, 34, 63, 102, 110, 125

Labor, division of. *See* Family, management in; Employees

Lam-iuⁿ, or Southeast Asia, 21

Land Ownership, by Chinese, 37, 57

La Paz town, as Chinese neighborhood, 11, 17

Laurel-Langley Act, 53-54

Lendiugoxofen, or adopted son-in-law, 166

Letters of Instruction, No. 270, 283, No. 292 (concerning naturalization of aliens), 183

Li Ch'i, 18

Lim Bun So Family, history of, 20

Lineages, 101-4, 112. *See also* Family associations

Lin Yueh-hua, on the history of a Chinese merchant family, 47

Liok Lim Hoe, or Chinese Masons Temple, 117

Lions Club, Iloilo, Chinese in, 115

Litigation, among Chinese, in Filipino courts, 75-76, 104

Lu kao, or rice porridge, 12

Luzon, Philippine island, Chinese on, 21, 25

Macao, 23; Chinese compradores in, 19

Macaos. See Cantonese

Magsaysay, President Ramon, 33

Manchuria, Japanese campaign in, 28

Manila Chinese: 2, 28, 39-40, 136 184-85; Iloilo Chinese economic relations with, 52-53, 63; Iloilo Chinese political relations with, 20, 100, 117, 118; marriage and migration from Iloilo, 10, 26, 126

Mannheim, Karl, on vein connections in business, 85, 108

Manufacturing, by Chinese in Iloilo, 77
Mao Tse-tung, 38, 184
Marcos, President Ferdinand, 38-39, 183-84
Marcos, Mrs. Imelda, 182
"Marginal Man," Chinese as, 47
Marginal trading community, Chinese as, 17, 42, 47
Marriage, 122-26, 128-33, 134, 230. *See also* Chinese-Filipino interaction, Postmarital residence patterns
Martial law, and Philippine Chinese, 38-39, 182-83
McBeath, Gerald, on political integration of Philippine Chinese, 185
Meng, or mongo beans, introduction of, 15
Merchant society, Philippine Chinese as, 3, 12, 185-86
Mestizos, Chinese-Filipino: in business, 16, 59-60; as ethnic group distinct from Chinese, 18, 41; marriage patterns of, 128-34, 188. *See also* Marriage, Intermarriage, Family
Middleman, political role of, 115-16, 182
Mindanao island, Chinese on, 25
Miss Chinatown, Contest controversy, Manila, 184
Mitchell, J. Clyde, on conceptual definitions of ethnicity, 4
Molo town, Chinese in, 10-11, 15, 17, 26
Muî^n-tsai. See Concubines
Muscovado, or brown sugar, mills as Chinese business, 15
Music Association of Iloilo, 43, 104-5
Mutual Aid Societies, 64
Nan-an County, Fukien province, 25
Nanking Assembly and Election of Senators of 1912, 18
Nash, Manning, on resident strangers as economic caste, 46
Nationalism, of Chinese, 18, 20, 41-42. *See also* China, Republic of; China, People's Republic
Nationalism, of Filipinos and economic nationalization, 34-36, 55, 59. *See also* Chinese-Filipino interaction
Naturalization, *See* Citizenship
Negros island, Chinese business with, 26, 119
Neolocal postmarital residence practices. *See* Households

Nixon, President Richard, 38, 182, 183
Olsen, Stephen, on commercial training of children, 86
Ongcu, 30
Ong Family Association (Tai Guan Tong), 20, 37, 127
Orient News, newspaper, 183
Oton town, Chinese gravesites in, 15
Overseas Chinese Cooperation Society, during Japanese Occupation (*Hoa-Kiau Hap Hoe*), 31
Overseas Trade Bank, 63
Pacific Economic and Cultural Centre, 183
Pacific Trade Co., in Iloilo, 18
Pagkakaisa sa Pagunlad, Inc., Iloilo, 108
Pak-iau, or provincial sales agent system, 55, 60
Panay island, map, 6
"Parent bazaars," 119. *See also* Cabacillo-agent system
Parian, or ghetto, 15, 17
Park, Robert, on the marginal man concept, 47
Partnerships, Chinese mercantile, 70-74, 170, 186
Passi town, Chinese in, 31
Patrilocal postmarital residence patterns. *See* Households
Patronage, 65. *See also* Immigration, Investment; Partnerships
Phah-thiap, or bonus share, in business and inheritance arrangements, 152
Philippine Constabulary, 33, 118
Philippine Constitution, 34
Philippine government, and Chinese, 7, 8
Philippine National Railway, 55
Philippine Securities and Exchange Commission, 75, 109
Phō-ê. *See* Adoption
Po Family Association, 108
Political clubs, 99-100
Polygyny. *See* Marriage
Population, estimates of. *See* Ethnic group
Postmarital residence patterns, 136-38
Presidential Decree No. 176 (concerning nationalization of Chinese alien schools, 185; No. 278 (concerning registration of aliens and naturalized citizens), No. 725 (concerning natur-

alization of aliens), 183. *See also* Citizenship, Chinese schools

Provincial agent system of Chinese commercial distribution, 55

Public relations, by Chinese with Filipinos, 36, 103

Race, Chinese population estimates by, 7

Reading clubs (*Tiong-hoa Ke-miā^n Tong*), 18

Real estate, investment by Chinese in, 78-80. *See also* Residence patterns

Residence patterns, 10-11, 15, 16, 25-26, 27-28, 176

Resident strangers, Chinese as, 46

Retail Trade Nationalization Law of 1955, 35, 151

Rice and Corn Dealers Association, Iloilo, 36

Rice and Corn Nationalization Act of 1960, 35, 36

Romer's Rule, of conservatism of change, 181

Roxas City, Chinese in, 26, 39, 55, 57, 89

Roxas, Sixto K., III, on urban trends in Iloilo, 39

Ryan, Edward, on Chinese in Java, 87

Sa^n-chiah-khì, or "mutual plumping up" loans, 68. *See also* Credit arrangements

Sahlins, Marshall, on predatory expansion of segmentary lineage, 106

Samar province, Chinese in, 15, 119

San Francisco City, Chinese acculturation in, 191

San Jose City, Antique province, Chinese in, 56-57

Santa Maria Catholic Church, 37, 131

Santa Maria School, 12, 34

Sara town, Chinese in, 10

Sarawak, Malaysia, Chinese in, 65

Sari-sari, or general store, Chinese in, 26, 37, 56, 98

Sari-sari Store Association, Iloilo, 98, 113

See, Chin-ben, on counting Chinese ethnics, 13n

Seng-liẽn, or mature man concept, 152

Shantung Incident, Philippine Chinese reaction to, 28, 30

Sib, or *tzu*, 101-4, 135. *See also* Tzu, Lineages

Singapore, Chinese in, 34

Sìn-iōng, or trust, 68, 71, 84. *See also* Credit arrangements

Siōng-kheh, or ideal credit client, 66. *See also* Credit arrangements

Sì-Tsong Chhin Hōe, or lineage association, 101. *See also* Family associations

Social stratification and class, 111-12

Spanish influence, on Chinese, 15-17, 40, 41-42

Sse-yap, or four dialect region, Kwangtung province, immigrants from, 24

Storefronts, as real estate investment, 78-80

"Store name," equal to family name, 18, 139

Sugar industry, Iloilo, 39-40, 53-54

Suki, or marketing mate relations, 82. *See also* Consumption patterns

Sulu province, trade with, 18

Sun Yat Sen, founder of Chinese Republic, 18

Sun Yat Sen School, 19, 18, 29-30, 34, 37, 39, 99, 108

Surnames, Chinese, and immigration patterns, 16, 25

Sy Family Association, 108

Tagalog language, 77

Tai Tung High School Building Fund, Bacolod, 112

Tan, Antonio, on twentieth century, history of Philippine Chinese nationalism, 16, 20, 28, 29

Tan Family Association, or Yu Uy Tong, 20, 26, 39, 100, 101

Tantoco family, history of in Iloilo, 20

Taxes, business, paid by Chinese merchants, 48, 49, 63, 96

Teng Hsiao-peng, Vice Premier, 183

"Three generation myth," 145-46

Tiam-tui, or goodwill payment for storefront, 78

Ti si, or association officers, 100

Tiu Gan Family Association, 20

Tocqueville, Alexis de, on the predicament of commercial life style, 87

Tong, or bribes and extortion, 36, 69, 97, 98

Tong association, or secret societies, 15

Tòng Hiong Hōe, or village associations, 101. *See also* Family associations

Transportation, commercial, by Iloilo
    Chinese, 53-56, 78
Tsong-phō, or ledger, 69. *See also*
    Accounting practices
Tùi-lāi, or inside partner, 72. 73. *See also*
    Partnerships
Tzu, or lineages, 26, 110, 112. *See also*
    Sib, Family associations
Ui-chiok, or last will and testament, 151.
    See also Inheritance
Unionization. *See* Employees
U.S. business firms in Philippines, 18,
    39, 52, 60
U.S. influence on Philippine Chinese,
    16-21, 32-33, 34, 43-44, 60
Utang, or debt relations, 36
Uxorilocal postmarital residence pattern.
    See Households
Uy Family Association, 37
Weightman, George, on history of Philip-
    pine Chinese as marginal trading com-
    munity, 2, 34, 47, 101, 116, 193
Wertheim, W. F., on "minority trading
    communities," 3

Wholesale-retail marketing, development
    of, 15, 18
Wickberg, Edgar, on Chinese in nine-
    teenth century Philippines, 16, 23,
    45n, 65
Wolf, Eric, on closed corporate commu-
    nities, 84
Women, and   family business, 143-
    45, 152, 165-66, 189,
Wu Family Association, 118
Yap Family, spatial-occupational cluster-
    ing in Iloilo, 26
Yap Kai-sing, honorary consul for Re-
    public of China, 45n
Yap Tico family, history of in Iloilo,
    20
YMCA, in Iloilo, 108
Yu family, spatial-occupational cluster-
    ing in Iloilo City, 26
Zamboanga City, Chinese in, 2, 18
Zarco, Ricardo M., on Chinese in Manila
    parian, 136